Reclaiming e
for future generations

Manchester University Press

The *Manchester Capitalism* book series

Manchester Capitalism is a series of books that follows the trail of money and power across the systems of our failing capitalism. The books make powerful interventions about who gets what and why in a research based and solidly argued way that is accessible for the concerned citizen. They go beyond critique of neo liberalism and its satellite knowledges to re-frame our problems and offer solutions about what is to be done.

Manchester was the city of Engels and Free Trade where the twin philosophies of collectivism and free market liberalism were elaborated. It is now the home of this venture in radical thinking that challenges self-serving elites. We see the provincial radicalism rooted here as the ideal place from which to cast a cold light on the big issues of economic renewal, financial reform and political mobilisation.

General editors: Julie Froud and Karel Williams

Already published:

The end of the experiment: From competition to the foundational economy

What a waste: Outsourcing and how it goes wrong

Licensed larceny: Infrastructure, financial extraction and the global South

The econocracy: The perils of leaving economics to the experts

Reckless opportunists: Elites at the end of the establishment

Foundational economy: The infrastructure of everyday life

Safe as houses: Private greed, political negligence and housing policy after Grenfell

The spatial contract: A new politics of provision for an urbanized planet

The pound and the fury: Why anger and confusion reign in an economy paralysed by myth

Praise for *Reclaiming economics for future generations*

'Here comes a book full of insightful challenges to the economic mindset that has been handed down through textbooks and classrooms worldwide. The authors clearly demonstrate the power of questioning and unlearning that inheritance. But they also show what it would mean to diversify, decolonise and democratise economics to make it fit for our times, and those that lie ahead. If future generations were here today, they'd surely urge us to read this book.'
Kate Raworth, author of *Doughnut Economics: Seven Ways to Think Like a 21st-Century Economist*

'*Reclaiming economics for future generations* exposes harmful hierarchies in the economics discipline and raises crucial questions about their origins, persistence, as well as how to challenge them. An important book for anyone looking to build a better economics.'
Ingrid Kvangraven, Assistant Professor in International Development, King's College, London, and co-author of *Decolonizing Economics: An Introduction*

'This book elucidates the impediments which confront women, people of colour and the marginalised in pursuing economics. More than that, it challenges the reader to understand these impediments as a vital step to overcoming them and becoming responsible agents for change. The political situation now requires such realism. Today, ever-growing numbers of people are more dissatisfied with the existing social conditions than before and more open to radical alternatives. Transforming society for the better has never been about simply accepting and working within existing constraints. We cannot create alternatives without first understanding the social impediments that deter us before dreaming, with eyes wide open, the conflicts we need to win. Indeed, now is the time to reclaim economics and offer transformative alternatives, and this book is a solid contribution.'

Dorothy Grace Guerrero, Head of Policy and Advocacy, Global Justice Now!

'For a long time, the discipline of economics has been challenged for not addressing society's most depressing outcomes. This challenge has finally been combined with a critique of the discipline's Eurocentrism, lack of diversity, elitism and blunt blindness towards structural inequalities. *Reclaiming economics for future generations* does a fantastic job leading this critique. A must-read for everyone who craves a better future.'

Carolina Alves, Research Fellow in Heterodox Economics, University of Cambridge, and co-author of *Decolonizing Economics: An Introduction*

'*Reclaiming economics for future generations* is a thought-provoking tour of the ways in which economics – both its study and its policy advice – does not represent the lives of people around the world and why it must change. It's a forceful book that deserves attention and debate within the profession.'

Claudia Sahm, Senior Fellow at Jain Family Institute, Founder of Stay-at-Home Macro Consulting, and former Federal Reserve and White House economist

'Through a meticulously argued, outrage-inducing narrative, the authors make a clear and compelling case for a radical overhaul of economics. A thoroughly readable, well-researched contribution to the field. The voices of economists and students throughout the book truly bring it to life.'

Marion Sharples, Head of International Partnerships and Training, UK Women's Budget Group

'For many decades, the economics discipline, particularly its mainstream vintage, has provided the intellectual scaffolding for much of the injustice we see in the world. The Rethinking Economics collective, with this new book, have provided a practical blueprint of how to reorient the discipline and align it with common sense notions of social justice. *Reclaiming economics for future generations* is essential reading for those of us who believe in the potential for economics to be a force for good in the world.'
Grieve Chelwa, Institute on Race, Power and Political Economy, The New School, New York

'Mainstream economic thinking is one of the main pillars of the hegemonic, uneven and unsustainable mode of living that has led to the multifaceted crisis human societies currently face. This book deconstructs it from different angles, shows its entanglements with several dimensions of social domination, and calls into question the imperative of economic growth and the modern-colonial development paradigm. Written in a collaborative way by representatives of a new generation of economists, it makes a significant contribution to imagining a liveable future for all.'
Miriam Lang, Professor of Environmental and Sustainability Studies, Universidad Andina Simón Bolívar, Ecuador

'This courageous book takes on the dominant economic theory, called neoclassical economic theory, that has played a crucial role in perpetuating the prevailing world economic order by refusing to question the structurally embedded racial, gender, class and international power imbalances that underpin it. Combining sophisticated theoretical criticisms, deep engagement with lived experiences and trenchant policy analyses, the book shows how everyone can – and should – participate in repurposing a discipline that is too important to be left to economists alone. It is a beacon for everyone who wants to make the world a better place.'

Ha-Joon Chang, Professor of Political Economy of Development, University of Cambridge, author of *23 Things They Don't Tell You About Capitalism* and *Economics: The User's Guide*

'These young economists show the way forward for a new economics apt for the pressing questions of the twenty-first century – an economics that is inclusive, ecological and diverse.'

Giorgos Kallis, ICREA Professor, Universitat Autònoma de Barcelona, author of *The Case for Degrowth*

Reclaiming economics for future generations

Lucy Ambler, Joe Earle and Nicola Scott

Manchester University Press

The right of Lucy Ambler, Joe Earle and Nicola Scott to be identified as
the authors of this work has been asserted by them in accordance with the
Copyright, Designs and Patents Act 1988.

Published by Manchester University Press
Oxford Road, Manchester M13 9PL
www.manchesteruniversitypress.co.uk

British Library Cataloguing-in-Publication Data
A catalogue record for this book is available from the British Library

ISBN 978 1 5261 6529 9 hardback
ISBN 978 1 5261 5986 1 paperback

First published 2022

The publisher has no responsibility for the persistence or accuracy of URLs
for any external or third-party internet websites referred to in this book,
and does not guarantee that any content on such websites is, or will remain,
accurate or appropriate.

Typeset by Newgen Publishing UK
Printed in Great Britain
by Bell & Bain Ltd, Glasgow

Contents

Contents

A note on how this book was written

Ariane Agunsoye
Lucy Ambler
Joe Earle
Michelle Groenewald
Danielle Guizzo
Kamal Ramburuth-Hurt
Francesca Rhys-Williams
Bruno Roberts-Dear
Brototi Roy
Nicola Scott

The writing of this book has been a collective effort, to which everyone on the list above has contributed. Over the course of eighteen months, each of the contributors shared their thinking, experience and research through written contributions and ongoing conversations. Specific contributions to each chapter are highlighted in the contents page, but the group has also significantly shaped the arguments and framing of the whole book, and therefore we wish to share credit as equally as possible. Of the group, Lucy, Joe and Nicola were paid by the international student movement Rethinking Economics (www.rethinkeconomics.org) to facilitate the research, writing and editing process. For this reason, they are the names on the front cover. Final drafting and editing was done in the first half of 2021 by Nicola and Joe who take full responsibility for any outstanding mistakes or misjudgements. The book also draws on focus group research with twenty students aged 13–17 and interviews with sixty-two economics students, professionals and academics, all of whom are united by a shared belief that economics can and must be better. We cite them throughout the book to understand better, in their own words, the challenges they face in the discipline, and their hopes for the future.

A note on power

We recognise that the structural inequalities which we highlight in academic economics and the global economy, are also reflected in the writing of this book, and in Rethinking Economics (RE). This means that there are tensions and contradictions in the book's argument that are important to consider.

For example, the book calls for economic knowledge production to be decentred away from Europe and the US. While we draw on interviews with a diverse range of students and professionals from across the world, the majority of the book's contributors are European, and the authors are all UK based. We also need to work on decentring economic knowledge produced by RE.

Similarly, we highlight the need for economics to become more diverse and inclusive. While seven out of ten of the contributors and authors are women, and this reverses the trend of male dominance in the discipline, the same number are White, which does not reflect the change we want to see.

Likewise, while the authors and contributors to this book come from a range of socioeconomic backgrounds, all have attended university. As a result, in this project, we haven't achieved our goal of taking economics out of academia and into society, where it can work more closely alongside communities who are marginalised and oppressed.

That this book reproduces some of the problems it is critiquing should not come as a surprise. The hierarchies and inequalities embedded in academic economics and the global economy are the environment in which RE and this book exist and so they become embedded in us too. The fact that RE student groups are often male dominated or that the authors of this book are UK based are examples of this.

For these reasons, the proposals we make about how to reclaim economics in Part II of this book apply as much to changing our own thinking and practice as they do to changing what others do. We completely recognise that this book is just a small first step of a much bigger process to diversify, decolonise and democratise economics and we are committed to continuing this work.

We hope that, despite the scale of work still to be done, this book makes those people who do feel sidelined in economics because of who they are, where they are from and the ideas they have, feel that they are not alone, and that they are supported by a growing international movement that sees them and values their presence in the discipline.

Foreword

For more than a decade now, dissatisfaction with the state of economics as a discipline has been growing within its ranks. Much of it has been driven by students and young people who are increasingly aware of the many limitations of what they are being taught at universities across the world, and much more willing to challenge existing dogmas and power structures.

This book is the outcome of a collective effort by such young people, to identify more precisely the source of their unhappiness with the current state of economics and, even more importantly, to highlight how this state of affairs can be changed.

It highlights a wide range of problems within the profession including a lack of diversity and inclusion; harmful hierarchies between countries; a dominant paradigm that fails to address structural inequalities, whitewashes histories of oppression, and undermines democracy and development; and incentive structures that punish economists who seek to venture beyond this paradigm. By presenting these concerns in clear-eyed and courageous ways, it also provides much hope for the future of economics.

We know that much of this dominant paradigm in economics is simply wrong and is being continuously exposed as being wrong: from being over-optimistic about how financial markets work and whether they are or can be 'efficient' without regulation,

to misplaced arguments in favour of fiscal austerity or the deregu-
lation of labour markets and wages. Critical relationships between
humans and nature that form the basis of most material production
are dismissed as 'externalities'. These are only some of the ways in
which mainstream economic thinking is either irrelevant or down-
right misleading in understanding contemporary economic processes and useless or counterproductive in addressing humanity's
most important challenges.

One reason is that much of the mainstream discipline has been
in the service of power, effectively the power of the wealthy, at
national and international levels. By 'assuming away' critical concerns, theoretical results and problematic empirical analyses effectively reinforce existing power structures and imbalances.

Deeper systemic issues like the exploitation of labour by
capital and the unsustainable exploitation of nature by forms of
economic activity, of labour market segmentation by social categories that allows for differential exploitation of different types
of workers, of the appropriation of value, of the abuse of market
power and rent-seeking behaviour by large capital, of the use of
political power to push economic interests including of cronies, of
the distributive impact of fiscal and monetary policies – all these
are swept aside, covered up and rarely brought out as the focus of
analysis.

This is associated with strict power hierarchies within the discipline as well, which suppress the emergence and spread of alternative theories, explanations and analysis. Economic models that do
not challenge existing power structures are promoted and valorised
by gatekeepers in the senior ranks of the profession. Alternative
theories and analyses are ignored, marginalised, rarely published in
the 'top' journals, and obliterated from textbooks and other teaching materials.

The disincentives for young economists to stray from the straight and narrow path are huge: academic jobs and other placements as economists are dependent on publications, which are 'ranked' according to the supposed quality of the journal they are in, in a system that demotes articles from alternative perspectives; promotions and further success in the profession depend on these markers.

This combines with the other pervasive forms of social discrimination by gender, racialised identity and location. A macho ethos permeates the mainstream discipline, with women routinely facing the consequences. Along with widespread patriarchy, the adverse impact of relational power affects other socially marginalised categories, according to class, racial and ethnic identities, and language. The impact of location is enormous, with the mainstream discipline completely dominated by the North Atlantic in terms of prestige, influence, and the ability to determine the content and direction of what is globally accepted. The enormous knowledge, insights and contributions to economic analysis made by economists located in the Global South in Asia, the Middle East, Africa, Latin America and the Caribbean are largely ignored.

Then there is disciplinary arrogance, expressed in insufficient attention to history and a reluctance to engage seriously with other social sciences and humanities, which has greatly impoverished economics. Arrogance is also evident in the tendency of economists to play God, to engage in social engineering, couched in technocratic terms which are incomprehensible to the majority of people who are told that particular economic strategies are the only possible choice, in an attitude that collapses into the unethical.

Fortunately, there is growing pushback against these tendencies, globally and within the current bastions of economics in the North Atlantic. This book is very much part of that response: challenging the rigidities and power structures within the mainstream discipline, and calling for a more varied, sophisticated, nuanced and relevant understanding of economies. This is, of course, greatly welcome; it is also hugely necessary and urgent, if economics is to reclaim its position as a relevant social science that had origins in both moral philosophy and statecraft.

Jayati Ghosh
Professor of Economics,
University of Massachusetts Amherst, USA;
formerly Professor of Economics,
Jawaharlal Nehru University, New Delhi, India

Introduction

Change is coming

Joelle Gamble is a Black American[1] woman and an economist in her early thirties. In December 2020, she was appointed Special Assistant to the President for Economic Policy by the Biden–Harris Administration.

This book is about all the barriers people like Joelle must overcome to succeed in economics. Being a woman in a male-dominated discipline is hard enough. Being a Black woman in a discipline that completely fails to engage meaningfully with racialised inequalities is even harder.

This book is also about the many people like Joelle, who have pursued careers in economics despite these barriers, because they see it is important, and believe it could be better. It is about how they are reclaiming economics. But first, here is Joelle's story.

Joelle was born in the US state of California in the early 1990s to a police officer and a preschool teacher – both former US Marines. Looking back on her childhood she remembers knowing 'that whatever I did with my life, I wanted it to be in the service of others. My parents did that, and they ingrained in me that it is an important way to live one's life.'[2]

'I'd say the thing that was a very dominant part of my childhood, was my parents trying to prepare me for college,' Joelle said. 'They did not graduate college, so they just knew it was very important for me to go to college, so I could have a good career and livelihood, and be successful.'

Joelle started at the University of California, Los Angeles (UCLA) in 2008. Shortly after, President Barack Obama was sworn in as president of a country in a deep economic recession. Her family was in that 'weird position' of not being poor enough for Joelle to be eligible for a grant to attend college but also not well off enough for her to afford it easily.

She struggled to afford college and became acutely aware of the impact of state revenues falling, people's incomes shrinking, and the subsequent budget cuts and tuition increases facing virtually all public universities. This experience made Joelle realise how much government policies shaped her life. 'That took me on a path of activism,' Gamble said. 'That's how I began to find my voice.' In addition to becoming an advocate for college affordability, Gamble also wanted to work on behalf of her friends who were undocumented migrants in the US. 'All these things were happening that were affecting my life, affecting my friends, so I got very involved in advocacy and student government.'

Though her original major was Eastern European languages and culture, Joelle ended up graduating with a degree in international development studies. Just four days after graduating in 2012 she moved to New York to start a job at the Roosevelt Institute, where she was able to fight for issues she cared about like college accessibility.

She remembers how her

> first boss out of college, Felicia Wong ... has been a huge, positive influence on my career and shaped how I think about the economy. Thinking about issues of inequality, the racial wealth gap, the

importance of market power, the importance of protecting working people: These are all things that I learned under her guidance, and she really helped me develop a passion for economic policy.

After five years working, Joelle went to Princeton to do a master's in Economics and Public Policy. A year after she graduated in 2020 George Floyd was murdered by a policeman who knelt on his neck for over nine minutes in an act of brutality that shocked the world.

Joelle recounts

thinking about how much I learned and how much I had to unlearn to be anti-racist in economic policy ... The economic crisis and the renewed attention on anti-racist movements are not two separate 'moments we're in.' One way to think of the two is to talk about economics' diversity problem. It's real and it's something I experienced first-hand. But, there are fundamental problems in economics that prevent it from promoting anti-racist public agendas.[3]

Joelle explains that

As a millennial in the United States, my life has been defined by crises; deep economic crises, climate change, the continual fight for racial justice, which has just been a constant in my life as a Black woman. And so for me, the need for change has been the default setting.[4]

Now she is part of the US President's team, she will work with colleagues across government to develop new economic policies. She has the biggest platform of all to promote anti-racist agendas within economics and the economy and deliver on the need for change to address the crises that have defined her life.

We, the authors, share Joelle's belief that it is necessary to reform our economies to address the many crises our generation faces. We chose to study economics because we wanted to understand the world we were inheriting and improve it but were left feeling deeply disappointed and uneasy.

We are from an international student movement called Rethinking Economics, with over a hundred groups in thirty countries across the world, all campaigning for reforms to university economics education.

That is because academic economics today is not fit for purpose. This book explores what has gone wrong with economics and how it can be reclaimed so that it becomes a force for good in the world.

Reclaiming economics is no easy task. The problems we highlight have long histories and are deeply embedded. The majority of the economics profession doesn't recognise the scale of reform that is needed. It is easy to give up hope. To feel that the change we need isn't possible.

That is why we wanted to start this book with Joelle's story. A Black American woman in a discipline that is all too often White[5] and dominated by men. An economist who has forcefully highlighted the deep-rooted problems with the discipline and how they can be addressed.

A millennial who has shared our experience of growing up in a world of existential crises. And now, an economist who is working to achieve change at the heart of the most powerful government in the world. Joelle is an example that change is possible. She inspires us.

What is economics and why does it matter?

Research, and our experience of conversations with friends and family, clearly highlights that for many people across the world, economics feels like a boring and difficult topic which is for politicians and experts, not for people like them. We are very conscious that part of reclaiming economics is about making it feel more relevant and accessible to people outside of the discipline.

For this reason, before we continue, we want to explain why we believe that economics is important to your life whoever and wherever you are, which we hope will convince you that you should join the growing global movement to reclaim it.

Economics is many things. Maybe, most basically it is the study of the economy. But what is the economy? The idea of 'the economy' is a fairly recent invention. It came into use around the 1930s as a label to describe the organisation of production, distribution and consumption of goods and services in a geographical area like a country or region.

Many people (including lots of economists) think of the economy as things that are bought and sold in exchange for money. In reality, the economy is much broader than that. All the unpaid care that goes into raising children who go on to become the next generation of workers is part of the economy. The living world that provides the natural resources and life support systems necessary for human life, and by extension economic activity, is part of the economy.

Today we live in highly globalised economies. This means that they connect humans on a planetary scale. Our food, energy, clothing, electronic devices, buildings, roads and almost everything human-made that we see around us, contain some component that someone from somewhere else has worked on.

Our economies also connect us with the earth, plants and animals, through the food and natural resources that we consume and the waste products we release back into the living world over the course of our lives.

We all take on many different roles in the economy as workers, unpaid carers, owners, investors, borrowers, citizens, consumers and savers. In all of these ways, we 'do economics' every day.

How economies are organised affect our lives in fundamental ways influencing our health, opportunities and the future of the planet. Understanding how our economies work, how they can be improved, and how we can thrive within them is vital for everybody.

Economies are not 'natural' nor governed by fixed laws. How they are organised is always the result of a particular history as well as a broader political and social context, and they are evolving all the time. The way they are now is not the way they have to be.

Most people in the world today feel that they have little or no influence on how economies are organised, the rules of the game or how things are valued. This fuels a sense of powerlessness and inevitability.

As a result, doing economics is about making the best you can out of the economic cards you are dealt. Where you are born, your racialised identity and gender, the jobs and income of your parents or carers all dictate the economic resources and power you have in life.

From that starting point we do the best we can, but often it feels we are powerless to change the economy around us. Is there a supply of housing we can access affordably? Is this housing linked up to water, energy and sewage systems? Can we access a nutritious and regular supply of food without having to sacrifice other essentials? Has past economic activity increased extreme weather events? The answers to all these questions are out of our control.

What shall we invest in? How do we regulate and distribute economic resources and power? These are all decisions about how the economies we live in are organised which are made by the powerful: governments, international institutions, businesses and experts.

The processes through which credible knowledge about 'the economy' is created are important because they shape the range of choices government, business and individuals have and what they ultimately do.

For example, if we 'know' that raising taxes or the minimum wage will lower overall taxes or jobs then we are less likely to do

6

it. And if we 'know' that low productivity is the cause of low wages for women or a particular racialised identity, not a lack of bargaining power, this shapes the solutions we develop. That is why the famous economist Paul Samuelson said, 'I don't care who writes a nation's laws or crafts its advanced treatises if I can write its economics textbooks'.[6]

Today, in many countries what is viewed as 'credible' economic knowledge stems from academic economics. The discipline of academic economics is based in universities across the world which employ economists who produce research which is published in academic journals, and educate students who then go into government, businesses and think tanks.

This is where we come back to Joelle's story and the international student movement Rethinking Economics. Through our experience of economics education, we have come to believe that academic economics in its current state does not provide us with the knowledge that we need to build thriving economies that allow people to flourish whatever their racialised identity,[7] gender or socioeconomic background, wherever they're from in the world. We must reclaim economics so that we can create a world of racial justice and gender equality to pass on to future generations.

We believe that economics is important to your life. We hope that this is enough to convince you to read on, and ultimately join the movement to reclaim economics.

Summary of Part I

Part I sets out what has gone wrong with economics and why it needs to be reclaimed. In Chapter 1, we demonstrate that academic economics in the United States and United Kingdom is undiverse and uninclusive. Women,[8] people of colour, and less socioeconomically privileged people are significantly underrepresented in the discipline and become more so further along the career ladder.

Barriers to studying economics include not knowing what economics is, not having family or friends who are economists, thinking it is going to be too mathematical, feeling it is not for people like you and not being able to access university. As a result, undergraduate economics is already highly unrepresentative of broader society.

Once at university, a whole new set of barriers to students from underrepresented backgrounds pursuing further study and careers in economics emerge. It can be a feeling that everyone else in the class is privileged or that students don't see themselves represented in their textbooks or teachers. Often classrooms are dominated by loud, confident, White men, and others feel marginalised.

Discrimination based on racialised identity and gender is widely reported in economics while sexual harassment is all too common. All of this fosters a sense of imposter syndrome for people from underrepresented backgrounds studying and working in economics.

We trace diverging pathways within economics in the UK depending on socioeconomic background and racialised identity, finding that privilege secures access to 'elite' universities and major employers such as the Government Economics Service.

Diversifying economics and fostering an inclusive culture is necessary for individuals from underrepresented backgrounds to have equal opportunity to study and practise economics; to be treated with dignity and respect by colleagues; and to be able to access the income, status and power that economists receive.

It is also necessary for economics as a discipline to be able to claim legitimately that it represents society and the public interest. It must be more diverse and representative in order to claim to understand the economic experience of different social groups. More broadly, a diverse and inclusive discipline of economics fosters greater social mobility and trust in experts, which in turn underpin democracy and social cohesion.

Chapter 2 takes a historical view of economics as an academic discipline and identifies deep and ingrained hierarchies in how it is structured. A particular approach, often called neoclassical economics, has become dominant in universities across the world, and while versatile, it prescribes the use of certain theories, methods, assumptions and values.

There are many alternative approaches which reject the foundations of neoclassical economics, with names like feminist, ecological, Marxist, institutional, post-Keynesian and stratification economics. However, these approaches are often deemed bad economics, or even different subjects entirely, by the mainstream of the discipline.

Economists who wish to pursue research using these perspectives are often told that they are not economists and find it more difficult to access funding and publish their research. It is clear that the discipline has become narrower and more hostile to different perspectives in the last fifty years. We are now at the point that any significant diversity of knowledge has been eradicated from many university economics departments entirely.

Peer-reviewed academic journals are supposed to guarantee the quality of published research in a discipline. Within economics they are deeply hierarchical, with the top five ranked journals commanding significant status and power. Many top-ranked universities globally will not hire economists who are not likely to publish, or have not already published, in these journals.

Economics journals police what is acceptable research, thereby determining who can get recruited and promoted in university economics departments. They also almost completely neglect to publish research which addresses issues of racialised identity and gender.

The 'specialist' journals that do focus on these topics are much lower ranked, which makes it harder for academics publishing in these journals to get jobs in university economics departments. This creates a systemic disincentive not to engage with racialised identity and gender, which is a key mechanism that drives the underrepresentation of these topics in academic economic research, theory and teaching.

Many neoclassical economists believe that they can be objective observers of the world and therefore that their identity does not matter. We highlight substantial evidence that the identity of economists influences how they think about the economy which in turn leads research, theory and teaching in certain directions and not others.

On this basis, the dominance of men in the global output of economic research, with women accounting for just one in six authorships since 1990, will have clearly influenced the topics, methods and findings of this research.

Tying the argument in this section together, we can see clear connections between the identity of economists, how the academic discipline operates, and the knowledge that is produced. In Chapter 6, we return to explore how reform can attempt to address the deeply embedded and harmful hierarchies in academic economics.

Then we go on to explore how the United States sits at the top of a global hierarchy of academic economics, with the UK and Europe following behind and large parts of the rest of the world not recognised at all.

Status and power in this hierarchy is gained and reproduced through being home to highly ranked economics journals and also through training foreign economists. The US in particular plays an important role in training students from across the world, and qualifications gained there give economists access to jobs in government and international institutions globally.

This role as a global trainer of economists highlights a key mechanism through which the undiverse, uninclusive and hierarchical culture of the discipline in the US influences the global culture of academic economics.

Tracing how economics became internationalised in the twentieth century, led first by Europe and later by the US, gives important historical context. It helps explain why the vast majority of recognised economic research today is created in, and focuses on, Europe and the US and the widespread assumption that this will be applicable to other parts of the world.

As a result, economists from many countries outside the US and Europe are marginalised, struggling to be recognised and to participate meaningfully in the discipline. These deep hierarchies in economics, which directly drive a systematic lack of focus in economic research on gender, racialised identity and countries outside the US and Europe, are not the result of scientific progress or luck. Economics developed in societies which were built on White, male, European supremacy and the status quo today has emerged from that.

In Chapter 3, we return to explore the neoclassical framework, which we have seen dominates academic economics globally, and argue that it is fundamentally unable to make visible, much less address, the structural inequalities which are one of the defining features of modern economies.

We begin by establishing the existence of structural economic inequality. This is not inequality as an outcome of economic competition; it is deep and often intergenerational inequalities in wealth, income and power between groups in society along racialised, gender, caste and class lines and between different countries.

The theoretical foundations of neoclassical economics are unsuitable for addressing structural inequality because they analyse the interaction of individuals in an ahistorical vacuum. As a result, they ignore the historical and social contexts which explain where inequalities come from and how they are reproduced. This means that neoclassical economics is strongly biased towards accepting the status quo. We illustrate these weaknesses and blind spots through considering how neoclassical economics attempts to explain the continued prevalence of racial and gender discrimination today.

Neoclassical economics undermines the case for redistribution by failing to differentiate between the value of consumption to meet basic needs and consumption of luxuries and so it falsely concludes that increasing total output increases social welfare. It explains the distribution of economic resources between different groups based on how productive they are but ignores the role that power, culture and history plays in determining what and who is productive.

Neoclassical economics claims that efficiency should be prioritised in economic management by rewarding different groups according to how much they contribute to production. However, it often fails to achieve this goal because a blind spot when it comes to land means that it doesn't make visible the extent to which modern economies reward simply owning land and other assets rather than any actual contribution to production.

Neoclassical economics conceptualises an equity v. efficiency trade-off, suggesting that efforts to increase equity will distort incentives and create inefficiencies that will decrease productivity and total output. This framing is harmful and has significantly undermined the scope of government economic policy to address structural inequalities. We argue that targeting economic policy to meet basic needs is a better way to achieve the neoclassical goal of maximising social welfare than increasing total output. As a result, there actually often isn't a meaningful trade-off between equity and efficiency.

We end the chapter by returning to the experiences of students who are told that this neoclassical framework is an objective description of the economy and yet realise very clearly how it is unable to describe their experiences of structural inequality.

Chapter 4 turns to the economic history of our world to understand better how today's structural inequality came to be. We begin in 1500, a time when, compared to today, there was much less difference between the material living standards of different regions and societies, across the world. We highlight a graph showing world GDP (Gross Domestic Product)[9] taking off at this point before increasing exponentially. This graph is often known as the hockey stick graph and is widely used in economics education.

The standard story of this transition is that around this time a shift took place, from an economic system called feudalism to capitalism, the system we have today, and it was this innovation which caused the extraordinary increase in economic activity.

The CORE textbook in economics[10] complicates this narrative by highlighting that not all countries took off at the same time or pace, and it highlights examples of countries which were substantially held back by colonial rule or interference by European nations. However, it does not consider the possibility that the economic success of the European countries at this point was a direct result of their violent oppression of other countries.

We argue that the transatlantic slave trade has played an important role in UK and US economic development and, later, the vast amount of land globally that was appropriated by European colonial powers has led to a distribution of resources and power which profoundly shape our global economies to this day. We note that gender and reproductive control were central to the economic organisation of colonies, creating or reinforcing hierarchies which are reproduced in modern structural gender inequalities.

Economic narratives around the two major phases of globalisation between the mid-nineteenth century and World War One, and then after World War Two to the present, highlight the prosperity gained from greater integration through trade, investment, financial markets and regulatory convergence.

In focusing on voluntary exchange for mutual benefit, these narratives underplay the historical role of real or threatened violence that the most powerful countries used to force others to become more integrated with global economies. They also highlight the role of liberal government and inclusivity in explaining a country's economic performance but ignore that for much of this period many European governments were liberal democracies at home and authoritarian, oppressive regimes outside their national borders.

When decolonisation movements won independence from their European colonisers in the twentieth century, former colonisers did all they could to protect the economic resources they had accrued from their colonies. This made it much harder for newly independent countries to compete in the global economy into which they were often forced to integrate.

We note that the phenomenon of reverse reparations, where compensation is provided to the perpetrator rather than the victim of oppression, is a recurring feature of our global economic history, further embedding existing structural inequalities.

Another, underexplored aspect of globalisation is the dynamic by which dominant countries are able to define acceptable economic policy and create systems in which certain behaviour is required in ways which prevent other countries from challenging structural inequalities which are the result of historical oppression.

By ignoring the role that oppression and violence has played in historical economic development, academic economics maintains a fiction that allows it to be ignored in the present. We argue that if

14

these histories are seriously considered then we are forced to reconsider how we think about our modern economies.

We need new economic theories that highlight how violence and oppression undermine people's freedom, the mechanisms through which those with power and wealth are able to protect, grow and pass these advantages across generations, and the deeply embedded racialised dimensions of historical oppression that explain why the wealthier countries in the world tend to be Whiter. Without this, a whitewashed history is being passed on to the next generation of economists through university economics education, and we must do better.

Chapter 5 turns to consider how academic economics undermines democracy and development. We begin by exploring the history of the subdiscipline of development economics, highlighting its birth in efforts to help the 'third world' free itself from 'backwardness', and then its evolution, often mirroring broader shifts in economics and politics, up to the present.

We argue that development economics has become too focused on internal explanations, such as corruption, for the poor economic performance of low-income countries. As a result, it tends to suggest interventions which focus on the symptoms and not root causes of poor economic performance which would require an analysis that incorporated how history and power have reproduced structural inequalities.

Randomised Control Trials (RCTs) are currently the vogue method in development economics having been popularised in the book *Poor Economics* and validated by a Nobel Prize for its authors. While advocates of RCTs claim they are a radical break from previous approaches, we find many continuities including the acceptance of underlying structures as fixed rather than open to challenge. This undermines the ability of RCTs to address poverty and inequality.

We suggest that the whole framework of development and underdevelopment is deeply rooted in a colonial mindset and has been a mechanism through which ideas and values from the US and Europe have been imposed on other parts of the world, through the internationalisation of economics we traced in Chapter 2.

Rather than being a single pathway predetermined by economists and powerful countries, economic development needs to have principles of democracy and self-determination at its core and be led by the people who are doing it so that it reflects their needs, priorities, values and culture.

This leads us to consider the relationship between academic economics and democracy, and we find five deep tensions between the two. They are:

- a tendency to support and legitimise the removal of economic decisions from the sphere of democratically elected government;
- positing that efficiency should be the primary goal of economic policymaking without democratic input;
- analysing democracy through individual choice and therefore ignoring the complex ways in which collective choices and action are debated and enacted in modern societies;
- framing government intervention as often necessary but always second best rather than recognising the key role governments play in the coordination of collective action;
- ignoring the connection between economic and political power which allows those with economic resources to influence economic rules and institutions and individual behaviour.

We end the chapter with three case studies that highlight different ways that economics has contributed to undermining democracy and development in practice. The first presents the economist Dani Rodrik's perspective on the lack of economic policy options available to the government of post-Apartheid South Africa, comparing this with analysis from the writer and campaigner Naomi Klein. Their strikingly different accounts of the same situation highlight clearly the ways in which economic narratives can obscure how a country's ability to determine its own path of economic development is often constrained.

The second considers how quantitative easing in the United States, a supposedly technical policy carried out by the country's independent central bank, deepened racial and gendered wealth inequality with little democratic debate or oversight. This highlights just one way in which economics bypasses democracy but contributes to highly political outcomes.

The third takes us to India to explore how the government and large energy companies justify the building of new coal mines using economic narratives of development in ways which bypass democracy. These decisions impose costs – displacement, ecological damage, loss of culture and community – on local communities and future generations who have no formal way to influence them and so resort to protest and resistance.

Summary of Part II

In Part II of the book, we turn to explore how economics can be reclaimed in order to address what has gone wrong and build a healthier discipline. Chapter 6 makes the case that it is necessary to diversify, decolonise and democratise academic economics (we call this the three Ds).

Diversifying economics is about broadening both the people involved with economics and the knowledge within the discipline. This requires moving from rigid hierarchies where certain groups and countries dominate, towards a more decentralised and egalitarian discipline in which economists better represent the societies they are from and knowledge production addresses local and specific realities including structural inequality and historical oppression. We suggest that this requires a pluralism of theories and methods and a much more interdisciplinary approach, which will require a deep shift in mindset from the current assumption that there is one right way to do economics.

Decolonising economics requires embedding an analysis of history, oppression and power at the foundations of our understanding about how economies operate, which will lead us to new ways of thinking and different economic policies. Decentring knowledge production should include actively seeking and incorporating perspectives from outside the US and Europe, including from Indigenous communities, which will broaden our collective understanding of how economies can be organised to achieve different goals.

We recognise that some argue that the attempt to decolonise knowledge is a distraction, and that attention should be focused on challenging and transforming structural inequalities caused by colonial and racial oppression. In the case of economics, we believe that decolonising knowledge is directly connected with this broader process of decolonisation as the redistribution of resources and power.

As we will see throughout this book, neoclassical economics has largely rejected economic policies which address structurally, the distribution of resources and power. Part of decolonising is to develop theories and policies which effectively and legitimately reset distribution, such as addressing the ownership of land, property, business and financial assets; accumulated wealth; incomes; access to essential goods and services like housing, food, education and health; and writing off debt.

It is also necessary for a decolonised economics to address the deeply unbalanced distribution of economic power because until it does, it leaves in place a key mechanism through which structural inequalities are deepened and reproduced.

At a national level, policies to rebalance power might include: rent controls and increasing the rights of renters to rebalance power between renters and landlords; promoting unions and developing sectoral bargaining, particularly in low wage and informal sectors to rebalance power between workers and employers; and developing wealth and inheritance taxation to prevent economic power accumulating over generations. Internationally, policies might include allowing countries to impose exchange and capital controls and provide subsidies.

A democratised economics would put the principles of democracy and self-determination at the core of economic development, setting goals and developing policies which represent the needs, priorities, values and cultures of the communities who will be affected. It requires recognising that if everyone plays multiple roles in the economy – including carer, worker, owner, saver, investor, citizen and public service user – then everyone has an expertise that stems from their economic experience.

Academic economics needs to engage seriously with this distributed economic knowledge and expertise through developing different research methods and building ongoing relationships and dialogue with different groups in society. This requires a new type of public-interest economist who recognises that decision-making is a social not technical process and therefore the need to 'do *with*, not to or for' citizens. We need a new social contract between experts, politicians and citizens which sets out these shared commitments.

Here it is important to consider power relations and historical oppression so that public interest economists can engage with, represent and advocate for groups with less power. In this way, they could play an important democratic role, scrutinising and redistributing economic power.

What we call for would be an enormous shift for academic economics and right now it feels like the discipline is making very little attempt to engage meaningfully with the issues we're raising here. Transformative change will not come unless the discipline recognises the scale and embeddedness of the problem and really commits to a deep and long-term process of reflection and change.

While we don't have control over the discipline, we acknowledge that change starts within and that there is significant work we are able to do to diversify, decolonise and democratise our own international student movement.

Finally, we turn to consider how the three Ds can be embedded into economics education so that the next generation of economists will be equipped with the knowledge, skills and values needed to transform the discipline and the global economy. This section aims to provide practically useful advice for teachers of economics which can provide a way in to what can otherwise feel like a daunting task.

We suggest eight questions to ask when we set out to teach economics. These are: Who are we teaching? What are we teaching? How do we teach? How do we assess? Who does the teaching? How does research influence our teaching? What challenges do we face? And what opportunities exist? We hope that teachers are excited and energised by this process and are motivated to join a growing international movement committed to embarking on this urgent journey.

In Chapter 7, we argue that it is necessary to reclaim economics as everyday democracy and we set out four possible building blocks or pathways to achieve this goal. First, we highlight how the framing of the economy and long experience of powerlessness and alienation within it are barriers to individuals and communities feeling like they might be able to have any influence over how the economy is organised.

We suggest that it is necessary to reframe the economy and our thinking about agency – the capacity of individuals to act independently and to make their own free choices – for people to believe that it is even possible for societies to decide how to organise their economies democratically.

Then we explore how people might build the power, resources and practices needed to be able to reorganise the economies they live in from the bottom up. We suggest that doing this will generate different economic knowledge and new narratives which will change how we think and act both about our economies and also about democracy.

We argue that this bottom-up approach must be combined with and supported by top-down efforts to build the democratic institutions and practices in local and national government and economic institutions which allow everyday collective decision-making about how to organise economies.

Finally, we explore how all of this needs to be underpinned by a principle of economics education for everyone extending across school and adult education, public service broadcasting and local media and a public-interest role for economists and universities.

The aim of all this is to build the democratic institutions, skills and practices that are necessary to enable everyone to participate in decisions about how the economy they live in is organised. This must be accompanied by decentralisation and redistribution of economic power and resources to ensure nobody is excluded from participating because they are struggling to survive, and to prevent anyone from buying political power they can use to manipulate economic rules and institutions.

Finally, in Chapter 8 we turn to the future. We explore how the organisation of our modern economies has driven some of the biggest global crises the world faces: pandemics and climate and ecological breakdown. We then demonstrate that structural economic inequalities play a significant role in determining who lives and who dies in these crises.

A root cause is part of a system that, at the fundamental level, explains why the system's natural behaviour produces the problem symptoms rather than some other behaviour. Our modern economies are a root cause of systemic racism and sexism, socioeconomic inequality and the ecological crisis.

When our economies are rooted in a set of principles that values whiteness, maleness and wealth, we should not be surprised by the inequalities that show up. Structural inequalities need systemic change, change that infiltrates through every level of the system, otherwise we risk reproducing and deepening them.

We conclude that our modern economies are unjust, illegitimate and destructive. This is particularly harmful for those who are deprived of the resources needed to secure a basic standard of living, but ultimately it harms us all. Transformational economic systems change is necessary to address the ecological crisis and the systemic inequality that is embedded deeply into our economies, both of which are tearing our world apart. It is necessary for our generation to survive and flourish and to have a world to pass on to our children and grandchildren.

In the past few years, young people and climate activists across generations worldwide have taken part in the Fridays For Future school climate strikes. They call for 'justice for those who have been the most affected by climate change' and clearly identify how structural inequalities impact who is harmed. They also highlight the importance of 'centring the voices of Black, Brown and Indigenous People, who for centuries have been resisting the systems that eventually led us to this situation today'.[11]

We wholeheartedly support the call to create economies that are built on regeneration and care, not extraction from people or the planet. To achieve this, we must all do battle where we are standing to reclaim economics for racial justice, gender equality and future generations.

Part I

What has gone wrong with economics?

Chapter 1

Undiverse and uninclusive

*With contributions from Ariane Agunsoye,
Michelle Groenewald, Danielle Guizzo
and Bruno Roberts-Dear*

At the age of sixteen, Francesca Rhys-Williams, a contributor to this book, decided she wanted to study economics; however, it was not a subject option available at her high school, so she went to another school for her economics course. She was surprised to find the class included few women.

The lack of gender diversity in economics is well documented. According to a basic search of the Research Papers in Economics database, women make up only a quarter of academic economists worldwide.[1]

Economics in government and international institutions is similarly dominated by men. For example, of 173 central banks globally, only fourteen were headed by women in 2019, up from twelve the previous year.[2]

In this chapter, we demonstrate that women, people of colour and less socioeconomically privileged people are significantly underrepresented in academic economics and become progressively less represented further along the career ladder from undergraduate to senior professor. For example, in US economics departments, one in three assistant professors are women but only one in six full professors are.[3]

We highlight the lived consequences of this lack of diversity and inclusivity through focus groups with high-school students and interviews with people at different life stages who are under-represented in the discipline, including university students and academic economists (a full list of interviewees is provided in the Appendices). Hearing people underrepresented in economics express their experience of and relationship with the subject helps us to understand the stories behind the statistics.

In highlighting this problem, we focus on the United States and the United Kingdom because, as we show in the next chapter, the former dominates the global discipline of economics today and the latter has historically. Practically, focusing our argument on two countries gives us the necessary space to go into more depth. However, throughout the chapter we weave in stories and statistics from other countries, which suggests that this pattern is repeated in economics globally, playing out in different ways according to local history and culture. This view is supported by the testimony of interviewees we spoke to from countries across the world including India, Chile, Finland, South Korea, South Africa, Guyana, Brazil and Malaysia.

In the next chapter we explore the mechanisms by which the lack of diversity and inclusivity in US economics is exported to other countries across the world because of the position of the US, at the top of a global hierarchy of economics.

Barriers to becoming an economist

In this section, we explore the barriers young people from backgrounds and identities that are underrepresented in economics face to study economics at university. Collectively, they are an important part of the reason that academic economics in the UK and US lacks diversity.

26

What is economics?

As an outsider, one of the first hurdles to becoming an economist is even knowing what it is. We held focus groups with ethnically diverse students from two non-fee-paying mixed-sex high schools in the UK who did have the opportunity to study A Level economics at their school (only about half of UK non-fee-paying and non-selective school students have that opportunity).[4]

Many focus group students only had a vague understanding of the subject, and consequently were deterred from opting to study it, such as fourteen-year-old Beth who remarked: 'I need more knowledge about it … what I think of immediately in my mind is a pie chart and a calculator … You have to commit yourself to something that you have not done, ever.'

Barbara, a seventeen-year-old student studying an A Level in Economics, also remarked how not knowing anyone in economics can affect a student's choice to study it and that, 'There's a lot of mainly White people in economics, because they have maybe family friends that study economics. They'll know more about the subject.' So even at this age, there's awareness of a lack of student diversity in the subject.

As students in the UK choose their first formal examined subjects (GCSEs) at age 13–14, with some choosing at age 12–13, those like Beth and Barbara have no way to find out whether economics is something they would enjoy or be good at, and often believe that they do not have sufficient knowledge about the subject to pursue its study.

We know that over two-thirds of British undergraduate economics students in 2018–2019 studied economics at A Level[5] and it is the key route into economics at university.[6] However, half of non-selective, non-fee-paying schools offered economics at A Level in

2017, compared to three-quarters of fee-paying schools and four-fifths of selective non-fee-paying grammar schools.[7] As a result, economics education is harder to access in the UK if you come from a less socioeconomically privileged background.

Our interviews with university economics students and professionals also highlight the role of a person's familial and social networks supporting them at the start of their study of economics (and this is potentially even more important for people from underrepresented backgrounds). For example, student interviewees from a range of identities[8] mentioned they had family members or knew of people (mostly men) who worked in economics or in a related field.

Alex from a low-income background in North America talked about their lack of understanding of what economics was when they were growing up:

> Economics, at least around where I grew up, was never taught in schools. Coming to university, economics was an entirely new thing [and] from a background of not having anyone in my life who had a professional career or who had been to university, it was very new … When I chose to study economics, I had no idea what an economist did. I just knew economics is resource allocation and that's what I wanted to do … I got into economics as I have this drive to relieve the barriers that people face to self-sufficiency and just living … And I knew I wanted to influence government public policy to make things easier for already marginalised people.

To become an economist, you need to know what economics is and seek it out. That most commonly happens through family networks and schools. Others, like Alex, are drawn to it through their life experiences. Young people often have a curiosity about the world and many of their questions are economic in nature. This can be a strong motivating factor to want to study economics, even if, as in Alex's case, they had not engaged with it in school.

Erika, who identifies as Japanese American and middle class with working-class family members, recalled the life her grandmother experienced on a low income with cancer as being a motivating factor for choosing economics, as she wondered at that time:

> How does she live? Until I realised 'Oh, she lives on social security. How does that work? How did she get her medical bills paid for? How does social security work and what, who gets it and what do we think about that?' I wanted to understand that more.

However, as we will see later, what is often taught in economics does not reflect the lives lived by people such as Erika's grandmother and Alex's family.

Economics is too mathematical

The idea that economics is very mathematical and technical is often cited as a barrier to increasing diversity in economics. Participants of our UK focus groups highlighted this feeling, describing economics as 'the maths side of business', 'the mathematical side of money', 'the money side of business' or focused on 'graphs, statistics and maths'. These views are also widely held by 15–17-year-olds across the UK according to recent research by the Royal Economic Society's Women's Committee.[9]

A minority in our focus groups defined economics in a broader way, suggesting that it is 'about our government, the people around us and what we and communities can control', and 'how people use money to influence how our environment is'.

The focus on maths, graphs and the language used in economics was perceived to be a barrier by some of the 16–17-year-old focus group participants who were studying economics. In their conversation, three students expressed their apprehensions.

Emmanuel: The graphs. We have about 50 different graphs. We studied it for about 6 weeks, and we've already got 50 different graphs ... There's a lot to remember ... So, if it's just been for six weeks, I would be doing that for two years. It's tough.

Barbara: I agree. There are quite a lot of graphs. It does make sense I'd want to then like the writing part of it.

Daniel: It's the terminology that they are using now which I do not understand ... When we are talking about demands – I just do not get it.

The sentiment of economics being 'too technical' or 'maths-focused' was also held by some undergraduate students in economics before they chose to study it at university. Emilia from Finland studying in the UK, Anna from Denmark, and Luis from Mexico who studied in the US, all highlighted this view.

While some suggest that girls and women are put off economics by the maths, this claim is not supported by the evidence.[10] Rather than innately disadvantaging any group, the mathematical and graphical reasoning in economics and the technical jargon are another barrier to entry, which certain groups are supported to master in school and family life, e.g. boys being told they are good at maths, while other groups of young people have much more to do individually or have to catch up when they get to university.

Economics isn't for people like me

Even if you find out what economics is and are drawn to it despite the maths, another barrier is feeling, or being told, that it isn't for people like you. Stereotypes about what kind of people are economists develop early in life. Many of our 13–14-year-old focus group students weren't aware of what economics was and yet still made links to particular gender and racial identities when they visualised an economist. Cara, aged 13–14 years old, observed, 'Well, whenever you go into central London, and you see all these people in suits, they are usually young White men, who you think have just come out of university, getting a job, and they are quite formal, they look intelligent.'

Images of men who are White and wealthy were prevalent among the 16–17-year-old focus groups as well as ideas about economists being intelligent, 'posh' and 'middle class'. When asked to draw an economist, Olivia explained her decision: 'I associate economics with businessmen. So I drew him in a suit because people working in business places are usually very professional, so they have suits and briefcases and smartphones because they're up to date with technology and stuff like that.'

Another student, Fiona, explained what shaped her view of economists. 'I saw this video that showed 100 of the top CEOs and it kept showing the faces of the CEOs and you could consecutively see them as a White, middle-aged man.' Nina, from this focus group, felt that the perceptions of economists as White, wealthy men could be a barrier or incentive for other groups:

People were saying how it was just middle-aged, White men [as] CEOs, people like other, younger, White males are likely to look up to them and want to be like them, or follow in their footsteps, and because there is no representation, then obviously people of colour might not be as inspired to follow in that path. But at the same time, because there are no ethnic role models in the industry, other ethnic people might want to get into that industry so they can be role models for other people.

While breaking through a glass ceiling can be a motivating factor to succeed in economics, as we shall see, underrepresented students and professionals face many challenges to thriving in the discipline.

Bea, a British economics postgraduate, went to an all-girls school. After she finished her high-school exams she was really interested in economics, but her school didn't teach it. She ended up going to the boys' school next door to study economics, the class was two-thirds boys, and while she eventually got used to their domination in class, she almost decided 'actually, I don't want to pursue economics'.

A British undergraduate student, Gina, further highlighted the dominance of men in economics as a potential barrier to studying it at university.

> In terms of being a woman, before I came to uni I read stuff about the percentage of women studying economics, so I thought 'in my course I'm probably going to be one of nine females who study economics' ... it's quite intimidating if you're in a class and there's just so many boys. In my high school classes, I barely ever talked in some of them because there were so many boys ... they just dominated!

Such views about the dominance of men in economics were not restricted to British students of economics, as Danish postgraduate student Anna remarked: 'Yes, the barriers [to economics] would be like being a woman studying in a field that is male-dominated.'

Priya, an Indian UK-based postdoctoral researcher, highlighted the doubts voiced because she was a woman who decided to pursue postgraduate studies in economics after her first degree in India. This occurred despite her identifying as coming from a privileged middle-class background:

> When I decided to do a master's the question would come up, 'Oh, so what do you want to do after? When do you want to settle down?

When are you going to get married?' In a way that's not the worst barrier in the world, it's just that as a social thing it happened so often that I feel that if I didn't have the support of my family, my parents and a few friends, then it's easy to kind of fall into that place of, 'okay I don't need to aspire to that much, I am okay with what I am doing.'

A pattern of courage and resilience emerges from the stories of these women who all decided to pursue economics despite the barriers they faced because of their gender identity.

This desire not to accept the dominance of men in economics was again highlighted by Erika who we heard from earlier. They spoke more of what made them choose to study economics at university:

it was not what I was supposed to do, or it was not something I was supposed to understand … I think I was really tired in high school of being in those political conversations like Leader Competitions and there'd be this condescending privileged White boy that would be like: 'Well you're wrong' and [I'm] like: 'Aargh!!!' I didn't want to be talked to in that way and I thought: 'Well maybe I should level up?'

Access to university

A concrete barrier for many people in the US, UK and across the world is accessing university education. For example, Isabel (an academic economist) highlighted that even when overcoming the lack of exposure to economics, individuals from lower-income backgrounds still face financial challenges in accessing university:

My older sister was in college at the time and so I was conscious of finances. And so, whereas I could have gone to an Ivy League school, I set my sights lower because I was worried about my parents' ability to finance college education, to have two students in college at the same time.

In many countries, going to university is simply not an affordable option for much of the population, and where material deprivation is correlated with a racialised identity, caste, tribe or religion then certain groups in society will be more excluded from accessing higher education.

In some countries, governments have increased fees and/or reduced the level of financial support they offer in recent years, making it more difficult for young people from historically excluded backgrounds to attend university.

Rachel, an academic economist, highlighted the impact of income and wealth inequality on who became an economist in their home country:

> the government of [where I was born] was starting to nebulise public education and so subsidies that had been available ... to lower income families like mine were no longer there and so the biggest challenge for me was more financial ... I'm sure that there were many other people who perhaps never went to university not because they weren't intellectually able, but because they couldn't afford to go ... that's something that sometimes gets lost in discussions around what kinds of barriers women or ethnic minorities face ... sometimes those barriers are not necessarily because of race or gender ... but also what the material constraints of being low-income just places on your ability to take advantage of a university education.

Access to education was the dominant motive of the #FMF (Fees Must Fall) protests that emerged in South Africa from 2015 because higher education significantly improves a young person's chance of finding employment in the country. The South African government was reducing funding to higher education while costs in the tertiary education sector were rising and students felt they were being squeezed out of the system. This inaccessibility hit Black students the hardest and therefore reproduced the same racial exclusion of low-income Black students as was the case during Apartheid.

Even when the university system offers free or relatively free education as in the case of Germany, there still remains the issue of being able to maintain oneself. This is highlighted by Sofia, a German professor of economics, in the case of families who have migrated to the country: 'From Germany, I know that a lot of immigrant children will probably not go to university, partly because if it's too far away from them, possibly they can't afford it.'

In some cases, financial insecurity means students take on several part-time jobs under which academic performance often suffers, reinforcing inequalities between wealthier and less wealthy students. One of the contributors to this book often teaches students struggling to keep up with coursework because they are juggling job responsibilities.

Financial issues at home affected Noel, now a professional economist, when he was at school:

> paying the bills, trying to stay afloat, so because of issues at home, sometimes I'd come late to class, and let's say my maths teacher, for example, rather than trying to think 'Why are you late?', they automatically assumed I wasn't interested, was disengaged and I didn't want to be here.

The same book contributor believes teachers should adjust to what responsibilities their students have and take this into consideration in coursework and deadlines as well as help where possible. However, they are clear that these individual solutions are ultimately not enough to enable many financially insecure students to succeed in their education and that they need more financial support.

Access to university is not just determined by finances. The extra-curricular activities like internships and volunteering that strengthen an application to study economics at university also often require resources and networks to access.

Gina, a Black economics student in the UK we heard from earlier, spoke about attending a school where these opportunities were not tailored to people like her.

> There is a scholarship from the Bank of England and it's an opportunity specifically for African and Caribbean students. And where I studied before university did not tell me about this. One of my friends sent me the link on social media. That's the downside of going to these quite elite schools. It was a non-fee-paying school, but it was very White, very middle-class and quite selective ... because you're a minority, they don't look for opportunities that are open to you.

These are the barriers to studying economics at university that our interviewees and focus group participants highlighted. There will inevitably be others we haven't covered and they'll affect different people in different countries in different ways. But collectively these barriers make it much harder for many young people from backgrounds and identities that are underrepresented in economics to ever make it to university to study the subject.

Economics at university

In this section, we explore the experience of economics at university for students and academics from backgrounds and identities that are underrepresented in the discipline. The experiences we share highlight an environment that is deeply uninclusive. They go a long way to explaining why economics becomes progressively less diverse the further along the career ladder you look, with White, relatively privileged men dominating the most senior, highest status, 'superstar' roles in the discipline.

Economics is for the privileged

A common barrier at university that emerged for some of the students interviewed was the theme that economics did not reflect the lived experiences of students from non-privileged backgrounds.

Erika, who we heard from earlier, spoke of the assumption that economics educators make about students' social class and lived experiences:

> being in a classroom … I feel often it's assumed that we come from and we'll go on to privileged places. So when professors are like: 'All of you guys in this economics classroom are going to probably get your banking jobs and you probably don't have any student loans, you probably come from wealthier backgrounds because most of the school does' … it's not really about the discussion of economics, but just the assumption of who makes up a classroom of economics students.

Alex highlighted how getting used to the privileged lifestyle embedded in university economics education was a challenge for someone coming from poverty and a working-class background.

> I was like trying to learn this new language … not just a new language of economics, but a new language of a privileged lifestyle … Economics education just does not account for those barriers that I've lived and that I know are barriers to living the kind of life that economics implies.

This failure to engage with or explain the economic experiences of certain groups in society was particularly difficult for many of our interviewees who were explicitly motivated to study economics to address these questions. Here is Erika again:

> Growing up going over to my aunt's house and my cousins and I would go on a round to the store to get the ingredients to get dinner … they would use their food stamps, tell me how they were embarrassed in

front of me and my brother, even though we were cousins … If there was just more of a conversation in the classroom that felt like you were really getting people from different lived experiences, so they'd see these topics at every angle. I don't really necessarily feel like we get this now. I feel like social security and all these welfare programs are talked about in a way that seems like it has nothing to do with anyone in the class. And I think that we could really gain from interacting with them more.

Jessica from Canada, who identified as being from a middle-class background, observed how the social backgrounds of their peers affected their experiences at university:

university is a place of privilege. There are people that would certainly not be here if they weren't on a scholarship. But then there are also kids that are: 'I'm here because like my rich dad forced me and all I do is smoke weed and never go to class.' So, everybody has a different story, but wealth plays into that … Then there are people that I know that go to the food bank every week because that's how they eat. They're in economics because they're super passionate about it and some international students are from a part of the world where it was a huge opportunity and a gift to come and study here which they recognise. But they just don't come from money and that affects their experience.

My education doesn't represent me

Linked to Erika's previous point, a lack of diversity in who studies and works in economics leaves some feeling underrepresented. One of our academic economist interviewees, Rachel, a US-based Black African woman, told us: 'In mainstream economics, I don't see myself represented at all, or if I do, it's very much a sort of caricature in terms of the "poor downtrodden African woman".'

Michelle, a contributor to this book, teaches economics in South Africa:

it is highly possible that economics students in South Africa can go their whole undergraduate [and sometimes] postgraduate degrees having never even heard of a single African economist, or for that matter even a single female economist. Having taught final year undergraduate development economics to a class of about 150 students, I had asked students at the beginning of the semester to name me a single female economist. In the majority of cases, they could not name a single female economist. When I had asked if they could name me a single economist from the Global South [lower income countries south of North America, Europe and Russia] they could not name any.

An economics graduate, Michaela, highlights this absence:

A lot of the economics that we are taught is one-dimensional ... it doesn't touch upon the intersections between race or gender or anything like that ... a lot of the focus is on Western countries ... when it comes to things like the African continent or places like South America or the Caribbean who are equally as important to the global economy, we're not taught about that. And if we are taught about that, it's an optional module. It's not a core subject.

Economics textbooks are generic and feature examples focused on Europe and the US. When exceptions do occur, as Hiba, a Sudanese postgraduate who studied in the UK put it, economics usually refers to the same stereotypical examples such as 'Kenyan coffee workers, or Ethiopian sugar farms ... They represent the farmers as a group or the workers as a group ... It wasn't necessarily very new because it's like the face of global poverty is definitely, you know, Africa!'

Gina, who we heard from earlier, studies the subject at a leading UK university:

To this day I haven't learned about a Black economist. Like I know Arthur Lewis was a Black economist, that's the only one I know of. I haven't heard of another Black economist, let alone a Black female economist! ... So I get why there aren't a lot of Black people in economics because there's no representation.

Seventy students from eleven universities and six provinces who participated in the annual Rethinking Economics for Africa Festival in 2019 shared their views on how economics is not adequately able to deal with a range of issues they experience. They felt that their education just wasn't relevant to a country like South Africa – the conference's host nation – where economic inequality is the highest in the world; more than half of the youth working age population are unemployed; and there are significant gender inequalities that continue to exclude women from the economy. We return to explore the failure of economics to address structural inequalities in more detail in Chapter 3.

My teachers don't represent me

Anila, a Sudanese student studying a master's in Economics in the UK, felt that their department was dominated by rich, White men, followed by White women, and that no professors were African nor of African origin, despite the inclusion of African-specific courses within the course programme. They firmly believed this was wrong as:

> there needs to be some sort of fair representation ... in the context of teaching students, the fact that [they] appoint a French professor really to teach African microeconomics, couldn't they find any better African professor who has done much research work and has the credentials because these people do exist. They're just not included in the same way in academia ... It feels like: 'Hey we're trying to help you and this is what we think you should do', but you're not even from there and you don't fully get the context.

Intersectional data on the gender, racialised identity and socio-economic background of academic economists in the US and UK illustrates clearly that many students will have no one from their background within economics to look up to or feel supported by.

For example, in the US one in four tenured or tenure-track economists is a woman, but only one in sixteen is either Black, Latinx or Native American.[11] Barriers faced by women and people of colour in economics are magnified for women of colour and have to be overcome at every stage through education to becoming a full professor.

Of all women who were awarded economics PhDs in 2018/19, only 8 per cent were from ethnic minorities, while about 30 per cent of all women in the US are from minorities.[12] The percentage of minority women who obtained PhDs that year drastically drops when it is related to the total number of PhDs awarded to all men, women and ethnicities, i.e. to just under 1 per cent.[13]

In India in 2018/2019 just under 50 per cent of all PhD students were women,[14] but a recent report has found that only 15 out of 512 faculty members of Indian Institutes of Management (where research focuses on finance, economics, marketing and management) came from the most socially marginalised groups in society and nobody was from an Indigenous background.[15] Therefore, it is very unlikely that women from more disadvantaged socioeconomic or caste backgrounds will be taught by or know of any economists with a similar identity.

In UK universities, intersectional data reveal similar gaps in representation in economic research roles (see Table 1.1). Black Caribbean and Pakistani people are also the least likely to teach economics in UK universities.[16]

As we write there are no Black women of African or Caribbean descent who are professors of economics at any UK university.[17] This is part of a systemic problem in UK universities in which there are only twenty-five Black British women professors.[18]

41

Table 1.1   *Diversity among research economists in UK universities by racialised identity and gender*

Identity	Percentage of research staff in UK universities
Black Caribbean men	0.12 per cent
Bangladeshi women	0.25 per cent
Pakistani women	0.58 per cent

Source: Advani, Sen and Warwick, *Ethnic Diversity in UK Economics*

Power in the classroom

We've already seen how the perception that economics is dominated by White men was a barrier to deciding to study the subject at university, but what was the reality like for our interviewees? For many the perceptions of a lack of gender diversity were confirmed. In the UK, only a quarter of academic staff in economics at twenty-four of the most prestigious universities (known as the Russell Group) during the 2018/2019 academic year were women.[19] Women undergraduates at a sample of sixteen of these universities represented just one third of students in 2018/2019.[20]

Hearing about women's experiences in a classroom and subject dominated by men can help us to understand why some of them do not pursue careers in economics and internalise gender-based discrimination. Nurul, a postgraduate Malaysian student in the UK, indicates below how the dominance of men in economics can create gender, power and knowledge imbalances in the classroom:

> Sometimes, in the lecture hall, when someone has a question and a guy says it, I feel like that has more weight than a girl raising her hand to say something that is equally right and equally true. I feel like the guy has much more credibility to what he's saying, whereas the girl, I feel like she's just putting her hand up and then she's saying something that is less functional.

This bias then shapes and reinforces ideas about who can be an economist. Laura, a postgraduate student in Austria, said:

> I had the feeling that we mostly had male professors and I don't know if consciously or not consciously, but that impacts the image for myself, like, the elderly White man still has the knowledge which they give to their students, the image of who can be or who represents economists. For me that's still mostly male.

In the US in 2016 nearly a quarter of economics professors and a third of undergraduate degree students were women, in a pattern that matches the UK's very closely.[21]

This dominance of men in US universities contributes to even women with a deep commitment to economics questioning whether they belong. Taylor, an undergraduate student in the US, explained:

> I feel like I belong because it's something that I'm very passionate about. But there's always the thought at the back of my head where it's like: 'Oh, but they're not going to listen to you, they're not going to actually take you seriously because you're a woman.'

A parallel experience of studying economics was reported by many student interviewees of colour. Here Lee, a student from South Korea studying in the US, voiced their feeling of how their sense of identity directly affects their sense of belonging in economics:

> So, I didn't feel welcomed in the major or welcomed in the classroom ... I think as a South-Korean male in the classroom, I often find myself ... asking questions and answering questions, sitting in the front row, to try to differentiate myself from the general population of the class-room. I often question whether I am fuelling the stereotype of Asian male, or Asian students in general in the classroom ... The fact that a part of my mental capacity has to be taken up with those thoughts is a loss on my academic progress in the classroom, and just how I spend my time in the class. I think that is something that a lot of people of colour, students deal with in these situations. It will be nicer if our

attention span could be spent elsewhere than simply thinking: 'Oh, am I being too stereotypical?'

Kim, a South East Asian student also studying in the US, noticed that as a person with her ethnic background she felt more accepted within her faculty compared to US-domiciled students of colour:

> Other people of colour that took economics and that I've talked to, like Latinx and Black students, have mentioned how uncomfortable they've been in classes. I can't really speak for them, but I feel like their experiences are much different to mine. It really ties in with the 'Asians being the model minority'. There is a connection between that and how professors treat me, like 'Asian versus other students of colour'.

The importance of peer support between students of colour or those who are generally less represented in economics was highlighted by interviewees. Anna, from an immigrant family of colour and working-class background, who had studied economics at postgraduate level, noted:

> I think barriers were more racial because they are not so used to seeing someone like me [at this university]. But it was easier because I've got some friends who are also people of colour, so [we] supported each other.

The overwhelming theme to come out from the majority of our interviews is that economics classrooms, departments, and the universities they sit within are experienced by women, people of colour and those from working-class backgrounds as predominantly White, populated by men, and economically privileged spaces.

Wealthy, White men are at the top of a clear and fixed hierarchy of people in economics. Emma from Denmark identified the dominance of White men in class during their postgraduate studies in the UK and the failure of teaching staff to challenge this:

Throughout the year I saw a development where we went from everyone is kind of active, to only or predominantly the White men in the room are active ... If I'm not in a classroom where [professors] are aware that some people walk in there with having the experience of being taught and congratulated when speaking up and others have been caricatured when speaking up ... if you don't try to deconstruct that and deal with that in the classroom, then people become silent, including myself, because it turned out to be yet another room where White men felt more comfortable speaking up.

Similarly, Hiba, a postgraduate in economics from Sudan previously quoted in this chapter, was aware of what they perceived to be an innate self-assurance by their peers who were White men and the effect this had upon their own studies in the UK:

I felt that other students who were White and male felt a lot more confident in class, whether to ask questions, or to answer questions, or to even argue ... I just didn't feel like that. But I don't know where to place that, whose fault is that?

Hiba and Emma's experiences highlight how important it is for faculty teaching staff to be trained to be able to support all students to feel their voice counts, especially those whose identities are underrepresented in economics.

Discrimination

A number of our interviewees highlighted witnessing and experiencing discrimination. Here's Emma again:

One particular professor ... not intentionally, but the consequences of his teaching was sexist ... whenever a woman was presenting, we would all get way more criticism. There was a particular experience where a classmate of mine, who maybe presents [themselves] as the most feminine and is also one of the only women of colour in the

45

classroom, studied a lot for a presentation. She gave a presentation with two White men from the UK who are both middle-class at least, I think maybe upper-middle class would be appropriate. She just got torn apart by this professor, while the two others got congratulated and got into an intellectual discussion with him.

Discrimination based on racialised identity is prevalent in the US. In 2019, the American Economic Association (AEA) surveyed just over ten thousand of its members[22] and found 'that nearly half (47 per cent) of Black economists [reported] being discriminated against or treated unfairly in the profession based on their racialised identity'. In comparison, one in four Asians, one in six Latinx, and one in twenty White survey respondents report discrimination or unfair treatment. Perceptions of having one's racialised identity respected within the field also contrasted greatly. While three out of four non-Black survey respondents believed that economists of their race/ethnicity are respected in the field, only one in five Black respondents believed the same.[23]

In the same survey, nearly half of women and one in three men said that they have witnessed gender-based discrimination.[24]

In 2020 the US macroeconomist Claudia Sahm published a viral blogpost[25] documenting a variety of abusive and discriminatory behaviours in the discipline, especially towards women and minoritised groups highlighting the toxic culture of economics.

The AEA has established a Code of Professional Conduct and several other initiatives recognising that the marginalisation of people based on their identity 'damages the field as a whole by limiting the diversity of perspectives and dissuading talented people from becoming economists'.[26] Claudia Sahm argues that the AEA's response is well-meaning but falls short in its implementation.[27]

Francis and Opoku-Agyeman argue that the AEA hasn't put enough priority or resources into these initiatives, pointing out that it 'spends more money on website upkeep than on a [summer] program that has accounted for nearly 20 per cent of all PhDs awarded to minorities in economics'.[28]

There is important acknowledgement of the toxic culture of economics in many parts of the discipline. In the US, more than 80 per cent of women respondents and 60 per cent of men respondents agree that economics would be a more vibrant discipline if it were more inclusive.[29]

However, considerable parts of the profession still refuse to acknowledge that there is a systemic problem, as highlighted by internet forums like the US Economics Job Market Rumors and this response to the AEA survey:

> I am saddened by the AEA's decision to undertake such a survey, with such loaded questions that seem aimed at a predetermined outcome, namely that we allegedly need to focus on anything other than determining economic truths, as best we can. I am concerned that the push that lies behind this survey will alter the climate in economics in a negative fashion, by discouraging the field's long-standing emphasis on challenging our colleagues to defend their work in seminars, etc. … The temperament behind this survey is not that of the discipline I entered almost … years ago, which had earned the title of Queen of the Social Sciences. Rather, the temperament behind this survey is that of the degraded, politicized, non-disciplinary departments and programs which have either been invented or corrupted over the last several decades …[30]

Similarly, it is concerning that while only one in six women economists in the US feel their gender is respected in economics, half of men feel that women are respected.[31] Men in economics, like many areas of life, appear unwilling to listen to the experiences and concerns of women.

It appears that there is rarely much pressure from universities for economics to clean up its act. One recent example of this is illustrative. Harald Uhlig is a professor of economics at Chicago University and the lead editor of a prestigious economics journal. After the Black Lives Matter protests in the US in 2020, Uhlig tweeted the following:

> Black Lives Matter just torpedoed itself, with its full-fledged support of 'defund the police'. George Floyd and his family really didn't deserve being taken advantage of by flat-earthers and creationists. Oh well. Time for sensible adults to enter back into the room and have serious, earnest, respectful conversations about it all.[32]

It later surfaced that Uhlig had written a blog in 2017 in which he compared pro-athletes taking a knee to 'football players waving the confederate flag and dressing in Ku Klux Klan garb' during the national anthem in what is an outrageous case of false equivalence.[33]

After these posts came to light, Professor Bocar Ba reported that when he was a student in Uhlig's class, Uhlig hosted a lecture on Martin Luther King Day (a federal holiday in the US), joked about it, and directed his joke at Ba. This was corroborated by others in the class and Uhlig was then suspended as editor of the *Journal of Political Economy* while the University of Chicago 'investigated' the problem for a week before he was reinstated. Uhlig later said that he was sorry that his tweet 'appears to have caused irritation'. This non-response from the University of Chicago is supported by its discrimination policy:

> A person's subjective belief that behavior is intimidating, hostile, or offensive does not make that behavior harassment. The behavior must be objectively unreasonable. Expression occurring in an academic, educational or research context is considered a special case and is broadly protected by academic freedom. Such expression will not constitute harassment unless (in addition to satisfying the above

definition) it is targeted at a specific person or persons, is abusive, and
serves no bona fide academic purpose.[34]

This definition is so restrictive that it cannot even address the racism in Uhlig's comments, much less the many more subtle forms of racism we have encountered in economics.

While universities are unequipped to address all forms of racism and other kinds of discrimination, the toxic culture of economics will continue to be reproduced.

Sexual harassment

Experiences of sexual harassment and gender-based violence (GBV) were raised by two women interviewees. The first, Carmella, an Italian professor of economics, remembers:

There was sexual harassment where I studied as an undergraduate, there was a lot of it, it was obvious. And there were a lot of professors, they were all male, pretty much, who were misbehaving massively, and I never really saw anything done in the system to make sure this didn't happen.

While an anonymous undergraduate in economics shared their story of GBV at university:

I was sexually assaulted by someone in the economics department. And even though it's happened off campus, it still very much impacts my campus experience ... I got a ton of support from the university, from the department ... because the perpetrator was in economics, it did make me feel really supported to be a woman who has faced this adversity but now with this support is able to overcome that and still exist as a woman in economics.

These two accounts contrast in the response from the university and economics department and illustrate the role culture and

institutions play in shaping the experience of women who are sub-
jected to sexual violence.

Worryingly, such experiences are not isolated. The 2019 AEA
survey found that one in fifty women economists who responded
said another economist or economics student had sexually
assaulted them, and one in twenty women respondents said
another economist or economics student had attempted to sexually
assault them.[35] Nearly a quarter of women respondents reported
that an economics colleague or students made unwanted attempts
to establish a dating, romantic, or sexual relationship with them
despite their efforts to discourage it.

Imposter syndrome

Even where there isn't explicit racism or sexism, the toxic culture
of economics appears to generate quite systematically a feeling
of imposter syndrome among many women and people of colour. When you are low status in a hierarchical group, you have to
do much more to prove yourself than those at the top and you're
always fighting for your right to be in the space.

To Nicola Scott, one of this book's contributors, she too felt this
imposter syndrome at university. When she was awarded her PhD,
scholarship related to international trade and economic policymaking, she was told by a White middle-class man she knew that
she probably received funding to fill a quota because of her minoritised ethnic status. In hindsight, she internalised that comment
throughout her PhD, especially as during it she saw no women of
colour role models in her faculty who were also the first in their
family to go to university. Nicola felt an imposter within academia,
that her research was not good enough – that she was not good
enough for it.

This sense of feeling inadequate within academia based on one's identity was highlighted by a few of the professional economists we interviewed. For example, Michaela, a Black British-African woman from a working-class background who is a UK Civil Service economist, explained 'You're second guessing yourself and you're not sure what you're producing is good enough.' While Zara, a White, middle-class woman, who is a UK based advisor on economics and equality issues stated:

> Whenever I try to talk to [people] that aren't specifically interested in feminist economics, there are all sorts of barriers … At some point [I] feel like I lack confidence because the first thing I said to you is: 'I'm not an economist'.

Diverging pathways in the UK

In the UK there is an 'elite' group of twenty-four universities called the Russell Group with their prestige coming from their histories and academic reputation. Most of these universities offer undergraduate economics education.

Our research has found that only 2.3 per cent of undergraduate economics students at Russell Group universities were from the lowest-income families[36] in 2018/2019 despite this group representing about 6 per cent of the population. In stark contrast, 41 per cent of undergraduate economics students at these universities came from the highest earning households in the country despite this group making up only 1 per cent of the population.

Economics students and academics in Russell Group universities are less likely to be people of colour. While half of White academic economists work in Russell Group universities, just one-third of Pakistani and Bangladeshi academic economists and less than one-fifth of Black academic economists do. Compared to their White peers, ethnic minority economists employed in Russell Group universities are 45 per cent less likely to hold a professorial or managerial role.[37]

Bangladeshi and Pakistani students are half as likely to study economics at Russell Group universities as White students are; Black students are about 60 per cent less likely to.[38] Our data for 2018/2019 from the London School of Economics shows that of all 729 economics undergraduate students, only seven were Black.[39] The number of Black students studying economics to master's or PhD level in the same year at this university was zero.

There are large and persistent 'attainment gaps' between White and ethnic minority economics students: ethnic minority students are 7 per cent less likely to get at least an upper-second-class honours degree and 11 per cent less likely to get a first-class honours degree.[40] These gaps have widened since 2012–2013 and clearly shape what further study and career options economics students from ethnic minorities have.

Here we highlight just one example of how these diverging pathways shape career opportunities for different students in the UK. The UK civil service has a Government Economic Service (GES), which has roughly trebled in size in the twenty-first century and now employs about 1,600 economists. It is the largest employer of economists in the UK and employs many graduates.

If we explore figures linked to the UK's Civil Service Fast Stream application process, the overrepresentation of Oxbridge graduates is evident among appointments made to its analytical schemes, which includes the GES.[41] The rate of such graduates with successful applications was one in five in 2018.[42] This compares to the success rate of applicants from Russell Group university graduates excluding Oxbridge totalling 1 in 20, and only 1 in 50 from non-Russell group universities in 2018.[43]

These figures from the Civil Service mirror those specifically from the GES's Fast Stream recruitment round of 2016. That year four-fifths of completed applications were received from those with a higher social class status, with 87 per cent of successful applicants coming from this group.[44]

Looking at the student experience in searching for jobs, GES recruitment data show that at every stage of the application process, ethnically minoritised applicants are less likely to be successful. In 2018, of those who passed the initial online test for the Fast Stream programme, only one in twelve ethnically minoritised candidates ended up receiving a job offer, compared with over one in five White candidates.[45]

It is clear that economics in the UK is two-tiered. There is an 'elite' track with a whiter and wealthier student cohort going to Russell Group universities and then on to jobs with higher wages, status and power, and a 'second class' track of poorer more ethnically diverse students studying economics at lower-status universities who subsequently find it harder to break into the world of academic and professional economics.

In recent years, the Government Economic Service has actively attempted to address diversity with its Gender in the GES and Apprenticeship Scheme set up in 2019, which aim to increase representation of women and people less likely to study economics at university respectively. These interventions are welcome, and we hope will lead to further change, but as we argue in Part II of this book, a deeper and more systemic approach is required to make economics truly diverse and inclusive.

Towards inclusion?

Diversifying economics and fostering an inclusive culture is necessary for individuals from underrepresented backgrounds to have equal opportunity to study and practise economics, to be treated with dignity and respect by colleagues, and to access the income, status and power that economists receive.

It is also necessary for economics as a discipline to be able to claim legitimately that it represents society and the public interest. It must be more diverse and representative to claim to be able to understand the economic experience of different social groups. More broadly, a diverse and inclusive discipline of economics fosters greater social mobility and trust in experts, which in turn underpin democracy and social cohesion.

We return to explore how economics can be made into a diverse and inclusive discipline in Part II of this book. Now we turn to consider how many economists are marginalised because of their choice of research or the country they are in, and explore how this is caused by deep and harmful hierarchies in academic economics.

Chapter 2

Harmful hierarchies

*With contributions from Ariane Agunsoye,
Michelle Groenewald and Danielle Guizzo*

In this chapter, we take a historical view of economics as an academic discipline and identify deep and ingrained hierarchies in how it is structured.

We argue that these hierarchies are harmful because they contribute to the marginalisation of large numbers of economists based on their identity, values, research choices or the country they work in. We highlight the lived consequences of this marginalisation by drawing on interviews with eighteen academic and professional economists from seven countries, with identities that are underrepresented in the discipline.

Another area of harm caused by these hierarchies is that they directly contribute to a deeply problematic lack of focus in economic research on gender, racialised identity and countries outside of the US and Europe. The result is that economics too often fails to understand or address the specific economic realities of different countries or how systemic racism and sexism are embedded in our economies.

These hierarchies are not the result of scientific progress or luck. They are unjust, as well as harmful, because economics has developed in societies that were built on White, male, European supremacy and the status quo today has emerged from that.

Knowledge hierarchies

Acceptable economics

Economics, like many academic disciplines, has different perspectives within it. These perspectives are built on certain assumptions about the object of study (in this case economies): how to define them, what to focus on, how humans behave within them, and what research methods are appropriate for undertaking this study.

In economics one perspective, widely known as neoclassical economics, has become almost completely dominant within university economics departments and academic research, and is consequently viewed as the mainstream.[1] D'Ippoliti estimates that just 8.1 per cent of economists publishing in academic economics journals worldwide are conducting research in perspectives outside of the mainstream.[2]

Similarly, most undergraduate and higher-level economics courses globally teach neoclassical economics.[3] Many other economic perspectives exist. Some university economics departments consciously recruit economists who use these perspectives in their research. However, as we show in this chapter, alternative perspectives are systematically marginalised within the academic discipline of economics, and as a result much non-neoclassical economic research takes place in other disciplines such as sociology, politics and human geography.

Before continuing, we need to briefly define some of the key aspects of neoclassical economics. In 1932, Lionel Robbins developed the neoclassical definition of economics that is still dominant today. He suggested that 'Economics is the science which studies human behaviour as a relationship between ends and scarce means which have alternative uses.'[4]

This definition focuses attention on scarcity, and choices about the allocation of resources under conditions of scarcity. It doesn't draw attention to economic production or how resources are distributed, which, as we will argue in the next chapter, are essential to making visible the mechanisms by which inequalities in wealth and power are created and reproduced.[5]

Neoclassical economics encourages a view of 'the economy' that is characterised by two main features. First, it is based on a mechanical view of the world. Economies are composed of individual agents who interact in a well-behaved way, based on predictable mathematical rules. This behaviour tends to produce a situation which, though not necessarily ideal, is stable and is known as equilibrium. In this sense economies are not unlike pendulums: they may experience short-term change and volatility but they eventually return to a stable state. Economists study how changes in the economy affect agents' optimal decisions and therefore the ultimate equilibrium they settle at to come to conclusions about different aspects of the economy.

Second, neoclassical economics paints a picture of the economy as a stand-alone, abstract system that emerges naturally from the actions of individual agents. It remains largely silent on questions of how the modern economy came about. In Chapter 4, we argue that, as a result, neoclassical economics whitewashes the role of historical oppression in economic development and the role of power relations in globalisation. This contributes to a lack of focus on how economic rules such as property rights, which are encoded in law, can – because of historical oppression – function as mechanisms by which unjustly accumulated wealth and power is handed down across generations (rather than simply as neutral rules that are necessary for economies to function).

One true knowledge

Neoclassical economics makes a distinction between 'positive' and 'normative' economics. It claims that much of economics is positive, which means it merely describes the world and is thus value free. Such a view was summarised by the writers of the popular book *Freakonomics*, Steven Levitt and Stephen Dubner, when they said that 'the economic approach isn't meant to describe the world as any of us might want it to be ... but rather explain what it actually is'.[6] This claim is repeated in virtually all economics textbooks and is a central pillar of modern economics.

As a result, many neoclassical economists believe that they can be objective observers of the world. The implication is that the dominance of economics by White men from relatively privileged backgrounds, which we explored in the last chapter, does not change economic knowledge in any way. In this chapter, we argue to the contrary that there has been a clear relationship between the identity of economists (including where they are from) and the development of economic knowledge, which has contributed to certain topics being seen as important and others being neglected.

This belief that neoclassical economics objectively describes reality underpins the widely held view that it is possible and desirable to aim to develop a single unified set of theories and methods to analyse the economy. If you believe this then the fact that academic economics has now become effectively monopolised by neoclassical economics is positive because it represents scientific progress.

On this view, modern neoclassical economics is the cutting edge of a singular journey of human progress towards developing a unified set of theories and methods which can understand and manipulate the economy. Neoclassical economics is dominant because it is right, anything relevant that was said in the past is assumed to be fully included in today's theories and what was lost is assumed to be unworthy of further research.[7]

Despite the widespread view that there is one true way to study the economy, economics has what Michael Reay calls a 'flexible unity'.[8] It has theoretical foundations, which we explore in more detail in the next chapter, which provide a fairly unified 'way of looking at the world' and an eminently recognisable style of reasoning, which can be applied to a wide range of human behaviour.[9]

However, it has also proved very able to adapt and incorporate theories and ideas from other economic perspectives. As a result, there are different and sometimes conflicting 'truths' within different parts of neoclassical economics. This ability to incorporate criticism has made neoclassical economics an adaptable and resilient paradigm and contributed to its continued ability to claim that its near monopoly of academic economics is legitimate.

Unacceptable economics

Despite the flexibility of neoclassical economics, there is a clear dividing line separating what is deemed to be legitimate and credible economic research and teaching, from what is not.

This dividing line isn't related to whether research focuses on the economy, which one might assume would be the definition of what is and isn't economics. The credibility of economic research is determined by the extent to which it is deemed to use neoclassical theory and research methods.

What is credible research isn't justified through open academic debate in which different perspectives are considered and then neoclassical economics is judged to have most explanatory power. As we show later in the chapter, neoclassical economists mainly ignore non-neoclassical economists in their research. This means there is very little dialogue in academic economics between economists with different perspectives.

Sometimes the line dividing acceptable and unacceptable economics is tacit and it's hard to tell exactly where it lies. It also moves over time, with certain theories and methods that were once rejected being incorporated into neoclassical economics or shifting in the other direction.

Nonetheless, the dividing line is there. In the rest of the chapter, we explore how this line is policed through various mechanisms. We see how those who are judged to be on the wrong side are deemed to not be economists and systematically marginalised. Therefore, they find it more difficult to fund and publish their research or get recruited and promoted in university economics departments.

First, we give a summary of the diversity of different economic perspectives beyond neoclassical economics, and how they provide fundamentally different ways of thinking about the economy from the ground up. They have different assumptions about human behaviour and the role of institutions, and how the two interact. They have different foci and priorities that represent value judgements about what is important and this means they ask different questions. They have different tools and approaches that lead them to different answers to economic questions. They are diverse and not all of equal validity but they all hold valuable insights (see Table 2.1).

Ranking subdisciplines

There is also a hierarchy of subdisciplines within neoclassical economics, which changes over time and in different places, but currently goes something like this.

At the top of the hierarchy of subfields within economics there is microeconomics and econometrics, below this there is macroeconomics of which the best is micro founded (consistent with the principles of microeconomics). Then there are vogue subfields like behavioural economics, and below this there are lower-status subfields like public, environmental, health, labour and development economics. All of these are better than the history of economic thought, and economic history, which like the alternative perspectives above are often deemed not economics.

There is a similar hierarchy of research methods. Applied quantitative approaches that combine theory and data are high status, as are quasi-experimental methods that seek to replicate scientific experiments (which we return to in Chapter 5), whereas most qualitative methods are not recognised as legitimate economics, as we will see in the next section.

In the US, a significant number of economists feel discriminated against on the basis of their views. The American Economic Association (AEA) survey we cited in the last chapter finds that one in five respondents felt their 'ideas and opinions are often ignored within the field of economics', and one in six have felt discriminated against or treated unfairly at least once based on their research topics.[10]

In the next section, we turn to explore how economists from underrepresented backgrounds experience discrimination when they choose to do research that draws on alternative perspectives or lower-status subdisciplines of neoclassical economics.

Marginalised for your research

A theme that came out across many of our professional interviews were interviewees being drawn to research areas that weren't explored much in academic neoclassical-dominated economics because they deemed them important to understanding poverty and inequality.

Advika, an Indian professor of economics in North America, told us that 'Questions of poverty and inequality and disadvantage have been the running thread of what propelled me ... agriculture was still – it still is very important'. Advika highlights the lack of

Reclaiming economics for future generations

Table 2.1 A brief introduction to different economic perspectives

	'New' neoclassical	Post-Keynesian	Classical	Marxist	Dependency
Humans ...	can optimise a variety of goals	use rules of thumb	act in their self-interest	do not have a pre-determined nature	do not have a pre-determined nature
Humans act within ...	a market context	a macro-economic context	a class context	a class and historical context	local economies which are embedded in the global economy
The economy is ...	stable in the absence of frictions and shocks	naturally volatile	largely self-stabilising	both volatile and exploitative	global with inequalities of wealth and power caused by colonial histories
Economic analysis should ...	be built up from individual optimisation	be descriptively realistic	be grounded in politics	recognise power relations	explore the mechanisms which constrain economic development
Implications for education	teach mostly models	teach models with realistic assumptions	ground education in broader social knowledge	ground education in broader social knowledge	highlight the role of power and exploitation in the history of globalisation
Analysis of income inequality	driven by market frictions	increased power of finance and capital	increased power of capitalists	increased power of capitalists	resources flow from poor to rich countries
Views on financial crises	caused by external shocks and frictions in financial markets	generated by financial markets	ambiguous	generated by a falling rate of profit	ambiguous

Note: To explore different economic perspectives in more depth, see the Exploring Economics website. Available at www.exploring-economics.org/en/ (accessed 13 June 2021).

62

Harmful hierarchies

Austrian	Institutional	Stratification	Feminist	Ecological
act according to their subjective knowledge and preferences	exhibit changeable behaviour	have group identities (race, ethnicity, gender, caste, sexuality, religion)	exhibit gendered behaviour	ambiguous
a market context	an institutional environment which shapes rules and social norms	group dynamics and power relations	a social context	a social and ecological context
volatile but this is often a sign of health	dependent on legal and social structures	an arena in which income and wealth inequalities are reproduced	ambiguous	embedded in the living world
be based on individual action	focus on the relationships between people and institutions	focus on group identity and discrimination	recognise more than just the 'economic'	recognise ecological constraint
teach economics without maths	ground education in historical context	teach about power and structural discrimination	ground education in broader social knowledge	ground education in ecological knowledge
caused by government intervention	changes to tax and regulatory structures	caused by structural discrimination against certain groups	highly gendered	ambiguous
generated by central banks	consequence of the concentration of firms and poor financial regulation	further widens inequality between groups	related to male domination in finance, and impact is stratified by gender	ambiguous

Source: based on a table in Earle, Moran and Ward-Perkins, *The Econocracy*, inspired by a similar table in Ha-Joon Chang, *Economics: The User's Guide*.

focus in neoclassical economics on rural farming, often carried out on an informal and micro basis, which is such a central part of understanding economic livelihoods, poverty and inequality in many countries across the world.

Another economics professor, Fatima, explained that she explores areas like law that are outside neoclassical economics to understand gender inequality better: '[my book is] very interdisciplinary. I didn't have a large data set to play with and so I went deep into the laws and the legal framework, the structural inequalities which are embedded in the law themselves …' In trying to gain a deeper understanding of how inequalities are formed and reproduced through laws, Fatima had to go into the realm of unacceptable economics.

One interviewee, Carmella, a professor of economics, explained that she wanted to work with 'women migrants' and try to 'understand their perspectives and reasoning' so that one day she might be able to influence economic policies that could improve their lives.

Another interviewee, Isabel, an academic economist, talked about conducting historical research on unpaid work done by Black American women. 'I ended up writing a paper on African American women who were domestic workers, but it was historical, so it was focused on women who were migrating from the south into the north.' Not only was Isabel's research historical and focused on an under-researched area but she looked at 'the unpaid work that they were performing, as a collective for their community'. In doing so, she rejected the view that economics is about exchange of goods and services for money and asserted the importance of unpaid labour, a domain mainly ignored by the discipline.

In economics today, all this research is judged not on its own merits but by the extent to which it contributes to advancing the frontiers of neoclassical economic knowledge. And, of course, it doesn't, because these economists are explicitly deciding to conduct research on topics which neoclassical economics does not focus on, using methods that it does not recognise as legitimate. The criterion for judging economic research is how much it tells us about neoclassical theories and methods, not the value of what it tells us about real economies or livelihoods.

Rachel, an economist, explained that 'when my qualitative work is not seen as economics, it's seen as sociology ... that's true of anybody who tries to [do] qualitative work, you get marginalised or re-categorised as not being a "real economist"'. She believes that part of this lack of acceptance is because her research has become more critical.

Isabel highlighted the challenge of getting research funding for her 'historical' and 'archival' research. She recounts 'colleagues who've made disparaging comments about the work I'm doing because it's qualitative work, and therefore not regarded as legitimate economics work'.

Isabel knows that in economics qualitative means old fashioned and experimental means modern. 'It's not research that I think is regarded in high esteem within the profession, because it's kind of old fashioned. It's not experimental, right?'

Isabel describes how her choice of research has led to discrimination, including from places one might not expect.

> I've had biases from Black economists, I've had biases from White feminist economists in terms of publishing in feminist economics .... There have been all kinds of biases. But I've kept at it because I know that it's really important to do.

Venturing beyond 'acceptable' research topics and methods can be isolating and Isabel has 'a difficult time finding someone who is able to read and understand what I'm talking about'. Practically, this also makes it harder to find peer reviewers who understand her work, which is a necessary part of getting research published in academic journals. Isabel has 'received a lot of feedback that tells me that the reviewers didn't understand what the hell I was talking about. And I think that the limitation is really due to their training'.

The arbitrary nature of marginalising economists for their choice of research topics and methods rather than any genuine evaluation of its quality is highlighted by the fact that this research is often recognised as valuable outside of the discipline. Isabel explained that

> [Currently I have a book deal] looking at women of colour who are active in the environmental justice movement. So, for me, the irony is that people outside of economics recognise the importance of this … but people within this academic community have a hard time thinking outside of the norm.

Narrowing of accepted economics

Many of our interviewees highlighted that academic economics has become narrower over the last fifty years in terms of what is accepted as legitimate research and teaching.

One interviewee, Ellen described the discipline when she entered it in the 1960s. 'Economics was a different kind of subject … it was long before the dominance of neoclassical economics … It wasn't the notion that you just did a very narrow curriculum in neoclassical mathematised economics.'

A decade later, in the 1970s, Fatima still felt economics was more open to different ideas: 'economics was less technically driven. It was much more interdisciplinary … It was much more open to political aspects and social aspects than it is now'. Fatima and Ellen both remember a time when economics accommodated many different, often conflicting ways of understanding the economy.

Aditi described her experience of this narrowing in the UK:

> I joined [a prestigious university in the 1980s] ... there was a lot of discussion about how we hadn't got with the times and because most universities in the UK by then, London School of Economics in particular, was already very much the neoclassical framework had won ... Around that time it was clear that – in economics at least – if you wanted to make a reputation then you would need publishing in certain journals, and for those journals it would be certain frameworks etc. ... it's the way in which you build empires in economics ... I think by the 1990s ... there was no longer even any discussion about the neoclassical framework, it was just accepted.

Aditi highlights the role of academic journals in policing what research is acceptable in economics, and we return to explore this in more detail in the next section. She goes on to highlight the impact this has on what is taught today and how it differed from her economics education:

> When we teach Micro and Macro Economics these days, there is a sense that there is a hegemonic truth that some framework has come out as more true than others. And therefore, there is less need for us to be pluralist in the sense of different frameworks in Economics. So I think that is definitely a step back, sadly, for Economics ... in the 1980s ... we were taught different schools of Economics and so we knew that no school was the truth, in that sense.

Aditi stresses here how the widespread belief within academic economics in the objectivity and universality of neoclassical theory underpins its transformation from one of many possible ways of understanding the economy into 'hegemonic truth'. We are now at the point that any significant diversity of knowledge has been eradicated from many university economics departments entirely.

The role of economics journals

Economics, like many other disciplines, has an ecosystem of academic journals. Journals are used in almost all academic disciplines to communicate their research. Usually, research articles published in academic journals have been peer reviewed. This means that experts in the field have reviewed the article and decided whether it is fit for publication, or whether it requires further refinement. This filtering process aims to ensure that only the best-quality articles are published.[11]

Journal editors, and the reviewers they select to peer-review articles, have a significant position of power. Their judgement of which articles to pick for publication based on their view of what is good and bad quality influences what economic research is recognised and valued.

In this way, what is published in economics journals both reflects existing views within economics and reinforces them. This is a key mechanism through which the near monopoly of neoclassical economics is reproduced.

Journals in economics are ranked by their 'impact', which is measured by the number of times articles published in them are cited by other research. The top five ranked journals hold a particularly important position at the top of the hierarchy of economics. They are the *American Economic Review* (AER), *Econometrica* (ECMA), the *Journal of Political Economy* (JPE), the *Quarterly Journal of Economics* (QJE) and the *Review of Economic Studies* (ReStud).

All of these journals are based in the United States, and we return to explore the implications of this later in the chapter. They are important, because many 'elite' universities globally will not hire economists who have not published, or cannot demonstrate that they are likely to publish, their research in these journals. Publishing in high-impact journals is increasingly necessary for recruitment and promotion in university economics departments.

The top five economics journals set the hierarchical culture of the discipline by focusing inward and towards other top journals. For example, between 2000 and 2009 two in five citations in the AER were of articles published in the top 25 economics journals. This number is much higher than other social sciences, which tend to cite other research in a less hierarchical and more interdisciplinary way.[12] In doing so, the top journals maintain each other's rankings, and act like a cartel – a group of independent market participants who collude with each other in order to dominate the market.

This hierarchical and inward-looking culture is further illustrated by how much less interdisciplinary economics is than other social sciences. In 1997, four in five of the citations in economics journals went to themselves (in comparison to around half for sociology, political science, etc.). Further research has found this trend continuing up to 2009 and we have no reason to believe it has changed in the last decade.[13]

The neoclassical mainstream of the profession is similarly inward-looking when it comes to engaging with research from other economic perspectives. D'Ippoliti suggests that fewer than one in ten citations in mainstream neoclassical economic research cite research done using different economic perspectives.[14]

In contrast, non-neoclassical economists have focused to a significant extent on criticising neoclassical economics and therefore end up citing the research they criticise! At one point, almost four in five citations in non-neoclassical economic research went to mainstream neoclassical research although this figure has started to fall in recent years.

D'Ippoliti notes that the number of neoclassical to alternative perspective citations has significantly declined from the 1980s when one in six citations in neoclassical economic research cited research done using different economic perspectives. This chimes with what we heard in the last section about the narrowing of economics, and it suggests that debate between different perspectives in economics has declined in recent decades.

Journal rankings and peer-review are the two central mechanisms for evaluating the quality of economic research and both appear to have contributed to the declining diversity of knowledge within the discipline.

As neoclassical economists are the majority of the discipline and they have an inward-looking culture, their work is cited more – including, as we have seen, by their critics. This majority and their dominance in top journals and departments also means that they are more likely to be called as referees. We've seen how this means it can be hard for non-neoclassical economists to find referees who understand their work.

These are the institutional mechanisms through which judgements that the neoclassical approach is rigorous, and other economic perspectives are inferior, are transformed into supposedly objective evaluations of quality.

As we saw in the last section, this makes it much harder for economists to research certain topics and use certain methods defined as outside the neoclassical mainstream. It also determines who gets recruited and promoted in university economics departments. This has the effect of denying economists academic freedom to make judgements about what they believe is important to research in economics.

Journals, racialised and gendered identities

The top economics journals almost completely neglect to publish research that addresses issues of racialised identity. Dania Francis and

Anna Gifty Opoku-Agyeman found that between 1990 and 2018 only 29 out of 7,567 economics research articles in the top five economics journals directly addressed issues related to race and/or ethnicity.[15]

The 'specialist' journals that do focus on these topics are much lower ranked, which makes it harder for academics publishing in these journals to get jobs in university economics departments. Research by Patrick Mason, Samuel Myers Jr, and William Darity identified that papers published in *The Review of Black Political Economy* (RBPE) – a Black academic-controlled economics journal – receive nearly four fewer citations than papers published in the average cited economics journals (in comparison to papers in top tier journals which receive on average eight more citations).[16]

In this way, racialised identity and ethnicity are erased from the top journals, and 'specialist' journals that focus on them are cited less and therefore judged to have a 'lower impact' factor in what becomes a self-reinforcing cycle.

A similar picture emerges with gender, for example when looking at the relatively low-impact factor of journals such as *Feminist Economics* (FE). Bea, a UK postgraduate student, had heard first-hand from a woman professor who had felt forced to move away from researching gender-wealth inequalities because it had taken years to get it published in any journal that wasn't FE. This made Bea realise that pursuing research on gender within economics would be a difficult path to take.

'Publish or perish' is a mantra faced by academics trying to progress up the career ladder in universities across the world. The low impact scores of journals that publish research on race and gender create a systemic disincentive for economists to do research on these topics. This is a key mechanism that drives the underrepresentation of racialised identity and gender in academic economic research, theory and teaching.

Identity, research and teaching

As we saw earlier in the chapter, many neoclassical economists believe that they can be objective observers of the world and therefore that their identity does not matter.

In our interviews we heard from many academic economists with identities that are underrepresented in the discipline, who were marginalised due to their choice of research topics and methods. For many of these interviewees, their identity and lived experience was an important source of their motivation to conduct the research they were doing, despite knowing full well it would lead to them being marginalised and discriminated against.

More broadly, there is growing evidence that economists with different identities think about, research and teach economics differently. A recent paper argued that Black authors are more likely to study race-related issues and are over 10 per cent more likely to report a finding of discrimination against Black people in their research.[17]

Similarly, researchers found that economists who are men are more likely than women economists to prefer market solutions over government intervention, are more sceptical of ecological protection, and are (slightly) less keen on redistribution.[18] In contrast, women economists are more likely to acknowledge labour market inequalities and tend to give more importance to social policy. Another study found that women economists are one-third more likely to support policies of income redistribution and making imports dependent on labour standards.[19]

It is important to examine the interplay between people's identity and the economic ideas they have. While men are less likely to support redistribution, as we will argue in the next chapter, neoclassical economics has foundations that are particularly unsuited to understanding, or even making visible, inequalities of wealth and power.

This suggests that, male dominance on the one hand, and the increasing monopoly of the neoclassical perspective on the other, have reinforced each other to mean that at times over the last fifty years academic economics has not been willing to even consider distribution as an important economic problem. This view is exemplified by the Nobel Laureate Robert Lucas who in 2004 said that 'of the tendencies that are harmful to sound economics, the most seductive, and in my opinion the most poisonous, is to focus on questions of distribution'.[20]

Similarly, women are far more likely to recognise and engage with problems associated with excluding unpaid household work from economic analysis.[21] However, the importance of unpaid labour in the economy is not considered within neoclassical economics. As a result, gender identity may not lead to women neoclassical economists incorporating household labour into their research even if women are on balance more likely to.

There is also evidence that economists with different identities teach the subject differently. In 2020 economists Ingrid Kvangraven and Surbhi Kesar conducted a survey of 500 academics from across the world.

They found that just over half of economists in wealthier, White majority countries such as those in North America and Europe reported teaching about racialised inequalities or the role of European colonialism.[22] In contrast, nearly nine out of ten economists based in countries which have been on the receiving end of racialised inequalities and European colonialism report teaching about them.

Likewise, respondents who felt excluded based on their racialised identity, ethnicity, nationality or religion were more likely to report that they taught these issues than those who didn't. And women were more likely to than men.[23]

On this evidence, it is quite clear that the identity of economists will shape how they think about the economy, which will in turn lead research, theory and teaching in certain directions and not others.

We saw in the last chapter that academic economics in the US and UK is dominated by White, relatively privileged men, particularly further along the career ladder.

Male dominance in economics globally is highlighted when we look at economic research output by identity. One analysis of published academic research found that women have accounted for under one in six authorships in economics since 1990.[24] Romania, Croatia and Bulgaria are the only countries in the world where women account for (just over) half of published research in economics.[25]

We can see clearly how women are less represented in research output even when they are well represented in the profession. In 2018/2019, just under half of all PhD students in India were women[26] but women accounted for only just over one-quarter of published economic research in the country.[27] This occurs because published research is often carried out by more senior, high-status economists and in India in economics only a little over one in five professors and one in three assistant professors are women.

On this basis, we believe that the historical and global dominance of men in producing economic research will have significantly influenced the topics, methods and findings of this research. Tying the argument in this section together, we can see clear connections between the identity of economists, how the academic discipline operates, and the knowledge which is produced. In Chapter 6, we return to explore how reform can attempt to address the deeply embedded and harmful hierarchies in all of these areas.

Global hierarchies

In this section, we explore the role the United States plays at the top of a global hierarchy of academic economics, with the UK and Europe following behind and large parts of the rest of the world not recognised at all.

We argue that status and power in this hierarchy is gained and reproduced through being home to highly ranked economics journals, which we discussed in the last section, and through training foreign economists. The US particularly plays an important role training students from across the world and qualifications gained there give economists access to jobs in government and international institutions globally.

We highlight how the role the US plays as a global trainer of economists is a key mechanism through which the undiverse, uninclusive and hierarchical culture of the discipline we have explored in this book so far influences the global culture of academic economics.

We trace how economics became internationalised in the twentieth century, led first by Europe and later by the US. This history helps to explain why today the vast majority of recognised economic research is created in, and focuses on, Europe and the US and the widespread assumption that this will be applicable to other parts of the world.

US dominance

The top journals, as we have seen, are all based in the US but the hierarchy of journals is international. The Social Science Citation Index (SSCI), which constitutes the most complete database for ranking the impact of journals, indexes only about 120 of the most cited economics journals worldwide. These are overwhelmingly from the US and Europe, and with a few exceptions they publish research in neoclassical economics. English is by far the dominant language of economics journals included in the SSCI, even among those from non-English-speaking countries.

When we talk of US dominance of academic economics, in practice this means the dominance of a small number of economics departments at 'elite' universities. The 2019 Economic Climate survey of economists in the US, which we cited in Chapter 1, finds that there is a strong feeling that US economics is dominated by a small elite.

Around 250 comments mentioned elitism and many referenced 'a strong sense that … the top journals – and de facto the profession – are controlled by economists from the top institutions'. About sixty comments referenced a network which economists are either in or out of, and if you are outside then your chances of succeeding in the profession are greatly diminished. They quote one respondent who felt that 'Those outside the top ten tend to be discounted, dismissed, and not taken seriously.' They highlight a 'strong feeling that those that obtained their degree, or work, outside the U.S. are not given the appropriate level of respect'.[28]

The top five journals we discussed earlier in the chapter play an important role here as they are closely connected with the top five university economics departments in the US. For example, around half of all authors of articles published in the *Journal of Political Economy* (JPE) and *Quarterly Journal of Economics* (QJE) received their PhD from one of the top five US economics departments.[29] The fact that the QJE is based at Harvard University and the JPE is based at Chicago University, both top five departments, further reinforces the closed, cartel-like nature of this dominance.

The nexus of top journals and departments at the top of the hierarchy of economics extends to dominance and control of the

American Economic Association (AEA). The AEA has 18,000 members but nearly three out of four of AEA council members are from the top five departments.[30] This is important because elected roles decide the programme of presentations for the annual meetings, and in this way have the power to showcase economists whose work they think is valuable.

All of this suggests that a small number of economists have a significant impact on the global discipline of academic economics and its culture.

A key mechanism through which this culture is spread is through economists from across the world training at US universities. Unlike law and medicine which can't legally be practised without gaining a licence through passing an exam, anyone can call themselves an economist. However, in practice most universities, government agencies and businesses will not hire 'economists' without a PhD, master's or undergraduate degree in economics, with PhDs required for academic and senior roles. To be a professional economist you need at a minimum an undergraduate degree, but to be an academic or senior economist a PhD is pretty much essential, and where you get it from matters.

In this way universities determine who can claim to be an economist and whether that claim is seen as credible by the wider economic community. Higher education degrees in economics are not all equally valuable in giving their holder the licence to be an economist.

The worlds of economic advising, international economics institutions, leading university economics departments and upper-level government economic positions of many countries, particularly in low- and middle-income countries, are dominated by economists who have received their PhDs from US or British universities. While a Brazilian PhD could make someone an economist in the United States, in practice such cases are unusual, whereas a US PhD in economics effectively gives one a licence to be an economist anywhere in the world.

This is a significant reason why in 2000, more foreign students received a PhD in economics in US universities than native-born students, with the largest contingents coming from Asia (South and East), Western Europe and Latin America.[31] In England, at the same time, an Economic and Social Research Council report stated that barely one in ten students enrolled in PhD programs in top-rated UK economics departments are British citizens.[32] In this way, training foreign economists can be seen as a core purpose for many 'elite' university economics departments in the US and UK.

This situation is both a result of and reinforces a strong country hierarchy in economics with the US at the top and completely dominant, the UK second (partly boosted by its historical influence on economics), European countries following, and many parts of Latin America, the Middle East, Africa and South Asia pretty much not recognised as significant players in economics.

Within these categories there are further hierarchies, with North and Western European countries higher status, then East and Southern European countries, and with India and South Africa higher status than other countries in South Asia and Sub-Saharan Africa respectively.

Given that the US is at the summit of the disciplinary hierarchy globally, we can suggest that its culture plays a disproportionate role in setting the culture of the whole discipline. This culture of economics both mirrors and reproduces broader global and historically embedded racialised, gendered, socioeconomic and geographic hierarchies.

Internationalisation of economics

Here we briefly outline the history of how economics has become a global discipline. The early internationalisation of economics took place in the European-dominated world of the late nineteenth and early twentieth century alongside a broader phase of globalisation we return to explore in Chapter 4. At this time, there were distinct traditions of organising the academic study of economics in French, German and English universities, which provided alternative models for other countries to draw from.

Egypt drew on both the French model with economics taught in law faculties and the English with economics taught in faculties of commerce. In India, the English politics, philosophy and economics (PPE) course was widely adopted, while in Indonesia, during the colonial period, economics was part of the law curriculum which reflected a more continental approach.

Other countries, including those which were never colonised, drew on different European approaches to economics for a range of ideological and strategic reasons. In Thailand, economics was focused on the state and government, many Latin American nations imitated the French and the German influence was prominent in Japanese economics education.[33] After the Russian Revolution in 1917, the Soviet Union developed another model of economics based on specialised institutes and academies connected to the state administration.[34]

It is important to note here that all these countries would have had pre-existing knowledge about how to manage economic production, distribution and exchange prior to the import of European approaches to economic research and education (one of which would include our current idea of 'the economy', which only developed in Europe in the 1930s[35]).

The economist Nicola Viegi suggests that for European colonis-ers 'education was an instrument of co-opting elites to the colonial project and a form of political and social control.'[36] This emphasises that the internationalisation of economics should always be seen in its broader historical contexts.

After World War Two, the centre of economics shifted decisively to the US, which from then on provided the main model for the organisation of economics education and expertise for Western countries during the Cold War. The US led the design of the post-war international economic system and its foreign policy was targeted at the containment of Communism and opening new markets.[37]

International institutions and American foundations organised economic curricula for government officials and other important actors in the Caribbean, Latin America, Africa, the Middle East and Asia. The United Nations' Economic Commission for Latin America was set up in 1948 and played an important role in educat-ing public sector technocrats in the region during the 1960s. In 1954 the World Bank established its Economic Development Institute, which provided ready-made teaching and training materials in the areas of macroeconomics and development policy.

The US-based Ford Foundation established an Economic Development and Administration Program in 1953 and it became 'the largest financial supporter of social science research in Latin America.'[38] It was also active across Asia providing grants to help create important research organisations in India, Pakistan and Indonesia. The Ford Foundation and others also supported univer-sities and social science research institutes in Africa such as the West African Institute of Social and Economic Research in Nigeria and the Uganda-based East African Institute for Social Research.

Direct financial involvement has played an important role in shaping the design and development of economics education, research and policy institutions in Latin America, Africa, the Middle East and South Asia, but its role as a global trainer of economics has been much more significant.

In the post-war period, graduates returning from the US played an important role developing economic policy institutions in their home countries often on the model of US organisations like the Brookings Institution, and staffing newly created development planning agencies. Among the two in three Brazilian central bank officials who did postgraduate work between 1965 and 1995, over half of them studied in the United States.

Marion Fourcade describes how 'between 1957 and 1970, about 100 Chilean students from the Universidad Catolica were educated at the economics department of the University of Chicago, partly sponsored by the American government.' These US-trained economists revolutionised the economics curriculum at the Universidad Catolica, influenced public debate on economic issues through their media work and occupied key positions in government after the Augusto Pinochet coup in 1973.

While the 'Chicago Boys', as these Chilean economists are known, are the most famous, there are many other examples of US-educated graduates playing a central role in shaping the economic policy of their home countries over the last seventy years. For example, in Indonesia, the economists who ran the country under the dictator Suharto's rule were known as the 'Berkeley mafia' because of their training at the University of California in Berkeley. These two examples highlight a sometimes-close relationship between economists and dictators, and we will in Chapter 5 turn to consider the tensions between economics and democracy.

Conflicts between US- and home-trained economists have been a regular occurrence in the second half of the twentieth century. Fourcade describes how US-educated economists tended to be more 'scientistic' in their methodological approach, believed in the universality of their knowledge and often recommended market-based economic policies. In contrast, economists trained in their own countries tended to be more 'nationalist' and 'interventionist'.

These theoretical and methodological differences, many of which we have explored earlier in the chapter, were more intense because they were often embedded in differences in social background. As studying in the US has always been an elite career path, US-educated economists were more likely to represent wealthier and more powerful sections of their home societies.

For example, back in 1996, more than four out of five 'of the professors at the two main economics departments in Rio de Janeiro (Brazil) had a North American doctorate'. In contrast, only about one in fourteen professors at the largest economics department in São Paulo had studied in the US and the numbers were even smaller at more provincial universities.[39]

Fourcade highlights similar patterns across the world. In 1985, thirty out of thirty-eight faculty members of the University of the Philippines School of Economics had received their PhD from an American university. In 1996, another study found that more than half the members of the Korean Economic Society holding a PhD were trained in the United States and that these US-trained economists were disproportionately based in the capital Seoul.[40]

Of course, these patterns have changed over time, and countries had differing relationships with US academic economics, but we can see clearly the ways in which the role the US has played in training economists globally has shaped the direction of the discipline and broader economic policymaking.

Latin America, Africa, the Middle East and South Asia have often served as a form of training ground for US academic economics where training local economists gives a chance to try out ideas which are otherwise confined to theory. Being able to demonstrate that these experiments are a 'success' then increases the intellectual status of certain economists and theories within the discipline. For example, the influence of the Chicago Boys in Chile boosted the status of the University of Chicago and the economic ideas they were developing at the time.

This influence is a sort of currency within academic economics. This can be seen in the boasts of Arnold Harberger, a professor at the University of Chicago for thirty-eight years, in an interview in 1999:

> I think my number of ministers is now crossing 25, and I know my number of central bank presidents has already crossed a dozen. Right now the central bank presidents of Chile, Argentina and Israel were my students, and the immediate former central bank presidents in Argentina, Chile and Costa Rica were also my students.[41]

In this way the process of gaining status in economics is multidirectional, with credibility at the top of the hierarchy of economics in the US gained through demonstrating legitimacy and influence among individuals and countries lower down the hierarchy, and vice versa.

These dynamics have driven a form of institutional and intellectual convergence between countries at the top of the hierarchy of academic economics and those lower down which has been key to forming the modern global discipline.

Where, and who, produces economic knowledge?

Flows of students travelling across borders, the dominance of neoclassical economics, the standardisation of education and the use of English all signal that academic economics is a globalised discipline.

However, the history and current organisation of the discipline we have outlined above mean that there are clear colonial hierarchies in where and who produces economic knowledge. These hierarchies in turn determine who has power to shape the discipline, and who has most economic credibility in the wider world.

Table 2.2 lists the countries that winners of the prestigious Nobel Prize for Economics have come from since it was first awarded in 1969.[42] As the most prestigious award in academic economics, it is an interesting indicator of what knowledge is most valued at the time.

Table 2.2   Recipients of the Nobel Prize in Economics by country

Country	Number of recipients of Nobel Prize in Economics*
US	56
UK	8.5
France	3.5
Norway	3
Canada	2
Sweden	2
Netherlands	1.5
Soviet Union	1.5
India	1.5
Germany	1
Italy	1
Israel	1
Finland	1
Austria	0.5
Cyprus	0.5
Hungary	0.5
Poland	0.5
St Lucia	0.5

*1 point sole country/half point where dual nationality listed. Calculated by the authors.

Source: compiled by the authors.

The table clearly illustrates that over the past fifty years the US has dominated economic knowledge production and only a small handful of mainly European countries have ever had an economist who has won the prize. Strikingly, of the eighty-six economics Nobel Prize winners up to 2020, only two are women and three are not White.

We have seen that the top-ranked economics journals internationally are mainly based in the US and Europe. Unsurprisingly, who produces economic knowledge, and where it is produced, influences its focus. As demonstrated by Figure 2.1, between 1985 and 2005 there were more papers about the United States than

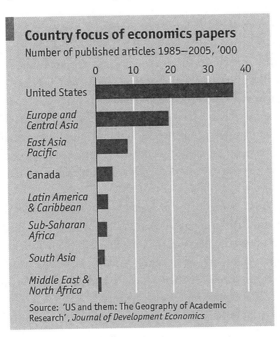

Figure 2.1 Country focus of economics papers

on Europe, Asia, Latin America, the Middle East and Africa combined.[43]

In this way, the belief of many economists that it is possible to objectively describe the economy obscures the reality that neoclassical economic knowledge has been developed historically mainly in the US and Europe, by White men from relatively privileged backgrounds.

We have seen that economics is built on abstract, universal reasoning which is divorced from broader historical and geographical contexts. Many academic economists assume that countries 'do not fundamentally differ from one another, and this allows for a similar treatment of the rich and the poor, the agricultural and the industrial, the open and the closed economies, and so on'.[44]

As a result, economists are much more likely to locate their claims to expertise in technical areas like monetary or fiscal policy than in individual countries or regions which are left to the less 'scientific' social sciences. In this way, economic knowledge produced in the US and Europe is presented as universally applicable. This has the effect of devaluing knowledge, expertise and priorities in countries where US and European economic knowledge is imposed from above. This is a theme we return to when considering economics and democracy in Chapter 5.

All of this highlights the prevalence of systemic power relations between different groups and parts of the world embedded in the practices of economic research. As the White British-American economist Angus Deaton notes, much economic research is 'done by better-heeled, better-educated and paler people on lower income, less-educated and darker people'.[45]

Even critiques of economics which centre the economic experience of women, people of colour and countries outside Europe and North America, tend to come from those who are more privileged and have been able to access university economics education. Those who are most negatively affected are often excluded because of the elite nature of economics and how this influences who is deemed to have a credible voice. We return to ask how we might more fundamentally democratise who has a voice in economics in Chapter 7.

It is important not to confuse the failure of economics to identify or value knowledge produced in Latin America, the Middle East, Africa and South Asia with the idea that this knowledge doesn't exist. Advika, professor of economics in North America who we heard from earlier, highlights that

> There is so much fascinating work going on in the Global South that people in the North just don't have any knowledge of. Everything is mediated through the North. What we are trying to do, part of our attempt at decolonising is just make us aware of all the fascinating and good work that is being done in different parts of the world.

This knowledge and the people producing it are currently invisible to the discipline of economics but it does exist. Decolonising economics requires making space for the knowledge and valuing the people who produce it. We return to how this task might be achieved in Chapter 6.

Struggling to be recognised

Wherever they are in the world, economists are forced to define themselves in relation to the dominant US and European centre of the discipline, which commands implicit, yet powerful, influence upon their immediate professional environment. Ndlovu-Gatsheni describes the students who pursue education and academics who seek to publish in journals in the US and Europe as struggling to receive 'affirmation and validation of their knowledge'.[46]

87

One of our interviewees, Juliana, a Brazilian student who had studied in two different European universities, highlighted the low status she felt. 'I felt disrespected as a Latin American, when it comes to the fact that a lot of professors have the feeling or the experience that Latin Americans are revolutionary'. She described feeling that she wasn't taken seriously because her professors thought 'Oh, Latin Americans are communists'. As a result, her nationality and regionality were the hardest experiences for her in terms of her identity in economics.

Hiba, a postgraduate from Sudan who studied in the UK, argued that economists in Africa were being sidelined from participating in developments within the discipline. 'We are kept out of the discussions that happen that are now popping up in Europe or in the US.' She explains, 'when there is a conference in … let's say London, what are the chances that people from African countries can attend? Given visa constraints, expensive airfare, and expensive accommodation, there's a systematic barrier that exists that disallows us to be part of that conversation.'

Because economics has developed and is structured with the US as the 'hub' and other countries mainly relating bilaterally to it as 'spokes', economists in Latin America, the Middle East, Africa and South Asia are sometimes not connected. Advika, who we heard from before, highlighted: 'Nobody is aware of, even with each other [the work that is being done by economists outside of Europe and the US] … So, I'm just saying it's not just that the North doesn't know about us, but we in the South don't know about each other.'

The majority of economists from Latin America, the Middle East, Africa and South Asia are either invisible or marginalised within academic economics unless they have studied or work at institutions in Europe or the US and many face a constant struggle to be recognised as legitimate economists with something valuable to contribute to the discipline.

Roots of economics

Economics has developed over the last 250 years in societies in which ideologies of White, male and European supremacy were deeply ingrained. Therefore, it should not be a surprise that academic economic knowledge, culture and institutions have racial, gender and geographical hierarchies embedded within them.

Here we highlight two examples of deeply racist views held by leading US economists in the late nineteenth and mid-twentieth centuries respectively. We do so because we want economics to face up to its history and really reflect on how it has contributed to the problems we've described in this book so far. But we recognise that they are upsetting and we completely understand if readers want to skip this section.

In 1903, Richard Ely, founder of the American Economic Association, stated that the 'problem is to keep the most unfit from reproduction, and to encourage the reproduction of those who are really the superior members of society'.[47] A few years earlier, he had made it clear who he believed was fit and who wasn't:

> there are classes in every modern community composed of those who are virtually children, and who require paternal and fostering care, the aim of which should be the highest development of which they are capable. We may instance the negroes, who are for the most part grownup children, and should be treated as such.[48]

More recently this writing by George Stigler in 1965 highlights similar views:

> Consider the Negro as a neighbor. He is frequently repelled and avoided by the White man, but is it only color prejudice? On the contrary, it is because the Negro family is, on average, a loose, morally lax, group, and brings with its presence a rapid rise in crime and vandalism. No statutes, no sermons, no demonstrations, will obtain for the Negro the liking and respect that sober virtues commend. And the

> leaders of Negro thought: they blame the crime and immorality upon
> the slums and the low-income – as if individual responsibility could be
> bought with a thousand dollars a year.[49]

Stigler went on to win the 1982 Nobel Prize in Economics just forty years ago.

A cursory glance at the standard histories of economic thought will show you how White, male and Euro-American the discipline has been. Adam Smith, David Ricardo, Karl Marx, Thorstein Veblen, John Maynard Keynes, Friedrich Hayek, Robert Solow, Alfred Marshall, Lionel Robbins, Paul Samuelson ... the list goes on.

While many of the other economic perspectives we highlighted earlier in the chapter have histories which are similarly White, male and Euro-American, there are important traditions of economics developed in other parts of the world and by women and people of colour.

Economics must commit to a long-term process of self-reflection and interrogation of how its knowledge, people, culture and institutions have been, and continue to be, shaped by these histories. We return in Chapter 6 to consider how this process can begin.

Chapter 3

Blind to structural inequality

One of this book's contributors, Brototi Roy, grew up in the small city (by Indian standards) of Bokaro in the east Indian state of Jharkhand, where schoolchildren who scored well were encouraged to take up one of two career options – engineer or doctor; social sciences were only for the ones who couldn't get into a science college.

Defying this convention, Brototi moved to Calcutta, India, to pursue a degree in economics, because she wanted to understand and address the socioeconomic inequalities she saw in her country. Straight away she became uncomfortable with what she was being taught without yet understanding why. Here we turn to explore the source of that discomfort, which so many economics students across the world share.

In the last chapter, we saw that that there is a systemic lack of focus in academic economic research on gender, racialised identities and countries outside the US and Europe. This lack of focus means that economics too often fails to understand or address the specific economic realities of different countries or how systemic racism, sexism, and elitism is embedded in our economies.

Now, we turn to explore the framework of neoclassical economics in more depth, arguing that it is fundamentally unable to make visible, much less address structural inequalities between and within countries and groups.

As a result, even if academic economics was to focus much more on the specific economic realities of different countries and how systemic racism, sexism and classism are embedded in our economies, it would not currently have the tools to do so effectively. This is an argument for diversifying the knowledge of economics and we return to it when exploring how to reform academic economics in Chapter 6.

The presence of structural inequality

Any adequate account of modern economies must engage with the presence of deep structural inequality. By this we mean that between and within countries, economic outcomes are mainly determined not by equality of opportunity, meritocracy, competition or any other legitimate system of selection but by systemic group advantages and disadvantages. These are deep and often intergenerational inequalities in wealth, income and power between groups in society distributed along racial, gender, religious, tribal, caste and class lines and between different countries.

If there was genuine equality of opportunity, then our life chances at birth and where we end up in the pecking order would be much less influenced by factors such as our identity or background. The reality is that, at a population level, how well or badly we do can often be predicted based on such markers as our gender, racialised identity, our able-bodiedness, the socioeconomic position of our parents/carers and where we are born in the world. There are many exceptions, but the general relationship is difficult to dispute.

Although the level of structural economic inequality within countries varies greatly, its presence is ubiquitous. Here we explore just a few illustrative examples.

In Guatemala, the majority of the population identify as Indigenous;[1] however, at least four out of five Indigenous

Guatemalans live in poverty, which is over twice as many as non-Indigenous Guatemalans.[2] One-third of Indigenous Guatemalans experience food insecurity.[3] Yet public expenditure (such as for health and education) for Indigenous People is less than half of that for the rest of the population.[4] For example, half of all Indigenous children do not attend school,[5] thus limiting their choices about the lives they will pursue.

In the US, the difference in rates of poverty among people with different identities is stark. Just under one in ten people who are White (non-Latinx) are classed as living in poverty, while for Black Americans the poverty rate quadruples in comparison to about four in ten.[6]

In India, the richest 10 per cent of Indians own 77 per cent of the country's total wealth.[7] A minimum wage worker in rural India will need 941 years to earn what the highest paid executive at a major Indian garment company earns in a year.[8]

In the UK nearly one in five Bangladeshi workers, one in ten Pakistani and Chinese workers, and one in twenty Black African and Indian workers are paid below the National Minimum Wage, compared to one in thirty-three White workers.[9]

Next we consider structural inequalities faced by women in the global economy. Women make up four in five of the 74 million textile workers worldwide.[10] Most work long days, some receive an hourly wage of just over US$1,[11] and have little job security. They serve a global industry mostly focused on producing cheap clothes for wealthier parts of the world at the expense of garment workers' livelihoods.

Despite accounting for almost one in three farm workers worldwide, a figure that rises to three in five in South Asia and Sub-Saharan Africa (not including self-employed and unpaid family farmers), only 13 per cent of women own land.[12] This leaves many women in precarious low-paid and informal agricultural jobs without a financial safety net.

Income inequality is compounded when gender and racialised identity interweave to disadvantage women in the labour market. Indigenous women and those of African origin, for example, are more likely than men from their ethnic group or men and women in the general population to earn $1 an hour or less in Bolivia, Brazil, Guatemala and Peru.[13]

The structural inequalities women face are further illustrated by the gender pay gap. UN Women reports that the global average gender pay gap results in women workers earning 16 per cent less than men do in their paid roles, with women in some countries paid up to 35 per cent less than men.[14]

The UK's Women's Budget Group[15] found that in 2019, since women had a lower employment rate than men and those who worked were subject to the gender wage gap, women received 43 per cent less than men from paid jobs that year. This is linked to global findings that women face limitations accessing paid work as their unpaid care and domestic work is estimated to be three times that of men.[16] The gender pay gap also has future repercussions for women to accumulate a sufficient pension and results in a gender pensions gap (where they have access to one).[17]

Structural inequalities are even starker between countries. The average income in the UK is around US$30,000 in contrast to about US$4,000 in Egypt.[18] Economic inequalities are everywhere correlated with health and social inequalities. For example, the life expectancy of a person from the low-income Central African Republic is 30 years less than someone in high-income France.[19] Of course, these two examples compare countries where the wealthier one was in a colonial relationship with the other. We turn to explore the histories of today's structural inequality in the next chapter.

Another example of the connection between economic and health inequalities is air pollution. The World Health Organization (WHO) estimates that nine out of ten people in the world now breathe polluted air, killing over seven million people every year.[20] To put that into context, fifty-five million people died from causes linked to air pollution in 2015, which is one in seven of all global deaths. It reports that 'More than 90% of air pollution-related deaths occur in low- and middle-income countries, mainly in Asia and Africa, followed by low- and middle-income countries of the Eastern Mediterranean region, Europe and the Americas.' This is directly linked to economic inequality because 'around 3 billion people – more than 40% of the world's population – still do not have access to clean cooking fuels and technologies in their homes, the main source of household air pollution'.

We argue in this chapter, that neoclassical economics inadequately identifies, explains, and addresses structural inequalities such as those presented above.

Unsuitable foundations

The neoclassical understanding of 'the economy' is built on three key theoretical 'prongs',[21] which taken together form the core of all neoclassical economics. They are:

- *Individualism*: Neoclassical theory focuses on the behaviour of individual agents, an 'agent' being defined as some sort of economic decision-maker. These include agents such as consumers who must decide what to buy, but also entails modelling the production decisions of firms or even the political decisions of governments as individual decisions. Neoclassical economics therefore has an 'atomistic' view of the world and tries to build an understanding of the economy wholly from the decisions of individuals.

- *Optimisation*: These agents seek to optimise explicit goals in their behaviour. The definition of 'optimise' is to 'make the best or most effective use of a situation or resource'. A consumer might want to use the money they have to buy the commodities they want the most; a firm might want to get the highest profit given the materials available and their technological prowess. The aims of agents can be wide ranging and they may even suffer from faulty decision-making, but in neoclassical economics agents almost always optimise some goal.

- *Equilibrium*: The decisions of individual agents must balance – a situation that is called 'equilibrium'. Agents make decisions about what to produce, buy, sell and invest in, and if these decisions are correct then no agent will have an incentive to change their behaviour. Agents adjust their behaviour until they have, based on their individual judgement, achieved the outcome that is best for them, and there is no reason for anyone to alter their behaviour, resulting in a stable equilibrium.

We saw in the last chapter how the subdisciplines of economics have different status in the discipline. Here we explore micro- and macroeconomics in a little more detail as they provide the theoretical foundations of neoclassical economics.

Microeconomics

Microeconomics is focused on the small: it is the study of individual households, firms, industries and markets.

Rational choice theory is the idea that overall or aggregate social behaviour results from the decisions and behaviour of individual actors.[22]

The term *homo economicus*, or economic man, refers to the representation of humans as reasoning, self-interested agents who strive to maximise their utility. In principle, economic agents can 'optimise' anything, but in practice the type of mathematics used by economists means that there is a focus on material sources of utility such as income and consumption over less tangible issues such as human rights, nature, job security and mental health.

The most basic world in microeconomics, and one to which all students will be introduced, is a smoothly functioning world where everyone behaves rationally and has all the relevant information; markets function perfectly, resulting in a 'socially optimal' (i.e. desirable, in the language of economists) outcome.

Such a situation can be represented using the types of maths and diagrams loved by neoclassical economists, as illustrated by the supply and demand graph in Figure 3.1. The basic idea is that in a given market – say, the one for shoes – the S curve represents the underlying decisions of producers about how many shoes they are willing to manufacture, while the D curve represents the decisions of consumers about how many they are willing to buy. Where these two curves meet – where the decisions of consumer and producers balance – is a stable and optimal equilibrium, showing how many shoes will be bought/sold (Q_1) and at what price (P_1).

After teaching the 'ideal' economy outlined above, microeconomics classes move on to discuss things which may prevent the economy from reaching a socially optimal outcome. It could be that consumers or firms do not have enough information about their potential choices and so make a decision which is objectively not in their best interests. A famous example that routinely pops up in economics education is the used-car market, where it is said

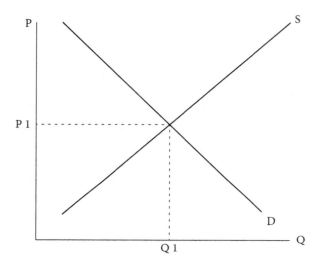

Figure 3.1 Basic supply and demand graph

that the risk that you might be buying a defective car will lead the market to break down, or 'market failure'. There are many types of these market imperfections, and economists study them to see how much of a problem they are and whether government policy might rectify them.[23]

Macroeconomics

Macroeconomics deals with bigger questions such as how countries can establish and sustain long-term economic growth, how they can control short-term economic fluctuations (commonly known as 'boom and bust') and how they can manage unemployment and rising prices or inflation.

Long-term growth macroeconomics such as the 'Solow Growth Model' attempt to show how different factors (such as technology or natural resources) contribute to the growth of economies. A modern variant called 'Endogenous Growth Theory' states that long-term sustained growth can be achieved by boosting skill levels and improving technology. This theory is the backbone for the current focus within government policy making on improving human capital.

Short-term macroeconomics looks at how policymakers can manage short-term economic fluctuations and influence unemployment and inflation. One approach entails the use of simple diagrams to represent the economy as a whole, the most famous of which is the IS-LM model.[24] As Figure 3.2 shows, it closely resembles the demand–supply diagram from microeconomics, but now the curves show how interactions between the market for goods and services and the market for money affect the GDP of the whole economy, rather than just how a particular market works.

Another, more advanced approach builds on the 'optimising agent' in the form of a 'representative agent' that is supposed to represent the economy as a whole. This agent lives for ever and makes optimal production and consumption decisions, predicting a path for GDP, prices and other economic variables such as unemployment over time.

Recessions are generally caused by 'exogenous shocks': sudden disturbances which come from outside of the model (such as the impacts of the Covid-19 crisis), affecting the agents' decisions and therefore the economy. As representative agent models use a single agent to represent the whole economy, they cannot model any type of inequality, because this requires interpersonal comparisons between different individuals and groups.[25]

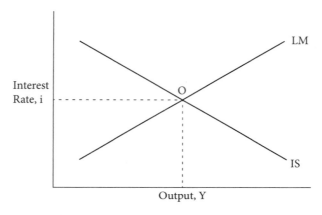

Figure 3.2 IS-LM model

Consequences

Here we can see that the core theoretical building blocks of micro- and macroeconomics focus on individuals not groups or systems and therefore cannot identify the way certain groups are structurally disadvantaged and then affected differently by economic events such as recessions and climate change.

Neoclassical economics presents a world of identical individuals making decisions in a vacuum not influenced in any way by their history or culture. In this way it makes invisible how the benefits and harms from historical oppression are distributed unequally in the world today. As a result of these histories, which we explore further in Chapter 4, different aspects of an individual's identity shape how they experience the economy; individuals enter the economy with structurally unequal resources and power which fundamentally shape the choice sets available to them.

While neoclassical economists will disagree endlessly about what kind of policies are best for different economies, at a more basic level, there is a striking consensus around what good and bad economic policy looks like. This includes consensus around the virtues of competition, the desirability of market mechanisms as opposed to public management, increased trade and specialisation, and the focus on efficiency as opposed to equity.[26]

The foundations of neoclassical economics lead to certain policies being framed as effective and common sense, and others as harmful and naïve. The dominance of this underlying neoclassical consensus has meant that many economic policies, such as exchange rate controls, import tariffs, land reform and rent controls, have been deemed ineffective or unacceptable when they might play a crucial role in addressing structural inequalities in wealth and power.

More broadly, the insistence that economists *are* objectively *just* describing the world, combined with the failure to engage with structural and historical analysis, means that neoclassical economics is strongly biased in favour of the status quo. The economist Ha-Joon Chang explains that 'In analysing individual choices, it [neoclassical economics] accepts as given the underlying social structure – the distribution of money and power, if you will.'[27] As a result, it only looks at 'choices that are possible without fundamental social changes'.

Chang points out that 'many neoclassical economists, even the "liberal" Paul Krugman, argue that we should not criticize low-wage factory jobs in poor countries because the alternative may be no job at all'. This is true if we accept that the underlying structure is inevitable, but if we are willing to change that structure itself, there are lots of alternatives to those low-wage jobs. For example, 'new labour laws that strengthen workers' rights, land reform that reduces the supply of cheap labour to factories (as more people stay in the countryside), or industrial policies that create high-skilled jobs' can mean that the choice for workers can be between low-wage jobs and higher-wage ones rather than between low-wage jobs and no jobs.[28]

Explaining discrimination

Reviewing the ways neoclassical economics attempts to explain discrimination clearly highlights the weaknesses and blind spots in its foundations that we have just described.

One approach is to describe *discrimination* as an issue of 'taste and preferences'.[29] Racist or sexist individuals may have a 'preference' for employing and targeting consumers of a certain racialised identity or socioeconomic background. As a result, they will lose customers and employees of the ethnicities and backgrounds they discriminate against and will, in the end, be priced out of the market. This approach is based on hardcore individualism (one of the pillars of neoclassical economics) and gives no account of the role played by discriminatory institutions and other political, economic, and social structures that create or perpetuate such identity-based discrimination.

Another approach is called *statistical discrimination*, which suggests there is some real basis for discrimination. For example, if on average certain identities are less likely to receive good quality education, which is likely to affect how good an employee they are, then, in absence of complete information about every individual, there is a rational basis for, say, an employer, to discriminate against an individual belonging to a specific identity based on this average statistical difference in their education.[30] This can also create a vicious cycle, as social groups which know they are going to face discrimination have less incentive to invest in education and so on, thus confirming the prejudice.

An open letter to the economics profession from the US economist Bill Spriggs in 2020 after the murder of George Floyd by a police
officer explains that 'To black economists, "statistical discrimination"
is a constant micro-aggression.' The idea that, despite 'the infinite
diversity of human beings', all employees somehow 'settle on "race"
as a meaningful marker' of 'negative attributes' and this has nothing
to do with 'history, laws, and social norms' is just 'stupefying'.

While 'far too many economists' are happy to accept statistical
analysis finding that 'negative attributes' are correlated with being
Black American, most don't 'accept that race is a social construct',
the purpose of which is 'to have a dominant group designate a
group to receive less of the goods of society'. For Bill Spriggs this
demonstrates that far too many economists still hold the assumption that Black Americans 'are inferior until proven otherwise'.[31]

This approach, by focusing on individuals, ignores broader systems that have been constructed in certain ways and reproduce certain outcomes and behaviours for different groups. Discrimination
operates across education, criminal justice, and employment in
ways that are connected and mutually reinforcing.[32] Discrimination
is embedded in the design, rules, norms and assumptions of institutions and structures in these systems, not just through individual
tastes, preferences or behaviour.

Discrimination is also intersectional along lines of racialised
identity, class and gender, shaping the experience and outcomes
of different individuals in our economies.[33] Neoclassical economics misses all of this by reducing racism to individual actions, and
racialised systemic inequalities to the personal or cultural insuf-
ficiencies of the marginalised group.[34]

Other economic perspectives highlight the role that racism can
play as a tool to maintain institutional arrangements that preserve
a dominant group's wealth and economic power – a point that

applies just as much to public health and police violence as it does to the labour market. In this section, we mainly draw on examples from the US, where these dynamics underpin the structural inequality between White and Black people. However, they also apply in other parts of the world to structural inequalities between all sorts of dominant and weaker social groups on the basis of religion, caste, tribe or gender, to name just a few.

In the context of the US, Kyle Moore highlights that 'for employers, racial wage or occupational differentiation among employees reduces their capacity for collective bargaining'. Here racism can benefit the powerful because if 'White workers maintain a higher wage or occupational rank relative to Black workers their relative superiority can be enough to suppress more extensive workplace demands'.[35]

Kyle Moore highlights an argument associated with *stratification economics* which we introduced in the table of economic perspectives in the last chapter (Table 2.1). Stratification economics views inter-group inequality as a result of long-term effects of dispossession of property brought about by historical factors.[36]

The differentiation among employees that Kyle describes is seen as a key part of the process by which certain groups maintain wealth and power because it reduces the possibility of an across-identities political front, lowers aspirations for certain identities, and weakens discontent with the institutions which reproduce the existing socioeconomic structure of society.[37]

The intentional stratification of racialised groups – to protect a dominant group's advantages and gains – creates intergenerational inequalities in wealth and, therefore, in economic and political power. This, in turn, shapes both individual behaviour and the design of our public institutions.[38] It is these dynamics that explain why, in the US, the wealth gap between Black and White families is as wide now as it was in 1968, the year when the Civil Rights Act was passed outlawing discrimination in housing.[39]

Consequently, the neoclassical framework for discrimination has resulted in policy proposals that are often limited to designing better mechanisms to ensure completeness of information, 'nudging' historically excluded identities to opt for more rational behaviour, or advocating for better opportunities such as schooling to increase the productivity of these socially disadvantaged identities.[40]

A prime example of this is the response of many economists to recent police brutality in the US in calling for more economic research to test various micro-oriented behavioural interventions, and expressing surprise that there isn't evidence that the use of body cams reduces police brutality.[41] This has led to a kind of colour-blindness and tacit belief that, by focusing on individuals, economics can sidestep having to address racialised structural inequalities.

Limiting the case for redistribution

We have seen already that neoclassical economics finds it hard to model inequality between individuals and groups because of its theoretical foundations. Neoclassical welfare analysis, which is used to evaluate the desirability of economic policies, is also inadequate in its consideration of redistribution, the decision to reallocate resources between individuals or groups to meet a particular goal.

One key idea from welfare economics is '*Pareto optimality*'. A situation is 'Pareto optimal' if nobody can be made better off without making at least one person worse off; any one person's gains must effectively be taken from another person. In other words, there are no unused resources available.[42]

In reality a broad range of situations can be Pareto optimal. Consider three people dividing a pie: whichever way they decide to do it, the outcome will be Pareto optimal as long as all of the pie is used. Whether they divide the pie equally or one person has the entire pie and the others have none, 'redistributing' the pie will involve taking it from one person and making them worse off. This effectively rules out any redistribution.

Another tool of welfare analysis is the *Social Welfare Function* (SWF). This tries to transplant the question of what an individual would do to maximise their utility (satisfaction) onto society as a whole. In other words, it asks which policy outcome 'we' would collectively prefer. The economist Amartya Sen has argued that since the SWF is concerned with maximising the total utility in a society, it is 'supremely unconcerned with the interpersonal distribution of that sum' and as a result is highly unsuitable for measuring or judging inequality.[43] SWFs don't give any information about which groups in society derive utility from a particular distribution of resources, which is necessary in order to decide whether that distribution is just or efficient, and to understand how redistribution could be used to improve an undesirable distribution.[44]

Failure to distinguish between wants and needs

All of this is about maximising utility, whether for an individual consumer or for society as a whole. Utility is a concept that is hard to pin down, which tries to describe the satisfaction gained from consuming a good or service. An economic good yields utility to the extent that it is useful for satisfying a consumer or society's want or need. In welfare economics, the concept of welfare is often used to describe the utility gained through the consumption of goods and services in a given society.

Embedded in this approach is a controversial judgement that consumption of the same good creates the same utility for every individual. In contrast, earlier economists[45] regarded the distribution of income as a major issue and were convinced that redistribution of wealth from those with many resources to those with less was the right thing to do because it increased overall welfare. Based on introspection and empirical evidence, they believed that at the level of high and low income groups, the latter derived more utility from gaining income to allow them to meet their basic needs than high income people lost from losing income.

This view was challenged by Vilfredo Pareto who argued that people with high and low-incomes might have such fundamentally different tastes that it would be impossible to compare their utilities. From this he developed his notion of Pareto optimality we've already seen (that an alternative is socially preferable if it makes one person better off and no one worse off).[46]

Then Lionel Robbins came along with his definition of economics in the 1930s,[47] which focused on *scarcity* and made no distinction between the consumption of goods to meet basic needs (food and shelter) and wants (fast cars, designer clothes), and the idea that meeting basic needs might have more impact on utility or welfare was lost. Neoclassical economics came to assume that *individual* differences of preference cannot be reliably compared and so it is pointless to consider how the actual distribution of resources affects the utility of different groups in society.

Another shift away from focusing on questions of distribution also began in the 1930s. Economics moved away from the concept of *marginal utility of consumption* (MUC), which highlighted that hungry people derive more utility from their first loaf of bread than their fifth. This was replaced by the *marginal rate of substitution* (MRS), which stated that hungry people would be willing to give up more of some other good, such as money, to obtain the first loaf of bread than they would to obtain the fifth loaf of bread.

In many ways, these two theories look the same. Both imply that a poor person would pay more for their first loaf of bread than their fifth. However, by replacing utility with money, MRS means we are no longer likely to conclude that a poor person would gain more utility from consuming a loaf of bread than a rich person. Here we explain why.

If we just compare the utility a poor and rich person derive from consuming a loaf of bread, as directed by MUC, it is hard to deny that more utility is derived by the poor person if they are hungry or less able to access other food. If, instead, we ask how much a poor or rich person is willing to pay for a loaf of bread, as directed by MRS, then a poor person isn't going to pay more because they have less money and they also need it more to meet their other basic needs. In this way, MRS implies that a poor person derives less utility consuming a loaf of bread than a rich person because they are willing to pay less. As a result, there is no case to distribute bread to poor people to maximise overall welfare.

Most people in most societies believe that consumption of basic necessities like food, water and housing has a greater moral and practical value to an individual than the consumption of luxuries. Neoclassical economics does not make this distinction, and so it perpetuates the existence of economies in which millions of people are not able to meet their basic needs by undermining the case for redistribution in the way described above.

Ignoring the role of history and power in who gets what

Now we move on to ask, how neoclassical theory explains economic distribution (who gets what, why) in the first place? The starting point is the four factors of production that are brought together to produce goods and services. These four factors are:

1. Land where the production takes place and the owners of which earn rent.
2. Capital such as a tractor or computer that is used to produce the output and the owners of which earns interest.
3. Labour, which is the workers who produce the output and who earn wages.
4. The entrepreneur who has the idea and brings together the other factors of production and who earns profits, which are the income from sales left over after the costs of all of the other factors of production are deducted.[48]

Neoclassical *marginal productivity theory* (MPT) states that each factor of production is rewarded in line with its contribution to production. Demand for any factor of production is determined by its productivity, the money value of what it produces minus its cost, and profit-maximising firms will hire an additional unit of a factor as long as it adds more to revenues than costs.

This theory explains that the reason top professional athletes earn more than surgeons who earn more than farm labourers and social care workers is because of the relative demand and supply for different jobs in competitive markets.

Differences in wages are explained by differences in acquired abilities like education and training and differences in inherent abilities; they compensate for danger or boredom, or because of barriers to entry such as licensing or regulations such as a minimum wage.

In this world, unions, through restricting the availability of labour, drive wages above equilibrium and therefore reduce demand (remember the supply and demand diagram earlier in the chapter). This benefits workers receiving the higher wage, but harms those who will now not be employed.

MPT is inadequate in at least two respects. First of all, it is patently clear that returns to factors of production are determined as much by power, institutions, and the rules of the game rather than any objective measure of their contribution to production. Societies have over time constructed ideas of 'skill' and 'value', which better reward work done by certain groups of people and not others.

Joelle Gamble explains that in the US they 'often classify work as low-skill that is actually high-skill, with a particular tendency to undervalue the work done by women and people of color.' She highlights care work as a prime example.

> Black workers are overrepresented in the childcare and social service professions, some of the fastest growing sectors in the country. Median hourly wages for home health and personal care aides were $11.37 in 2018. Yet these are jobs that require a high level of emotional intelligence, hours of training, and, in some states, an occupational license or certificate.[49]

Second, it implies that resources should be allocated to each according to their contribution. As the economist Joan Robinson pointed out:

> The theory purports to explain the difference between skilled and unskilled wages, not how the chance to acquire skills is limited. It purports to explain rent per acre, not the size of estates; the rate of interest, not the possession of capital … It says nothing about how [the ownership] of factors are distributed amongst people.[50]

As a result this theory has nothing to say about the justice of current patterns of ownership, which as we argue in the next chapter is often the result of historical oppression and therefore unjust.

The influence of neoclassical economics and MPT has encouraged governments to try to tackle inequality by increasing education and training opportunities. According to MPT, this will increase skills across the population, and for targeted groups such as low income workers, which will, in turn, increase productivity and therefore wages.

While education and training may be valuable, a focus on the productivity deficiencies of low-income workers obscures alternative external causes of their economic position including historical oppression and a lack of economic bargaining power.[51] We return in Chapter 5 to explore in more detail how neoclassical economics often explains the causes of poverty in ways which locate the causes in the deficiencies of poor people and countries (e.g. poor productivity, culture or corruption) rather than broader external or historical factors.

Today, though, MPT isn't justified because it directly leads to a fair allocation of resources but because it is efficient, and therefore maximises total output, which as we have already seen is assumed to maximise social welfare. According to this view, the huge wage inequalities, and increasing returns to land and capital, which characterise many modern economies across the world are argued to be necessary because they make up the structure of incentives which guide the efficient allocation of resources that maximises total output.

Misunderstanding land (a key driver of structural inequality)

Neoclassical economics recognises that land is a factor of production, but largely fails to treat it as a separate topic of analysis and therefore misses a key driver of structural inequality.

In macroeconomics, the standard neoclassical production function describes how total real gross domestic product (real GDP) in an economy depends on available inputs but is made up simply of capital and labour with one substitutable for the other; land is treated simply as one type of capital. Microeconomics still includes land as a factor of production but again treats it in the same way as labour and capital.

This ignores several fundamental differences between land and capital. Land is permanent, fixed and immobile, while capital is temporary, variable and mobile.

We cannot create land or the atmosphere or sunlight or water but can only acquire the rights to use it and improve or worsen its condition. Land can be used for many different things over time and its use for some things restricts its use for others. As populations grow, and capital stocks increase, land remains fixed and its value increases. As a result, land value appreciates rather than depreciates as capital does.

Land is fixed in geographical spaces and political jurisdictions and its value depends not just on it but what happens around it, e.g. improved transport links nearby or designating land for development increase the value of land without its owner doing anything.[52]

Neoclassical economics largely fails to make visible how the different ways land is treated in law play an important role either reproducing structural inequalities or challenging them. For example, the 1961 Land Compensation Act (UK) stipulates that land in England can be 'compulsory purchased' by public bodies without the consent of its owner, provided the landowner is compensated for it.

The compensation that must be paid for land isn't based on its current actual value. It is based on its 'potential' value from future development of the land and its surroundings, which by definition have nothing to do with the current owner. This approach substantially benefits existing owners of land at the expense of others who might benefit from alternative uses for that land, such as public sector home building which become less affordable as a result.[53] In this way, this law embeds and reproduces structural inequalities in land ownership in the UK.

Neither efficiency nor fairness

Before neoclassical economics erased the meaningful study of land, economists recognised that land was unique in that it was fixed in supply and had no cost of production. This means that increases in demand for land will only be reflected in an increase in its demand, not its quantity. Owners of land possess a good that is not subject to the normal laws of market competition, and are able to benefit from additional unearned income, called *economic rent* (not to be confused with the everyday use of rent). Rent in economics refers to any benefit that is derived from exclusive possession of a scarce resource or exclusive factor of production.[54] In the twentieth century, oil-rich countries became known as 'rentier states' due to their unique access to this scarce resource which everyone needed.

Brett Christophers explains the concept of economic rentier as the individual or, more typically, the corporation that controls the asset, while rentier capitalism is an economic order based on income-generating assets in which rents dominate overall incomes, and rentiers dominate economic life.[55] He argues that many economies today have become 'fundamentally orientated to "having" rather than "doing"' and in this way have become 'based on a proprietorial rather than entrepreneurial ethos'.[56]

In misunderstanding land, neoclassical economics conceals a central mechanism by which certain groups benefit from 'having' rather than 'doing', obscuring questions about the justice of how land was acquired, and structural inequality is reproduced. In the next chapter, we return to explore in more detail how the historical dispossession of land has shaped modern economies.

The neoclassical theory of distribution that underpins MPT is 'to each according to their contribution' (which emphasises productivity). However, the neoclassical lens fails to make visible the ways in which our modern economies are organised according to the principle 'to each according to what you have' because they provide unearned income to owners of assets like land which don't contribute to any economic production. This failure undermines its claim to allocate resource efficiently in a way that will maximise total output or by extension welfare. Therefore, neoclassical economics is ineffective as a guide to build economies which achieve fairness or efficiency.

Denies the possibility of both equity and efficiency

Neoclassical economics frames the ideas of equity and efficiency in a particular way that presents them as mutually exclusive goals. For example, the introductory textbook *Economics* by John Sloman and Alison Wride argues that 'there are two major [social] objectives that we can identify: efficiency and equity'.[57] The textbook begins by showing 'how a perfect market economy could under certain conditions lead to "social efficiency" [but] how markets in practice fail to meet social goals'. It then states that 'if the government is to replace the market and provide goods and services directly, it will need some way of establishing their costs and benefits', which can be done by using *cost benefit analysis* (CBA).[58]

This framing has a direct influence on government economic policy across the world. For example, in the UK the Green Book, a document produced by the Treasury which sets out the framework for the appraisal and evaluation of all government policies, programmes and projects, reads remarkably like an economics textbook in places.[59] It specifies the use of CBA to determine different ways of achieving market and welfare 'efficiency', defined as Pareto optimality, a concept we discussed earlier in the chapter.

CBA is portrayed as a hard-headed and pragmatic acknowledgement that we can't have all the good things that we want (a big pie and one that is equitably distributed), because the pattern of distribution is a natural outcome of dynamic economies, and redistribution distorts incentives and creates inefficiencies. But this framing is political, implying that we can't achieve one social objective without getting further from the other, which creates paralysing inertia and locks in the status quo. It implies that it would be great to address systemic inequality, but we just can't afford to because it will make everyone worse off.

However, it is not clear that this trade-off exists and it can just as easily be argued that there is an efficiency–inequity trade-off where increasing inequity reduces efficiency.[60] At a deeper level, efficiency is only a means to increasing total output or its rate of growth, not an end in itself. Likewise, increasing total output is only a goal because, as we saw earlier in this chapter, neoclassical economic theory claims that this is the best way to maximise social welfare. Understanding this allows us to reframe the trade-off as one between equity and social welfare (which is the end goal of increasing efficiency). However, we've already argued that increasing equity is one of the most effective ways to increase social welfare. If this argument is accepted, then actually there is no trade-off at all!

As Cahal Moran argues, economics needs 'a shift in perspective to the baseline assumption that needs are not at odds with economic aims but are instead a key foundation upon which an economy (and society) is built'.[61] If government policymakers thought in this way, they would be much better equipped to address structural inequalities.

Economics students recognise this failure

As we saw at the beginning of this chapter, Brototi, like many students, had a strong gut feeling that her neoclassical economics education was not equipping her to understand or address the structural inequalities she witnessed in her home country India. The economics students we interviewed for this book repeatedly highlighted the way that economic knowledge sidelines so many of the important details that explain structural inequality.

Alex, a North American postgraduate student from a low-income background who we heard from in Chapter 1, felt: 'It was a very idyllic picture that my economics education painted. If people work hard, they earn money, and that means they're good. If they're poor, that means they've made bad choices.' Alex remembered how examples like: 'Johnny started a business and makes this much revenue, has this much costs – calculate profits along those lines' made someone like them think, 'Where did he get that money? Did he get it from a bank? Did his parents give it to him?'

They further explained: 'I come from a background where every minute had to be occupied by doing something, otherwise I would be homeless. Economics education just does not account for those barriers that I've lived and that I know are barriers to living the kind of life that economics implies. People like me can't just start a business.'

Related specifically to racialised identity, Gina, a Black British undergraduate, believes that: 'Nowhere in economics do they ever acknowledge that the experience of a Black person is going to be different to that of a White person. You're just *homoeconomicus*. It doesn't matter what your race is.'

In contrast, Emilia, a UK-based Finnish undergraduate, commented on how what she learns in economics mirrors her life experiences as someone from a financially privileged background. She feels that: 'the more capitalist liberal Western economics course definitely tailors to the way my lifestyle has been where I've never had to worry about money ... but that makes me reflect on and question the course less because it suits my identity and what my lifestyle has been like'.

As is clear from the insights of Alex, Gina and Emilia, neoclassical economics struggles to account for the complex interrelationships between structural inequalities, people's identity and their lived experience and this is particularly jarring for students from backgrounds underrepresented in the discipline.

Chapter 4

Whitewashes history

Now we turn to consider the economic history of our world to understand better how today's structural inequality came to be.

In the last chapter, we argued that the theoretical foundations of neoclassical economics are unsuitable for addressing structural inequality because they analyse the interaction of individuals in an ahistorical vacuum.

As a result, when mainstream economic research and education seeks to explain why some countries today are rich and others are poor, it draws on an idealised and oversimplified historical narrative. This story whitewashes the role of historical oppression, such as the transatlantic slave trade, colonial land theft and reproductive control by men over women, in economic development.

Likewise, economic research and education about globalisation, a process by which the economies of countries become more integrated, often frames it as an increase in voluntary exchange for mutual benefit and increased prosperity. This glosses over the many historical examples of powerful countries using real or threatened violence to coerce others into becoming more integrated in global economies.

By ignoring the role that oppression and violence has played in historical economic development, academic economics maintains a fiction that allows it to be ignored in the present. If these histories are seriously considered then we are forced to reconsider how we think about our modern economies.

We need new understandings of our economies that highlight how violence and oppression undermine people's freedom; the mechanisms used by those with power and wealth to protect and pass it on across generations; and the deeply embedded racialised dimensions of historical oppression, which explain why the wealthier countries in the world tend to be Whiter.

The story of the great take-off

Embedded, structural inequalities of the type we see today are a specific feature of modern economies. In the words of economic anthropologist Jason Hickel, 'in the year 1500 [just over five hundred years ago], there was no appreciable difference in incomes and living standards between Europe and the rest of the world.' He highlights 'that people in some regions' of Latin America, Africa, the Middle East and Asia 'were a good deal better off than their counterparts in Europe.'[1] This is not to say that there weren't economic inequalities both within and across social groups but just that they weren't of the same scale and they weren't structural in the same way they are now.

So how does academic economics explain the transition from this period to the present day? A simple version of the story goes like this. Feudalism was the dominant socioeconomic system in medieval Europe, in which the nobility were given lands by the Crown in exchange for military service. In turn, loyal servants (vassals) were tenants of the nobles, while peasants were obliged to live on their lord's land and honour him, provide labour and a share of their produce, notionally in exchange for military protection.

During the seventeenth century (1600–1700), merchants gradually became more involved in the production of goods by supplying materials and paying wages. At this time, the institutions of private

119

property, markets and firms developed to resemble their modern form. This was called mercantile capitalism.

This combination of institutions created the conditions for the Industrial Revolution in the eighteenth century (1700–1800), which was characterised by the shift to using coal as a source of energy. This facilitated a transition from hand production methods to machine production, the improved efficiency of water power and the increasing use of steam power which significantly increased productivity.

It also saw the development of the factory system of manufacturing, characterised by a complex division of labour between and within work processes and the routinisation of work tasks. This was industrial capitalism, and it provided the impetus for the extraordinary economic growth we see in the famous 'hockey stick' graph (see Figure 4.1).

This narrative explains that economic growth made everyone better off but some countries did better than others and it increased inequality. In this story, we regret historical happenings like slavery and colonialism, but they are independent of the development of our modern economic system and the structural inequality we see today.

There is some economic research that complicates that narrative, exploring how historical events have influenced today's economic outcomes in quantitative terms. Economists have explored how 250 years of forced labour imposed by Spain in Peru has influenced regional differences in income and consumption today,[2] the long-lasting effects of slavery on economic outcomes in different parts of Africa,[3] and the increased level of conflict caused by the partition of ethnic groups as colonial powers were dividing Africa up between them.[4] This is positive, but importantly it only focuses on the harm done to people who were enslaved and the countries

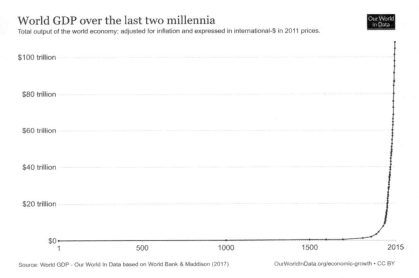

Figure 4.1 World GDP over the last two millennia: total output of the world economy; adjusted for inflation and expressed in international-$ in 2011 prices

that were colonised, not the economic benefits for the slave owners and colonisers. In this way, it misses a crucial part of the picture.

Similarly, economics education is slowly engaging with the role of slavery and colonisation in holding back the 'take-off' of economic growth for certain countries. For example, the first chapter of the new digital open-access economics textbook CORE presents an adapted version of the hockey stick graph by country (see Figure 4.2). It explains that 'not every capitalist country is the kind of economic success story exemplified ... by Britain, later Japan, and the other countries *that caught up* [our italics]'.

CORE highlights that, 'in some economies, substantial improvements in people's living standards did not occur until they gained

History's hockey stick: Worldwide historical real gross domestic product per capita (1000–2016)

Unit 1 'The capitalist revolution' in The CORE Team, The Economy. Available at: https://tinyco.re/19274920 [Figure 1.1a]

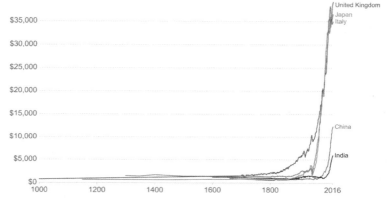

Source: Maddison Project Database (2018)
tinyco.re/19274920 • Powered by ourworldindata.org
Note: The units of measurement is 2011 US dollar which is used to compare Purchasing Power Parity and GDP across countries over time.

Figure 4.2 The CORE economics education curriculum's representation of economic development over a millennium

independence from colonial rule or interference by European nations'.[5] It cites three examples of this:[6]

- *India*: According to Angus Deaton, an economist who specialises in the analysis of poverty, when 300 years of British rule of India ended in 1947: 'It is possible that the deprivation in childhood of Indians … was as severe as that of any large group in history'. In the closing years of British rule, a child born in India could expect to live for twenty-seven years. Fifty years on, life expectancy at birth in India had risen to sixty-five years.

- *China*: It had once been richer than Britain, but by the middle of the twentieth century GDP per capita in China was one-fifteenth that of Britain.

- *Latin America*: Neither Spanish colonial rule, nor its aftermath following the independence of most Latin American nations early in the nineteenth century, saw anything resembling the hockey-stick upturn in living standards experienced by the countries in Figure 4.2.

CORE acknowledges harm done to people in these places, but like the research cited above, it doesn't focus on the economic benefits that accrued to Britain and other European colonial powers or how these benefits contributed to their economic development.

Without acknowledgement of the economic benefits of slavery and colonisation, economics education and mainstream academic research reproduces the harmful and offensive framing of economic development as a race in which low-income countries must 'catch up'.

What is missing from this story?

Slavery as central to European and US economic development

The transatlantic slave trade involved the enslavement of almost 13 million Africans, taken from their homelands to work for the benefit of Europeans and Americans, taking place over three hundred years, between the sixteenth and nineteenth centuries (1500–1800).[7]

For much of this period the UK controlled the trade transporting enslaved Africans to the US, exchanging them for cotton which was shipped to Liverpool and distributed across the UK where it was used in the textile industry which played a central role in the birth of industrial capitalism.

Even after the UK outlawed the slave trade in 1807, right up until the American Civil War in 1861, 85 per cent of its imports of cotton came from the US slave plantations and it was the country's single largest import (it was also the US's largest export).[8] This trade also included other core commodities produced on slave plantations in the US and Caribbean including tobacco, sugar and cocoa.

In *Capitalism and Slavery*, published in 1944, Eric Williams, a young historian who later became the first prime minister of an independent Trinidad and Tobago, forcefully argued that slavery was central to the transition from feudalism to our modern economic system of capitalism.[9] This argument challenged the commonly held view that the 'slave economy' of the Southern US States represented an alternative economic system to the industrial capitalism of the Northern US States and Britain.

Putting slavery at the heart of our analysis of the economic system forces us to reassess the basic concepts we use. While we normally distinguish between labour on one hand (workers paid wages to work) and capital (the goods used in production) on the other, slaves were both labour and capital. Their value in 1860 was equal to all of the capital invested in American railroads, manufacturing, and agricultural land combined.[10]

A gendered aspect of this economic system was that it depended on the capacity of enslaved women to give birth and so reproduce its capital. As a result, women slaves were subject to horrific sexual violence, coerced reproduction and forced separation from their children who were cut off from their histories and cultures.

The transatlantic slave trade also played a major role in the development of two central finance and insurance institutions in our modern economic systems. Donald E. Grant Jr demonstrates the links between many major financial and insurance institutions today including Lehman Brothers, Lloyd's of London, Aetna Insurance, Barclays, JPMorgan Chase and the slave-driven cotton industry. He explains that 'narratives and litigation records show

how these organisations monetised the African slave trade to lever-age resources for the building of their personal empires and global brands'.[11]

The historian Walter Johnson explains the role of credit and col-lateral, two distinct features of our modern financial systems, in the slave trade. 'Every year the cotton merchants of Great Britain made tremendous advances to the cotton planters of the South.' Then the planters used this money (credit) to 'purchase seeds and tools and slaves and the food to feed them, and they planned to use those slaves to plant and pick and pack and ship the cotton that would cover the money that had been advanced to them, and then some'.[12]

Walter Johnson quotes the pro-slavery political economist Thomas Kettel who, writing in 1860, explained how the slave-based cotton trade operated. The cotton 'is ready but once a year' when it is harvested but cotton producers need to 'buy supplies year round' and the 'whole banking system of the country' is set up to loan cot-ton producers the money (credit) they need to operate.[13]

Johnson explains the risk if 'the cotton proved too scant or poor to cover the amount that had been advanced against its eventual sale', or if 'the cotton market dipped' and cotton producers weren't able to earn enough to pay their loans back. As a result, the cotton merchants who were loaning the money required a security which they could take ownership of if the cotton producers couldn't pay them back. 'That security was the value of the enslaved ... [they] were the collateral upon which the entire system depended.'[14] In this way, the slave-based cotton trade was very much a modern capitalist economy and it is important that we acknowledge it as such, rather than try to distance ourselves from it.

Philip Roscoe describes that the 'obscene novelty of the slav-ers' banking system was that this financial value was secured on human bodies'. He argues that the 'slaves were exploited twice: their freedom and labour stolen from them; their captured "economic value" leveraged by cutting edge financial instruments'.

He also relates the story of the captain of the slave ship *Zong*. On a voyage in 1781 he realised he was unlikely to land his cargo of sickening and malnourished slaves, so he ordered 133 people to be thrown overboard. The perverse legal logic was that if part of the cargo had to be jettisoned to save the ship, it would be covered by the insurance. Insurance made the value of this human capital real and bankable.[15]

Not only have financial and insurance companies that exist today benefited economically from slavery as outlined above. Important finance and insurance practices were developed in this period that are widely used today. Slavery has been central to US, European and global economic development, not separate or opposed to it.

Colonial land appropriation as the foundation of modern economies

From 1500 to the twentieth century, almost every country on Earth came under the direct or indirect control of European colonial powers. By 1913 the British Empire alone held sway over 412 million people, nearly a quarter of the world's population at the time, and by 1920 it covered a quarter of the Earth's total land area.[16]

A key part of colonialism was the declaration of ownership of land backed by military force. In the US, the land on which enslaved people planted cotton was originally Native American land. It had been expropriated from Native American groups such as the Creek, Cherokee, Choctaw, Chickasaw and Seminole.

Walter Johnson argues that this initial dispossession was a key part of the transition to modern capitalist economies. In 1823, the United States Supreme Court in the case of Johnson v. McIntosh deliberated over 'whether White settlers could purchase land directly from native inhabitants'.

The Supreme Court decided this wasn't legal and that Native American lands 'must be passed through the public domain of the United States before being converted into the private property of White inhabitants'.[17]

Land needed to first be invaded by the US government before it could be given to White settlers as legal private property, which could then become the basis of a modern economic system based on property ownership and market exchange.

This process of invasion and turning of land into the foundation of economic systems occurred across the world. Indigenous Peoples were killed by colonisers and the germs they brought and forced to the peripheries of the new colonies.

When European settlers arrived in North America, historians estimate there were over ten million Native Americans living there.[18] By 1900, their estimated population was under 300,000.[19] European settlement of Latin America led to the death of 50–100 million people or 95 per cent of the Latin American population from 1492 to the mid-1600s.[20]

The scale of violence involved in these processes of dispossession are almost incomprehensible and certainly not accounted for in any way in mainstream understandings of European, US and global economic development.

When neoclassical academic economics does rarely attempt to understand the legacies of racialised oppression on the global economy, it often uses inappropriate methods. For example, one paper[21] has argued that regions in former French West Africa where colonial investment in education was higher still have more schools today. Another explores the extent to which colonial-era railway construction explains present-day inequalities in African urbanisation. A third suggests that literacy increased faster in British than French Togo and that this difference persisted after independence.[22]

This research highlights that there were negative and positive aspects of colonial policies and that some former colonies did better than others post-independence which is certainly true. However, Yannick Dupraz and Valeria Rueda argue that the approach this research takes does not allow us to evaluate the economic impacts of colonialism more holistically because they compare different colonised regions, rather than comparing colonised regions to non-colonised ones.

Moreover, it is impossible to compare colonised regions to non-colonised ones because there is no counterfactual of a world without colonialism to compare against. Dupraz and Rueda argue that

> Picking a place with no European settlers is no counterfactual for colonisation because colonisation was more than the presence of Europeans. It was the way everything was organised, from local economies to the international trade and finance. Therefore, any exercise aimed at measuring the effects of *colonialism* relies on the construction of artificial, shaky, comparison points.[23]

The starting point instead has to be that the violence and dispossession associated with colonialism has fundamentally shaped our global economies today and the structural inequalities which define it. Table 4.1 lists the UN's list of 'least developed countries' in 2020 and their former colonial rulers. What it tells us is no coincidence and must not be forgotten.

Economic benefits from colonialism

As we highlighted earlier in the chapter, it is important to understand how former colonial powers continue to benefit economically

Table 4.1   United Nations list of 'least developed countries' and their former colonial rulers

Country	Colonised by	Country	Colonised by
1. Afghanistan	Britain	24. Madagascar	France
2. Angola	Portugal	25. Malawi	Britain
3. Bangladesh	Britain	26. Mali	France
4. Benin	France	27. Mauritania	France
5. Bhutan	British protectorate, i.e. indirect rule	28. Mozambique	Portugal
6. Burkina Faso	France	29. Myanmar	Britain
7. Burundi	Belgium	30. Nepal	British protectorate, i.e. indirect rule (Nepal relinquished some territory)
8. Cambodia	French protectorate, i.e. indirect rule	31. Niger	France
9. Central African Republic	France	32. Rwanda	Germany then Belgium post WWI
10. Chad	France	33. São Tomé and Principe	Portugal
11. Comoros	France	34. Senegal	France
12. Democratic Republic of the Congo	Belgium	35. Sierra Leone	Britain
13. Djibouti	France	36. Solomon Islands	Britain
14. Eritrea	Italy up to 1941, then Britain	37. Somalia	Italian colony/ British protectorate, i.e. indirect rule

(continued)

Table 4.1 (continued)

Country	Colonised by	Country	Colonised by
15. Ethiopia	Italy (occupied more so than colonised) – 1941 full independence (see note 24)	38. South Sudan	Britain
16. Gambia	Britain	39. Sudan	Britain
17. Guinea	France	40. Timor-Leste	Portugal
18. Guinea-Bissau	Portugal	41. Togo	Germany until 1918, then France until independence
19. Haiti	France	42. Tuvalu	Britain
20. Kiribati	Britain	43. Uganda	Britain
21. Lao People's Democratic Republic	France	44. United Republic of Tanzania	Britain
22. Lesotho	Britain	45. Yemen	Britain
23. Liberia	Never formally colonised by Europeans[24]	46. Zambia	Britain

Source: adapted from Gargi Bhattacharyya, *Rethinking Racial Capitalism: Questions of Reproduction and Survival.*

today from the legacies of oppression. Gurminder Bhambra recounts:

> Richard Temple presented the general statistics of the British Empire to the Royal Statistical Society meeting in 1884. Of the £203 million pounds at the disposal of the British state for general government £89 million came from the UK, £74 million came from India and £40 million came from British territories and the rest of Empire.

At this time, 'Over half of revenue came from the wider Empire beyond the nation and two thirds of that came from India alone.'[25]

In Glasgow at the same time, the 1866 City Improvement Act was passed, introducing a scheme to bring a clean water supply into the city with the opening of the Loch Katrine project. Gas and electricity systems followed. In Birmingham, under Joseph Chamberlain (Mayor from 1873 to 1875), provision was made for gas and water supplies controlled by the government. They also cleared slums and introduced a city park system.[26]

The British Empire and the era of what is often called Municipal Socialism in the UK are usually viewed separately but we can see they are intimately connected. It is clear that the revenue extracted from the Empire contributed in large part to the development of publicly funded health systems, a national infrastructure of gas, water and electricity, and a social welfare system in Britain.[27]

In contrast, many former colonised countries have struggled to develop their own social and health systems in this way and their populations today live without access to clean water, sanitation or electricity. These structural inequalities are a direct result of the histories of oppression that connects descendants of those who were colonised and those who did the colonising.

Walter Rodney, a Guyanese historian and political economist, began to critique the benefits of Western-centric capitalist development with ideas linked to postcolonial scholarship that emerged in the 1960s.[28] He explained how structural inequalities within the global economy manifested in Africa in his book *How Europe Underdeveloped Africa*.[29] It presents a compelling case for Africa's contribution to Europe's 'developed' state, and Europe's contribution to Africa's 'underdeveloped' state through colonialism.

Bhambra argues that most European states were not nations but empires and that colonial populations were an *unequal* part of their coloniser's political community. She argues that by failing to acknowledge this, we do not recognise the legitimacy of claims by 'immigrants' today to settle in Europe and access education, health and social security. Rights to access these services tend to be associated with being able to demonstrate historical belonging to the nation, but, of course, many people all over the world can demonstrate this belonging to European nations through virtue of their country being colonised.[30] As a result, economics must engage with expanded notions of citizenship and the implications of this when considering immigration in modern economies.

Gender and reproductive control were central to the economic organisation of colonies

In the same way, gender and reproductive control over women played a central role in European expansion and oppression between the sixteenth and twentieth centuries (1500–1900).

The anthropologist Ann Laura Stoler argues that: 'The regulation of sexual relations was central to the development of particular kinds of colonial settlements and to the allocation of economic activity within them.' She points out that:

> Who bedded and wedded whom in the colonies of France, England, Holland, and Iberia was never left to chance. Unions between Annamite women and French men, between Portuguese women and Dutch men, between Inca women and Spanish men produced offspring with claims to privilege, whose rights and status had to be determined and prescribed.[31]

Nancy Folbre documents how Spain and Portugal limited women immigrants to the Americas in the 1500s to maintain their home populations, but this meant European men far outnumbered European women in Latin America.[32] The subsequent domination and violence by European men over Indigenous women, who had survived death through European illnesses and killings, resulted in a growing *mestizo* population and the Catholic church suspending religious rules around sex outside of marriage.[33] In the mid-sixteenth century, Spain legally prevented anyone with native ancestry from inheriting land grants and the term *mestizo* in essence meant illegitimate, while European men's financial contributions to their children mothered by Indigenous women were voluntary.[34]

Similarly, European companies operating in the Pacific since the 1600s, such as the Dutch East Indies Company, only employed single men from Europe and actively prevented European women from joining them.[35] The company encouraged sexual relations between their Dutch employees and local women, *concubinage*, but not Euro-Asian marriages as its government outlawed its men returning to the Netherlands with their colonised wives and children.

From a Dutch view of maintaining colonial dominance in the region, these long-term relations between Dutch men and colonised women meant that such men were more likely to remain as settlers, while these women were viewed as demanding less of these men financially and emotionally compared to Dutch women; this also saved Dutch employees money by having their concubines carry out domestic duties.[36] Concubinage continued so that by the 1880s almost half of all Dutch Indies' European men lived with Asian women outside of marriage, with such arrangements only being denounced a few decades later.[37]

These histories highlight the importance of identifying how historical violence and dispossession has occurred across intersections of racialised and gender identities, as well as considering how they have shaped the structural inequalities that characterise our modern economies.

The story of globalisation

Economic globalisation describes a process by which the economies of countries become more integrated through increased trade and investment as well as the increased alignment of laws, regulations and institutions which facilitate this integration.

There have been two major periods of globalisation, the first beginning in the mid-nineteenth century up until World War One, and the second beginning after World War Two up to the present.

In both cases, economics has provided the intellectual legitimisation for globalisation. The foundational argument is that increased trade will increase total wealth and therefore be mutually beneficial.

This argument is based on two concepts. First, specialisation, which is the idea that countries should focus on the goods and services they can produce most efficiently.

Second, comparative advantage, a theory that argues that even if one country can produce all goods more efficiently than another, total output and welfare will be increased if they each focus on producing the good they were most productive in and simply trade.

Neoclassical economics distinguishes between open economies, which are more integrated with the world economy, and closed economies, which are less.

Countries have a balance of payments that measures the value of all economic transactions between a country and the rest of the world, and some countries have a surplus – they gain income from the rest of the world – while others have a deficit – they accrue debt.

A country's exchange rate signifies the amount of a unit of its currency that can be exchanged for another. Neoclassical economics argues that exchange rates should be set through market mechanisms and not 'manipulated' or 'set' by government policy.

From this starting point economic reasoning has been used to discredit tariffs (taxes on imports) or quotas (rules limiting import/ export), capital controls (rules/taxes that limit the flow of capital) and any government policies or regulation that might give its national businesses an unfair advantage.

This reasoning invokes the standard neoclassical economic framing of voluntary exchange for mutual benefit and the alignment of laws and regulations between countries to reduce 'frictions' that make economic exchange more costly and create a level playing field to facilitate competition.

Writing in 1920, after World War One (1914–1918) had ended the first 'golden age' of globalisation, the famous British economist J. M. Keynes vividly described the benefits of that international economic system from his perspective, in a quote that is reproduced in many economics textbooks.

He explained how globalisation meant 'any man of capacity or character at all exceeding the average' could 'at a low cost and with the least trouble' consume 'comforts, and amenities' beyond the imagination 'of the richest and most powerful monarchs of other ages'.

'The inhabitant of London could order by telephone, sipping his morning tea in bed, the various products of the whole earth, in such quantity as he might see fit, and reasonably expect their early delivery upon his doorstep.' Swap the phone for the internet and many readers will recognise this is a feature of today's globalised economy.

Keynes described being able to invest 'wealth in the natural resources and new enterprises of any quarter of the world, and share, without exertion or even trouble, in their prospective fruits and advantages'.

135

He explained how globalisation had made the world feel smaller and more connected. This was facilitated because of the 'comfortable means of transit to any country or climate without passport or other formality'; the common use of currency which allowed travel to 'foreign quarters, without knowledge of their religion, language, or customs, bearing coined wealth upon his person', and the greater security which meant you were 'much surprised at the least interference'.[38]

What is missing from this story?

Nineteenth-century gunboat globalisation

In focusing on voluntary exchange for mutual benefit, globalisation narratives underplay the fact that the most powerful countries have repeatedly used military force or the threat of it to coerce less powerful countries to become more integrated in global economies.

The first global economic system developed in the nineteenth century with the European powers at the centre each connected in a web of economic relationships with their colonies, with raw materials flowing towards Europe and manufactured goods flowing back.

The financial system also became global with the levels of international movement of capital, before it was halted by World War One, not reached again until very recently.[39] Prior to World War One, the European Powers owned more than three-quarters of industrial capital in Africa and Asia.[40]

Thomas Piketty summarises the global system of the time in this way.

The rest of the world worked to increase consumption for the colonial powers and at the same time became more and more indebted to those same powers ... The advantage of owning things is that one can continue to consume and accumulate without having to work ... The same was true on an international scale in the age of colonialism.[41]

Putting colonial power relations at the heart of our analysis of the global economic system at this time forces us to reassess what we have tended to think of as the era of small government and globalised trade and finance.

Dani Rodrik highlights how European colonial powers used military force or the threat of it to compel other countries to agree to trade deals, honour contracts and pay back debts. He explains that when the Ottoman Empire defaulted on paying back its debt to its mainly British and French creditors in 1875, the Sultan was forced to let them set up a debt agency to collect Ottoman tax revenues. As a result, 'The Ottoman Public Debt Administration (which began operations in 1881) became a vast bureaucracy within the Ottoman state with the primary purpose of paying foreign creditors.'[42]

Rodrik recounts that 'when agitation in Egypt threatened British financial interests in 1882, the British invaded the country to "restore political stability" and ensure that foreign debts would continue to be repaid'. The British Prime Minister at the time had lots of his personal wealth invested in Egypt and, in this case, there was a particularly clear link between 'financial globalisation and military power.'[43]

These are just two examples that complicate the narrative that globalisation happened because of a voluntary increase in trade for the mutual benefit of all parties. They draw attention to the role of powerful states in constructing and enforcing the rules of global economic systems through military force or the threat of it, in ways that further their interests at the time.

Liberalism or social democracy at home and authoritarianism abroad

Mainstream economic narratives highlight the role of liberal government and inclusivity in explaining a country's economic performance but ignore that for much of this period European governments were liberal democracies at home and authoritarian, oppressive regimes outside their national borders.

In *Why Nations Fail*, economists Daron Acemoglu and James Robinson take what has been called a new institutional approach to explaining 'the Origins of Power, Prosperity, and Poverty'.[44] They see political and economic institutions as the reasons for differences in the economic and social development of different states. These institutions are either 'extractive' – excluding the majority of society from the process of political decision-making and income distribution – or 'inclusive' – including the widest possible strata of society in economic and political life. Countries with inclusive institutions are those that are prosperous today.

This framing equates economic success with democracy and inclusivity, while ignoring the way European economic development was built on 'inclusive' institutions at home and highly 'extractive' institutions in their colonies.

Historians Hall *et al.* argue that 'while the British state [in the nineteenth century] may be characterised as "liberal", what constituted "liberalism", seen in an imperial context, has to be severely qualified'. They suggest that

> The liberal state may have appeared to rest on consent but coercion remains critical to its operations; it may have been laissez-faire but interventionism was a central and persistent strategy; it may have stressed the enlargement of liberties and constitutional freedoms but it required the suppression of indigenous peoples and the cultural re-formation of its subject peoples; it may have been shaped by a belief

in the rule of 'free markets' but it also depended on state-driven economic policies in relation to Indian cotton or Irish agriculture.[45]

The same applies to other European states with violent treatment of colonial populations contrasting with social democratic type economic policy for the home country. France in the 1920s was a parliamentary democracy whose government would vote for the most progressive workers' rights in history just a decade later; and yet, an estimated 20,000 forced labourers died in the construction of the Congo-Océan railway in French Congo in that decade.[46] These contradictions ran right to the heart of the political-economic-social systems of the time and still lie, mostly unexamined, embedded in our societies and economies today.

Acemoglu, Johnson and Robinson themselves point out that some colonies such as Australia and New Zealand were built on inclusive institutions and have economically benefited accordingly. However, here there is inadequate recognition that 'inclusive' in these cases rested upon the dispossession and oppression of Indigenous Peoples.[47]

Another flaw in this approach is that it focuses on the inclusive or extractive nature of national institutions and ignores how a globalised economic system and rules were set up during both periods of globalisation and how these systems were often 'extractive' for less powerful countries.

Political but not economic decolonisation

Over the course of the twentieth century, many peoples fought and won independence from their colonisers, in what were often bloody wars. Hundreds of thousands of people died during the independence wars in Algeria, Indochina and Cameroon just a little over fifty years ago.

Although each country's journey towards and into independence has been different, a common theme has arisen. Newly independent people and academics have drawn attention to the fact that political sovereignty has not been combined with economic sovereignty. They are given the right to form a government and hold elections but economic control over their country's resources is limited using various techniques and strategies.[48]

The process of decolonisation in many countries saw a transitory period during which White settlers, businessmen, and officials attempted to transfer assets they owned into a form that could be moved out of the country, or at the very least shielded from newly independent governments.

For example, United Nations Conference on Trade and Development (UNCTAD) researchers found that large unrecorded flows from the overseas franc area to metropolitan France in the 1960s 'reflected primarily transfers by French residents in Algeria and elsewhere in Africa'. UNCTAD estimated about 4 billion French francs to have left the French colonial world for metropolitan France between 1957 and 1961, with another large outflow following in 1962. It mentioned considerable difficulties in ascertaining the exact magnitude of this outflow and acknowledged that the volume of flight capital might be considerably larger owing to these uncertainties: much of it had either not passed through official channels 'or has been in a form which renders identification difficult'.[49]

Rather than returning to European countries where tax rates were high, lots of this money was moved to tax havens, legal jurisdictions that allow individuals and businesses to escape the rule of law in the countries where they operate and live, and to pay less tax than they should in those countries.[50] This led to a substantial growth in tax havens across the world and today we are unable to understand the global economy without understanding their role.

Historian Vanessa Ogle describes this process in the case of Kenya, explaining that the movement of assets out of the country began to intensify in 1960 (independence was declared in 1963). 'The Times reported that from February to April about £3.4 million had left the territory' (equivalent to about £80.3 million in 2021 prices).

She explains how banks had recently developed products that allowed customers to move assets to tax havens. For example, a Bahamian discretionary trust was often recommended. A 'trust' is a legal relationship in which the legal title to property is entrusted to a person or legal entity who then has a duty to hold and use it for another's benefit (and have long been used to avoid inheritance or estate taxes).

'Discretionary' meant that control of the trust lay with the directors of a company the bank had set up for this purpose. 'Bahamian' just meant that the trust was set up in the Bahamas, which was a tax haven and at that point was still a British colony.[51]

All of this meant that the trust was 'legally far enough removed from the actual owner of the assets … so as not to become liable to taxes on the income that the trust earned … since the nominal owner was located in the tax haven of the Bahamas'. Because 'the actual owner could claim to have no legal control over the trust, he or she could not be forced by a government to hand over assets held abroad'.

Combined with other legal instruments such as a holding company and investment company, trusts could be used to shield assets in a variety of ways. They

> could acquire funds previously held in a Kenyan (or other) company, including real estate; could hold the shares of a Kenyan company

engaged in farming; and could receive as a gift securities [assets such as stocks and bonds] of UK residents that would be exempt from estate tax if the beneficial owner (the Bahamas company) was domiciled outside the United Kingdom.[52]

Ogle quotes Kleinwort Benson's bankers in the Bahamas (a leading UK investment bank at the time) reflecting on how it could attract new business to the recently launched trust company Arawak:

> As a result of political developments in the above-mentioned countries [Kenya and the West Indies], and possibly others, it is suggested that Arawak should give consideration to sending a knowledgeable representative to such areas with a view to getting business in the trust field as there seems to be an obvious need for residents of such areas to take some sort of evasive action against future legislation in their countries of residence in order to preserve their foreign assets.[53]

She then outlines the threat colonial asset holders were running from. 'Newly independent governments could resort to various instruments and measures to assume control over capital and foreign exchange.' Their options included 'ordering private banks to hand over gold and foreign currencies, forcing banks to register the full details of funds and securities held in banks abroad; requiring residents to exchange all foreign currencies, gold bars and negotiables in their possession for the new official currency'.[54]

One question to ask here is who bought the assets that could not be moved out of countries on the verge of independence? It is likely that those who were able to benefit were national elites with wealth who had good relationships with the former colonial power. Preferential access to the assets of departing colonisers for national elites may contribute to explaining why in 2017 ten of the nineteen most unequal countries in the world were in Sub-Saharan Africa.[55]

This process may also have contributed to a gradual shift from direct ownership of companies based in colonies, to indirect ownership of companies in newly independent nations, through stocks and bonds. Ogle explains that, indirect ownership 'allowed multinational corporations in particular to avoid the political risks that came with direct ownership of production abroad' including hostile independent governments and discontented 'workers and their unions'.[56]

One consequence of this history is that many governments are increasingly unable to effectively collect taxation. In 2020, the Tax Justice Network (TJN) reported that countries are losing a total of over $427 billion in tax each year. Of this 57 per cent is directly lost to corporate tax abuse by multinational corporations and the rest is lost to private tax evasion by individuals.

TJN explain some of the mechanisms through which this took place. 'Multinational corporations paid billions less in tax than they should have by shifting $1.38 trillion worth of profit out of the countries where they were generated and into tax havens, where corporate tax rates are extremely low or non-existent'. Similarly, 'Private tax evaders paid less tax than they should have by storing a total of over $10 trillion in financial assets offshore.'

While North America and Europe lose larger amounts in tax than Latin America and Africa, the size of their economies are much bigger. As a result, 'North America and Europe's tax losses are equivalent to 5.7 per cent and 12.6 per cent of the regions' public health budgets respectively, while Latin America and Africa's tax losses are equivalent to 20.4 per cent and 52.5 per cent of the regions' public health budgets respectively.'

Strikingly, the 'five jurisdictions most responsible for countries' tax losses' are the Cayman Islands, a British Overseas Territory (16.5 per cent of global tax losses), the UK (10 per cent), the Netherlands (8.5 per cent), Luxembourg (6.5 per cent) and the US (5.53 per cent).[57] Europe, the US and one British Overseas Territory are the five tax havens most responsible for global tax losses!

As these examples demonstrate, in many cases decolonisation hasn't led to any fundamental rebalancing of power or resources in national and global economies. To the contrary, wealth has continued to be extracted from countries, long after independence, through a global system of tax havens, the largest of which are in Europe and the US. This has made it much harder for newly independent countries to develop thriving economies that could compete in the global economy into which they were often forced to integrate.

Reverse reparations

The definition of reparation is the action of making amends for a wrong one has done, by providing payment or other assistance to those who have been wronged. One consequence of the failure to adequately address the injustice of slavery and colonialism at the point they ended is the phenomena of reverse reparations.

Here compensation is provided to the perpetrator rather than the victim of oppression. Reverse reparations are a repeated feature of our global economic history, and this led to the reproduction and deepening of existing structural inequalities.

The Abolition of Slavery Act was passed in Britain in 1833 outlawing the purchase or ownership of slaves in some parts of the British Empire (India, Sri Lanka and St Helena were excluded); 800,000 slaves were to be freed but not immediately. All slaves who worked in the fields were forced to continue working unpaid for their owner for six further years, in what is known as indentured labour.[58]

The UK government raised twenty million pounds, a sum that represented 40 per cent of government spending that year and is the equivalent of £17 billion today, to compensate slave owners for their loss of property. Up until the response to Covid-19, the Slave

Compensation Scheme was the second largest government bailout in the UK's history after the bailout of the banks during the 2008 financial crisis.[59]

Forcing former slaves into indentured labour and paying reparations to slave owners entrenched and widened the impossibly deep economic inequality that had been created by 300 years of slavery. To this day the British Government has resisted calls for reparations for those descended from slaves.

To rub salt in the wound, the loan the UK government took out to pay compensation to the slaveowners was only settled in 2015 and up until that point was being paid by British taxpayers, including descendants of the formerly enslaved.

More recently, after the end of Apartheid in South Africa in 1994 the new democratic government set up a Truth and Reconciliation Commission. It made the recommendation of a one-time 1 per cent corporate tax to raise money for the victims of Apartheid, what it called 'a solidarity tax', but this was rejected by the ruling African National Congress (ANC) party for fear of sending an anti-business message to the market. Yasmin Sooka, one of the jurors on the Commission, felt that while the hearings dealt with what she described as 'outward manifestations of apartheid such as torture, severe ill treatment and disappearances', it left the economic system served by those abuses 'completely untouched'.[60]

At the same time, in the early years after independence, the ANC was paying 30 billion rand annually (about $4.5 billion) to pay the interest on debt inherited from the Apartheid government – clearly another form of reverse reparation. Contrast this figure with the small in comparison $85 million that the government ultimately paid to more than 19,000 victims of Apartheid killings and torture and their families, which works out at around $4,500 each on average. While there was a strong legal case that this debt was illegitimately borrowed and therefore didn't have to be repaid (known as odious debt), the ANC didn't want to risk undermining the confidence of international investors, which could lead to an economic crisis.[61]

The racialised structural inequality that characterised Apartheid South Africa was widened through the reverse reparations described above and is locked-in to this day by the government's inability to collect tax. The Tax Justice Network (TJN) explains that nearly 'half of South Africa's adult population lives in poverty, with more women (52 per cent) in poverty, than men (46 per cent)'. TJN calculates that 'If the $3.39 billion in tax that South Africa loses every year to tax abuse was instead given as direct cash transfers of $85 per month [the minimum income the government says is needed to not live in poverty] to people living in poverty, over 3 million people could be lifted out of poverty.'[62]

Time and time again during periods of decolonisation, and in the broader development of the global economy, we see reverse reparations being paid to the perpetrators of oppression, and denied to the victims. The inequalities created are then locked in through the design of our modern economies, meaning that over time, they become deeply entrenched and structural.

Undermining national sovereignty

Another aspect of globalisation that mainstream academic economics underplays is the dynamic by which dominant countries are able to define acceptable economic policy and create systems in which certain behaviour is required. This often effectively prevents countries challenging structural inequalities which are the result of historical oppression.

What constitutes 'appropriate' economic behaviour, and what the 'right' economic institutions and policies are for implementing it, are very much the result of broader social contexts which are dominated by powerful actors and countries. We have seen in previous chapters how economic knowledge and training has been a central mechanism by which certain narrow economic ideas have been spread across the world and become widely accepted as universal.

What is deemed acceptable economics changes over time as a result of internal change at the top of the hierarchy of economics, which in turn is closely connected with broader political and economic shifts. Within economics a widespread rejection of national planning, criticism of public management and growing arguments for greater global integration of economies have progressively undermined the sovereign nation-state, which had previously been a central vehicle for the discipline of economics (and by extension economists) to gain the global influence they have today.

While economics has turned away from economic planning and shifted to a more market-based approach, the idea that this no longer involves government intervention is misleading. In practice, government intervention has been a central mechanism through which to construct markets, repurpose institutions and re-regulate economic systems to promote different activity and behaviour. Fourcade describes how, as a result of this shift, the role and goals of national economic institutions globally have shifted from being explicitly political to being about efficient technical management.[63]

Whatever the acceptable economics at a particular point, the structure of the global economy and the discipline of economics both exert a strong pressure on countries and economists to conform. For national political elites, demonstrating adherence to economic rules and norms to the rest of the world is important to present the image of a responsible state, legitimate trading partner, sound international borrower or an attractive location for foreign direct investment, and internally helps secure their legitimacy as political rulers.

A few countries, such as China, have had the power or circumstances to be able to adopt their own model of development, but most haven't. Economics has played a key role in developing and legitimising a form of globalisation that undermines national sovereignty and democracy, and narrows economic policy space. This often prevents or makes it more difficult for countries to build up their economic capabilities (including independent expertise and ideas).

Dani Rodrik argues that it is only possible to have two of either the 'nation-state', 'democracy' or 'hyper-globalisation', but not all three. You can have hyper-globalisation and some form of global democracy, but not nation states, the nation-state and democracy but not hyper-globalisation, or hyper-globalisation and nation states but not democracy. Rodrik demonstrates convincingly that over the past thirty years, we have been gradually moving towards hyper-globalisation, and nations which are only responsive to the needs of the global economy, not democracy. This alarming trend has been legitimised by economics.[64]

Defining capitalism

The broad term that most people use to describe our modern economies is capitalism, of which there are a number of varieties in existence around the world.[65] Like most things of importance there is disagreement about how exactly to define the key features of capitalism. In this section, we consider a mainstream economic definition from a popular undergraduate textbook. We argue that when the history we have outlined above is considered, it becomes clear this definition is inaccurate and fails to describe key aspects of our modern economies.

The online open-access CORE economics textbook is now used as the basis for introductory economics courses in universities across the world. It claims to teach economics 'as if the last three decades had happened' (in a veiled criticism of other textbooks that don't) and it promises to use more real-world data. The CORE textbook defines capitalism as an economic system based on the following three features:

- Private property is legal ownership over something that allows you to enjoy your possessions in a way that you choose, exclude others from its use if you wish and dispose of them by gift or sale to someone else who becomes their owner.
- Markets are a means of transferring goods or services from one person to another. They are reciprocal, because one thing is transferred for money or another thing, and voluntary, because the things being exchanged are private property and so the exchange must be mutually beneficial.
- Firms are productive profit-making organisations that are owned by private individuals who own the assets of the firm and employ others to work there.[66]

These are all institutions, which CORE defines as 'the different sets of laws and social customs regulating production and distribution' in capitalist societies.

What is missing?

Coercion

CORE's approach is symptomatic of a wider failure in economics. In the rare case, when mainstream economics does engage with economic history, which is low status in the discipline, it does so in a way that is oversimplified and inadequate. In this chapter, we've demonstrated these inadequacies, through exploring how economics understands the shift from feudalism to capitalism and globalisation.

As a result, the way economics defines our modern economies is limited. An accurate definition of our modern economies needs to recognise that large amounts of the economic wealth and power accumulated by Europe was not through markets underpinned by voluntary exchange and private property, but through slavery and colonialism which made humans property and was premised on the theft of land and people.

Many historians recognise this. In *Empire of Cotton*, Sven Beckert describes how Britain constructed a global cotton trade and uses the term war capitalism to describe this economic system.[67] Similarly, Nick Robbins describes how in India trade with Britain was known colloquially as 'unrequited trade' to highlight how so much was taken and so little returned.[68]

To their credit, some economists such as Dani Rodrik do highlight the gunboat diplomacy that backed up the first wave of globalisation in the nineteenth century, but this approach is not widespread, and the lasting outcomes of these events are not systemically incorporated into economic thinking.[69]

The way that neoclassical economics conceptualises freedom and individual choice further prevents us from seeing the effects of systemic inequality. The basic idea is that markets as institutions promote freedom because they rest on voluntary exchange as described here in the CORE textbook:

> Markets are a means of transferring goods or services from one person to another. There are other ways, such as by theft, a gift, or a government order. **Markets** differ from these in three respects:
>
> They are reciprocated: unlike gifts and theft, one person's transfer of a good or service to another is directly reciprocated by a transfer in the other direction (either of another good or service as in barter

exchange, or money, or a promise of a later transfer when one buys on credit). They are voluntary: Both transfers – by the buyer and the seller – are voluntary because the things being exchanged are private property. So the exchange must be beneficial in the opinion of both parties. In this, markets differ from theft, and also from the transfers of goods and services in a centrally planned economy.

In most markets there is competition. A seller charging a high price, for example, will find that buyers prefer to buy from other competing sellers.[70]

Without a focus on distribution, this framing erases the unequal power relationships that exist between different groups in society and how they influence the terms of market exchange. Many people in the world today are unable to meet their basic needs through market exchange and therefore have little agency. If the alternative is starving, being made homeless, or not being able to give your child a better life, then agreeing to dangerous or menial work for low wages is only voluntary in the narrowest sense of the word and talk of choice and freedom through markets is largely meaningless. Poverty is coercive, and its widespread existence in the world today means that those with economic power are often able to dictate the terms of exchange.

Neoclassical economics doesn't pay enough attention to how people's freedom is limited in modern economic systems. Private property, exchanged through markets, plays a role in economic production and provides freedom for its owners, but it also restricts the freedom of those who don't have it by excluding them from land and other important resources.[71] Property can be both liberty and theft, but neoclassical economics makes no attempt to theorise the latter, and this is particularly egregious in our modern economies where structural inequalities mean that ownership is so unequally distributed.

Violence

Even where economic accounts have a strong historical analysis like Dani Rodrik's *The Globalization Paradox* there is often an idyllic focus on trade, and the violence done by Europeans towards Indigenous People is seen as separate and unrelated to the economic analysis.

Rodrik describes how in 1670 what later became the Canadian Hudson Bay Company was given a charter by Charles II giving it a monopoly over trade and commerce as well as ownership of all land around Hudson Bay that wasn't already owned by another 'Christian prince or state'.[72] This, he says, illustrates the close relationship between 'power and economic exchange'.[73] Today the Hudson Bay company is HBC, Canada's largest general retailer, which makes it the world's oldest joint stock company.

Rodrik then returns to the standard economic definition of trade as mutually beneficial voluntary exchange. 'Whatever a country has plenty of can be exchanged for things that it lacks.' In this case, 'Cree Indians along Hudson's Bay certainly had plenty of beaver. But they were short of blankets, kettles and of course the rifles and brandy that they didn't even know they needed before they encountered White men.' Because there was 'high demand for beaver fur in Europe, the potential gains from trade were huge'.

Rodrik differentiates his approach from 'textbook renditions of trade', highlighting that in 'the real world, things are not that simple'. The 'heroes' of the Hudson Bay Company 'and their associates … had to engage in a dangerous venture – with risks to both purse and life – to reach the Indians through a new, maritime route'.

Hudson Bay Company had to

open and maintain channels of communication, build trust, and convince the Indians of their peaceful intentions. They had to do the 'market research' to figure out what the Indians would buy in return for fur.

> Above all else, they had to provide a safe and secured environment
> within which trade could be carried out. That in turn required laws
> and regulations backed up by force (if needed).[74]

Rodrik's story is strong on heroic bravery and very light on violence with just a brief mention at the end of backing up rules with
force (if needed). It fails to incorporate what Rodrik had previously
highlighted, which is that this was all built on the unilateral appropriation of land from Indigenous People in that territory which in
following years would be expanded to become the Dominion of
Canada in 1867.

On this basis, their intentions very much were not peaceful, and
while voluntary exchange between Indigenous People and colo-
nists did take place, it was within a broader context of conquest and
violence, which Rodrik's description of heroes, trust and market
research sanitises and erases.

Historians and other social scientists debate the extent to which
European settler colonialism constituted genocide of Indigenous
People but, whatever you label it, this systemic violence is inescap-
ably a fundamental part of this story which economics needs to
incorporate.[75]

One response might be that this is all in the past and not relevant to understanding our economies today. Again, this belief
can only be maintained if one goes to great lengths to separate any
links between economic activity and occurrences of violence in the
world today.

For example, over the last forty years, two billion people in
Latin America, Africa, the Middle East and Asia have been displaced from their ancestral homelands.[76] In India, the marginalised
Indigenous communities, known as Adivasi, who at a population
of 104 million account for just under 9 per cent of the population,
are disproportionately displaced.[77] According to one report, they

account for 60 per cent of all the displaced population of the country, often without any compensation, and in many cases facing multiple displacements.[78]

Major global food producers play a pivotal role in land grabs in areas populated by Indigenous Peoples[79] as well as pushing the uptake of ecologically damaging inputs such as chemical fertilisers and pesticides.[80] It is predicted that forecasted agricultural expansion up to 2050 will lead to habitat loss for nearly 90 per cent of 19,859 species of land animals.[81] This will have a devastating impact on many ecosystems and the planet.

These examples illustrate that violence occurs in different ways and at different levels and is much more than just direct physical violence. The damage done to the living world by food production, often in regions like Asia and Latin America for consumption in Europe and the US, is a form of structural, ecological and slow violence.

It is felt over years and generations due to the loss of forests and soil fertility, the destruction of cultural identities and loss of sense of belonging when people are forcibly displaced from their ancestral lands. Currently, mainstream academic economics has no conceptual framework to even begin to make visible this kind of violence, much less understand it.

More broadly, economics needs to engage with the possibility that there might be a deeper relationship between violence, coercion and capitalism. Writing in 1944, the historian Karl Polanyi identified three shifts that together had led to the great transformation which produced capitalism.

The first was that human life could be subordinated to market dynamics and be reborn as labour. The second was that nature could be translated into the market and reborn as land. The third was that exchange could be reborn as money.[82]

The philosopher Hannah Arendt saw these transformations, not as a one-off historical event, but as repeating cycles of commodification, as ownership is asserted over more aspects of the social and natural world, which were then imbued with monetary value and could be exchanged through markets.

If the thing that connects all these transformations is that different forms of coercion, violence and power, real or threatened, are required to assert ownership over something for the first time, then this should be part of how we define capitalism.

Capital

While private property, markets and firms are clearly all aspects of capitalism, CORE follows a broader failure in mainstream academic economics to engage seriously with how capital operates in modern economies. As might be suggested by the fact that capitalism takes its name from capital, it is not possible to understand our modern economic system without more of a focus on capital.

Importantly, a deeper analysis of capital helps us understand how modern legal and financial systems have developed to help those with power and wealth to protect their capital and pass it on across generations. This is a key mechanism by which structural inequalities formed by historical oppression, including slavery and colonialism, are embedded and reproduced in our global economy today.

The legal theorist Katharina Pistor explains that 'capital is made from two ingredients: an asset and the legal code'. She uses 'the term "asset" broadly to denote any object, claim, skill, or idea regardless of its form. In their unadulterated appearance, these simple assets are just that: a piece of dirt, a building, a promise to receive payment at a future date, an idea for a new drug, or a string of digital code.'[83]

However, with 'the right legal coding, any of these assets can be turned into capital and thereby increase its propensity to create wealth for its holder(s)'. Pistor notes that which assets are coded in law to be turned into capital 'has changed over time and will likely continue to do so'.[84] This reminds us of the transformations Polanyi and Arendt described in the last section, which they believed have been crucial to the development of capitalism.

Land, businesses, debt and know-how have all been coded as capital. Some capital, such as land, is tangible and can be used to produce food or provide shelter even in the absence of legal coding. But financial instruments, like the Bahamian discretionary trusts we explored earlier in the chapter, or the intellectual property rights for a medicine, are intangible and exist only in law.

Mainstream academic economics has largely ignored the law as an area important to understanding modern economies. Yet, contract law, property rights, collateral law, trust, corporate and bankruptcy all play a central role in facilitating the process by which assets are turned into capital, which itself is arguably the defining feature of capitalism.

Who has the power and expertise to select which assets are coded as capital, how this is done, by whom and for whose benefit are questions that go right to the heart of capital and the political economy of capitalism and yet mainstream academic economics never asks them.

Until it does, economics will continue to obscure that the coercive power of the state is essential for the accumulation and protection of wealth over long stretches of time. Pistor highlights that

> the fact that capital is linked to and dependent on state power is often lost in debates about market economies. Contracts and property rights support free markets, but capitalism requires

more – the legal privileging of some assets, which gives their holders a comparative advantage in accumulating wealth over others.[85]

Economics will also continue to obscure why conventional forms of redistribution have become ineffective. As we saw earlier in the chapter, a global network of tax havens has created a system which facilitates industrial scale tax avoidance and evasion. As a result, most 'of the gains from capital do not trickle down; they trickle up to capital holders who repatriate their gains or place them behind the legal shields other jurisdictions afford them to protect their wealth from tax and other creditors'.[86]

Until academic economics reincorporates a deeper analysis of capital into its definition of capitalism, it will not be able to explain the world we live in, much less meaningfully address structural inequalities.

Racialised identities

Economics also needs to acknowledge the racialised nature of the history of capitalism and the implications this has for understanding today why richer countries globally tend to be Whiter countries.

Writing in the 1980s, Cedric Robinson criticised Karl Marx and Marxism more broadly for assuming that European categories of class could be applied universally and locating the agency to create change in the White, male industrial working class.

While this group was exploited, they were formally equal to the White, male capitalist class unlike women or people of colour who were placed outside of the analysis. As a result, this approach failed to account for the reliance of the economic system on other structures of exploitation including the uncompensated labour of women in the domestic sphere, racialised colonial dispossession, and the coerced extraction of value from slaves, serfs and peasants. Robinson argued that Marx's analysis also failed to recognise the agency of groups who weren't the White, male working class to resist exploitation and create change.[87]

Robinson aimed to demonstrate how the global economic system was intrinsically racialised by studying its roots. He challenged the idea that capitalism was a radical departure from the previous socioeconomic system feudalism. He points out that racist ideologies were present before capitalism, highlighting the idea of Herrenvolk (governance by an ethnic majority) that drove the German colonisation of central Europe and 'Slavic' territories, and the role that British racism played a role in the colonisation of Ireland. In his view, the 'tendency of European civilization through capitalism was thus not to homogenize but to differentiate – to exaggerate regional, subcultural, and dialectical differences into "racial" ones'.[88]

For Robinson, our modern economic system developed in the social environment of a Western civilisation already deeply racist, and evolved to produce a system built on slavery, colonialism and imperialism. Complicating this sense of moving from the 'dark ages' to modernity as a linear process of moral and economic development is important because it is at the root of a tacit belief across much of society, and economics, that the West having gone through this journey is superior to other countries. We return to this in the next chapter when we explore the concept of development in economics.

Walter Johnson summarises the connection between our modern economic system and the transatlantic slave trade. In his view, 'the history of capitalism makes no sense separate from the history of the slave trade and its aftermath. There was no such thing as capitalism without slavery: the history of Manchester never happened without the history of Mississippi.'[89]

The legacies of slavery and empire remain at the centre of life today, and societies that don't understand their history can't understand their present. Some of our families benefited from slavery and empire, while others were dispossessed and brutalised.[90] If you can inherit wealth then you should also be able to inherit the debts that accrue when it is accumulated through oppression.

If we accept that slavery and colonialism are foundational institutions of our national and global economies then we see how racial hierarchy and economic exploitation are embedded deep within them. We also see that our modern economies did not develop in isolation in Europe or the US but were always connected with and dependent on the oppression of people in colonies.[91] Any understanding of our modern economies must rest on an understanding of this historical oppression and its continued effects today.

Misrepresenting history

In 2019, Suse Steed wrote a blog about why she couldn't teach economics any more.

> It's because we were never able to really deal with violence in the past and how it helped make some countries wealthy, that we don't seem that able to deal with it now. Why neat tables of economic statistics show how productive workers in China are, but news outlets show they are putting Muslims into camps. That some of the most productive countries have used massive violence and oppression, usually of other populations, but sometimes of their own people. We don't have any metrics in economics to marry these worlds together. If it doesn't show up on the balance sheet it

doesn't matter. It's this silence about violence which is my major beef with economics.

Economics creates a parallel view of the world which is a lot more palatable than the real world. In this parallel world the wealth of countries like the UK and the US is [because] we are more productive than other countries. This means in Britain we can tell ourselves we are rich because we work hard, we're industrious and inventive.[92]

Returning to Ingrid Kvangraven's and Surbhi Kesar's survey from Chapter 2, they asked 500 academic economists whether they teach courses that allow for an understanding of racialised inequalities and/or the role of European colonialism in shaping economic outcomes. Only two in five of 268 respondents from mainstream economics departments said yes.[93]

A concerning finding is that junior economists are least likely to answer yes to this question. This may be because younger economists are less likely to have been taught about racialised inequalities and the role of European colonialism in shaping economic outcomes and therefore less likely both to prioritise and have the knowledge to teach it. Or it may be because younger economists tend to be assigned to teaching the basic compulsory courses which are less likely to cover these topics.

As we know that most economics students globally receive a mainstream neoclassical education, these findings suggest that a considerable majority are never being exposed to issues of racialised inequalities or colonialism at any point in their studies. The whitewashed history of our modern economies we have challenged in this chapter is being passed on to the next generation of economists through university economics education and we must do better.

Chapter 5

Undermining democracy and development

With contributions from Brototi Roy and Francesca Rhys-Williams

In this chapter, we argue that economics has not done enough to prioritise democracy or self-determination in economic development.

This builds on our argument in the last chapter, that globalisation has for many countries prescribed a single predetermined pathway from 'poor' to 'developed', rather than supporting countries to chart their own course and decide how far they want to integrate with the global economic system.

The subdiscipline of development economics repeats many aspects of the oversimplified historical narrative we saw in the last chapter. It whitewashes the role of historical oppression in economic development and the unbalanced power relations between countries in increasingly global economic systems.

This often leads it to a focus on the defects of poor countries, such as corruption and poor education, as the main reasons for their poverty and underdevelopment.

It doesn't question whether the global distribution of wealth is an unjust result of historical oppression, or whether current trade and investment rules reduced the ability of less wealthy and powerful countries to develop economically.

In sum, development economics tends to accept the way things are now as fixed and inevitable and encourages countries to do the best they can given the cards they are dealt, rather than seriously considering whether the status quo is fair, efficient or sustainable. As a result, it legitimises and reproduces vast inequalities in wealth and power between countries which are unfair, inefficient and unsustainable.

To effectively address the root causes of problems and barriers to economic development rather than the symptoms requires an analysis, like the one we sketched in the last chapter, which incorporates how particular histories have embedded and reproduced structural inequalities in wealth and power between countries.

History of development economics

Here we turn our focus to development economics, a subdiscipline that focuses on low-income countries and prescribes methods to improve economic and social conditions. We begin by briefly outlining the history of development economics and argue that it is not fit for purpose because it focuses on the internal inadequacies of poor countries at the expense of external economic power relations between countries.

This leads development economics to propose interventions that address individual behaviour and outcomes rather than anything that attempts to change underlying economic structures and rules.

First, we briefly trace the intellectual history of modern development economics. In the post-World War Two period, economists grappled with challenges including the reconstruction of Europe, which had been devastated by war, industrialisation in South and Eastern Europe and economic development in the colonies, an increasing number of which were winning their independence.

This took on an urgency in the context of the emerging Cold War between the US and Soviet Union with economic security and development seen as key to preventing the spread of Communism.

The economist Grieve Chelwa, whose history we draw extensively from, quotes Albert Hirschman, a pioneer of development economics, who wrote that it 'started out as the spearhead of an effort that was to bring all-around emancipation from backwardness'.[1] In this first stage, the goal of development economics was very clearly to achieve 'sustained increases in income per head' and the 'vehicle that was to deliver this was industrialisation'.

By the early 1970s many failed attempts at industrialisation across the world led to a crisis of confidence within development economics. 'Countries that should have been well on their way to "take-off" did not do so and those that had taken off crashed only moments after.' The context of the 1970s was a decade of much geopolitical and economic upheaval.

The 1973 oil crisis led to the US pulling out of the Bretton Woods system of monetary management, which had been agreed after World War Two and had been a key feature of the post-war economic consensus. After this the US dollar was no longer pegged to gold and its value was left to 'float' (rise and fall according to market demand). One economic consensus was unravelling and it wasn't clear yet what would take its place.

In universities at this time academic economics was becoming increasingly mathematical, and this meant that 'the pioneers of development economics, many of whom were not trained in the new orthodoxy, could not adequately respond to the charge levelled by neoclassical economists that false starts were the result of government-inspired resource misallocations'.

Development economists were also criticised by more radical colleagues such as 'neo-marxists [who] pointed out that rather than bridge inequalities, as hypothesised by the classical development economists, whatever little industrialisation that had taken place had had the actual effect of deepening intra- and inter-country inequalities'. A third area of criticism was that often industrialisation had appeared to happen 'at the expense of political and democratic progress under authoritarian regimes' and this concerning trend had been neglected by development economics. Hirschman suggests that all of these factors contributed to the decline of this first classic phase of development economics.[2]

By the 1980s many poor countries across the world were in the midst of economic crisis. The World Bank, an international financial institution set up after World War Two that provides loans and grants to the governments of low- and middle-income countries for developing infrastructure, attributed the blame for crises in Sub-Saharan Africa on the policies suggested by development economists.

'The prescription of the World Bank and other allied institutions was, therefore, straight forward: poor countries, especially those in Sub-Saharan Africa, needed to structurally adjust their economies in favour of market-based allocations coupled with a minimal role for the state.' By the late 1990s the consensus began to change again, swinging away from structural adjustment policies that it became clear were not facilitating economic development and often had devastating results, especially for the poor.[3]

At the start of the twenty-first century, the international financial institutions (IFIs) such as the World Bank and International Monetary Fund, which acts as a lender of last resort to countries facing financial crises but often imposes stringent social and economic conditions on bailouts, recognised that 'the singular focus on markets inherent in structural adjustment policies (SAPs) had adversely impacted the lives of the poor'.[4]

They started to require 'governments in Africa to prepare Poverty Reduction Strategy Papers (PRSPs) that were to articulate how governments would protect the welfare of the poor'. Chelwa highlights that 'the IFIs and many in the [international development] donor community still held the view that statist policies were to blame for the crisis'.

This belief in the incompetence and corruption of the African state meant that the donor community insisted that their funding support direct provision of aid to needy communities. 'Government involvement in this process, if any at all was to be kept to a minimum.' Chelwa calls this 'the era of Non-Governmental Organisations (NGOs) and Project Aid'.

This was the context in which today's mainstream version of development economics was born. 'Inspired by the Millennium Development Goals (MDGs), donors identified micro-interventions in mostly health and education as these were considered to be important inputs into development.'

The large amount of funding for these interventions required rigorous evaluations to figure out 'what works'. 'Knowing what works is not only important for the purposes of accounting for tax dollars on the part of donors, but for the transplanting of this knowledge to other settings in the developing world.'

As we see in the next section, mainstream economists, armed with cutting-edge research methods like Randomised Control Trials, convinced donors that they could find out what works. Over time, the two groups 'formed a symbiotic relationship whereby donors supplied financial resources and economists provided credible answers as to which interventions worked'.

Chelwa concludes that 'Development economics was no longer concerned with the large macro-question of how to permanently increase income per head but with micro-level questions around whether certain interventions (mosquito nets, deworming tablets, iodised salt, teaching negotiation skills to girls, et cetera) improved some narrow measure of the poor's welfare.'[5]

Through Chelwa's history we can see that development economics frames underdevelopment in terms of internal deficiencies, not power relations between countries, or historical oppression. Ideas like the resource curse, which suggests that countries with more natural resources are more likely to have worse economic growth, democracy and development outcomes. Acemoglu and Robinson's 'extractive' institutions, which we discussed in the last chapter, is an example of an approach that stems from and reproduces this internal deficiency framing.

The other striking shift this history highlights is from a focus on structural approaches to economic development to more micro-level behavioural change approaches that address the symptoms not the root causes of poverty. As Ha-Joon Chang and others have pointed out, countries in Europe, the US and parts of Asia did not develop through micro-level behaviour change approaches.[6]

The historical record shows that these countries developed their productive capabilities (often using economic policies, like exchange controls and industrial subsidies, which are prohibited today) first and then often with the help of resource extraction from their colonies, built large-scale public infrastructures including sanitation, housing, electricity, health and education, which had a transformative impact on health and wellbeing and facilitated further economic development.

It is important not to idealise the top-down and centralised approaches of the first post-war stage of economic development.

Even if we wanted to, we couldn't return to this approach because our global economic system is very different now.

However, development economics urgently needs to reconnect with its historical ambition and a systemic focus, including, as we highlighted in the last chapter, an understanding of how historical oppression has contributed to systemic inequalities.

There is a need to review what worked and didn't in the different phases of development economics since World War Two. For example, Thandika Mkandawire argues that many African countries did develop considerably in the first twenty years after independence, and so we should re-evaluate the efficacy of the policies they used.[7]

Development economics also needs to challenge the clearly racist and colonial assumptions and attitudes which have seen African states discredited and thus bypassed by the international donor community. As we see in the next section, this is not something mainstream development economics looks likely to do at present.

Limitations of the RCT agenda

We have just heard how development economists using Randomised Control Trials (RCT) have formed a symbiotic relationship with the international development sector providing the valuable service of finding out 'what works'.

This success has raised the status within the discipline of economists such as Abhijit Banerjee, Esther Duflo and Michael Kremer who pioneered the use of RCTs in economics, which culminated in their receipt of the Nobel Prize for Economics in 2019.

Banerjee and Duflo have also popularised the RCT approach with their book *Poor Economics: A Radical Rethinking of the Way to*

Fight Global Poverty, which is now taught in development economics classes across the world.

Like medicine, where RCTs have been used most widely, in economics they allocate 'an economic treatment' to some members of a group and compare the outcomes against the other members who did not receive this treatment.

For example, to test whether providing credit helps to grow small firms or increase their likelihood of success, a researcher might partner with a financial institution and randomly allocate credit to applicants that meet certain basic requirements. Then a year later the researcher would compare changes in sales or employment in small firms that received the credit to those that did not.[8]

Like neoclassical economics, advocates of economic RCTs claim that they are an objective way to discover the world and find out 'what works'. However, the RCT approach does not attempt to identify or explain the structures and histories which shape individual behaviour and interaction. RCTs take people's preferences as given rather than considering how they might be formed by the economic and social position of different groups in society including along gender and racial lines.[9]

As a result, Duflo accepts that policy attention should be focused on men 'on the grounds that the economic returns will be larger', rather than acknowledging that the distortions she identifies 'relate to the historical structures that have curtailed women's productive potential and protected male privilege'.[10]

RCTs as a method are only capable of measuring certain things and this limits their value. To run an RCT you need a precise, well-specified question, a tried and tested intervention, a large and stable population to test, and a set of outcomes that can be measured in a relatively short period.

These are pretty restrictive conditions that exclude large areas of individual and social life from study. The more dominant RCTs become in development economics and the field of international development, the more research becomes skewed towards answering certain questions (while ignoring others that are not amenable to be studied through this method).

The key thing is that research using an RCT is anything but a 'natural' experiment or 'objective' description of the world because they involve the researcher, selecting bits of reality that can be studied and excluding messy bits, often in a broader context of working with governments and international economic institutions who are actively trying to change people's behaviour in ways that align with their interests and beliefs.[11]

The messy realities that tend to get removed – power, historical trajectories, wider social change, and economic structures that influence national development – are exactly the things that we have argued in this book are essential to understand and reduce poverty and structural inequality.

The continuity throughout the history of development economics has been that experts, often men, mainly White and relatively privileged, from Europe and the US have done research *on not with* subjects of research deemed 'in need' who are mainly people of colour and often women in Latin America, Africa, the Middle East, Asia and the Caribbean.

Ingrid Kvangraven cites research highlighting how few economic RCTs ask for or even consider the issue of informed consent to participating in economic RCTs, what should be an absolutely basic ethical principle of all research involving people. It found that only one in three participants in economic RCTs reviewed in Africa, Asia and Latin America were aware that they were participating.

Strikingly, this figure rose to two in three for economic RCTs conducted in Europe.[12]

In published research on economic RCTs carried out in former colonies, four out of five authors did not even discuss whether they asked for informed consent or not. 'While some state that participants were intentionally left ignorant and some indicate informed consent for parts of the study, not a single study indicates that participants were explicitly aware' of being part of an economic RCT.[13]

In this way, many RCTs are reproducing a colonial practice of research on human subjects violating the personhood of participants by treating them as passive subjects to be studied.

The widespread practice of withholding consent is only one of many ethical issues that are rarely addressed in research published on RCTs including the practice of lying, who researchers are accountable to, and how the choice of deciding who gets the treatment and who doesn't is made when it might have a significant difference on people's quality of life.

All too often, people who are deemed as in need of economic development and chosen to participate in economic RCTs are not treated as people, much less as citizens who can actively participate in the production of economic knowledge or collective action to shape their economies.

The rapid rise in influence of RCTs, highlighted earlier by Chelwa, is exemplified by the Abdul Latif Jameel Poverty Action Lab (J-PAL), which by 2018, fifteen years after it was founded, had conducted 876 policy experiments in eighty countries.[14] One estimate suggests that in this time it has received around $300 million in income from institutions including the World Bank, Britain's Department for International Development and the Bill and Melinda Gates Foundation.[15]

The success of J-Pal appears to have influenced the World Bank's decision to set up a specialised impact evaluation unit, consisting largely of former J-Pal associates, and the number of RCTs used in World Bank evaluations increased from zero in 2000 to two-thirds of all evaluations in 2010.[16]

Ingrid Kvangraven has analysed this rise in status. She argues that initially, economists advocating RCTs disputed the effectiveness of aid and development programmes, and criticised the validity of existing knowledge about economic development. In this way, they contributed to a sense that there was a problem which required experts and funding to conduct experiments.

Once RCTs were being used more widely, this gradually created a hierarchy of knowledge in which economic RCTs were at the top and the 'gold standard'. Other approaches are not able to make the same claims to scientifically identify 'what works' and so are delegitimised, with the risk of excluding centuries of insights and research about economic development from other disciplines and cultures. This hierarchy also contributes to limiting what 'credible' policy options are available to government to those which can be demonstrated to work through an economic RCT.

Advocates of RCTs in development economics have presented themselves as rebels who are telling difficult truths to the aid and international development industry. On this narrative they are focusing on pragmatically improving outcomes in the face of resistance and hostility. However, they also position themselves in such a way as not to be a threat to powerful governments, international financial institutions and donors.

In an interview with *The Financial Times*, Esther Duflo explains that the approach she advocates 'is less depressing than the view that it is a big conspiracy against the poor. Name your favourite enemy – capitalism, corruption … Our view is easier. You think hard about the problems, and you can solve them. That is why I feel generally a happy person, not at all discouraged.'[17]

Advocates of RCTs walk a fine line between presenting constructive solutions to global poverty while at the same time dismissing critics who point to broader structural problems. In doing so, they actively contribute to the marginalisation of more critical voices in the development field.

Rethinking development

At a deeper level, development economics represents a profoundly US- and European-centric perspective of what development (and underdevelopment) means. After World War Two, and in the context of former colonies becoming independent, the labels of "developed" and "undeveloped" provided a way to describe the respective roles different countries played in the global economic system, in a way that legitimised the presence of deep structural inequalities.

Rachel, a US-based academic economist of colour we interviewed, explained:

> I had the opportunity to see the ways in which mainstream economics was and is definitely grounded in a Western view of the world, a Western-dominated view of the world and in particular ways of thinking about non-Western societies, particular assumptions about the reason Western societies function and also particular ways of privileging Western forms of knowledge and ways of knowing.

Economics has at times intentionally, and at others accidentally, devalued other ways of life, social relationships and knowledge systems that exist outside of Europe and the US, which might be classified explicitly or tacitly as 'anecdotal', 'backward' or 'underdeveloped'.

This has long been highlighted by other disciplines. For example, community-based research in rural West Africa (and South

172

India) published in 1986 by economic anthropologist Polly Hill argued that most of development economists' theoretical work was based on unreliable and Western-biased assumptions.[18]

In the next chapter, we explore what economics needs to do to decolonise itself and how it might contribute more positively to a version of development defined and led from the bottom up.

Tensions between economics and democracy

Rather than being a single pathway predetermined by economists and powerful countries, economic development needs to have principles of democracy and self-determination at its core.

Self-determination is the ability for countries and people to make choices and manage their own economies in ways which reflect their needs, priorities, values and culture, and democracy is a key mechanism for achieving this.

In this section we consider the relationship between economics and democracy and argue that there are five tensions, many of which will be familiar from earlier chapters, that work together to prevent the discipline effectively promoting democracy and self-determination.

Removing decisions from the sphere of democracy

Economics has provided the intellectual legitimacy and practical support to de-democratise large areas of collective decision-making around the design of economic rules and institutions which underpin the organisation of our economies and the distribution of resources.

A prime example is the rise of independent central banks across the world. Central banks conduct monetary policy to achieve low and stable inflation and manage economic fluctuations, which in turn influences the interest rate charged on mortgages and savings and the level of money in the economy.

Independent central banks are run by unelected policymakers and designed in such a way to be free from direct political influence. The rationale is that these are technical decisions and politicians can't be trusted not to politicise them, for example by using monetary policy to boost economic activity before an election.

The neoclassical economic framework provides the intellectual underpinnings of the claim that experts are able to manage the economy in a way which is consistent with democracy. That argument goes something like this:

The economy is characterised by *knowable, predictable forces*, underpinned by the certainty of optimisation and equilibrium – this means economic experts believe they can model a situation, often mathematically, to make a prediction of how some policy will affect the economy. This view rests on the assumption that there are fixed mechanical relationships between variables like unemployment and inflation, or taxes and investment.

This is not the same as saying that everything in neoclassical economics is certain: there will almost always be probabilities and potential errors attached to any prediction. But it does mean that if policymakers want to achieve particular political goals, economists can claim to design policy scientifically to achieve those goals. Economic experts can therefore take the objectives set by politicians through democratic mechanisms and objectively work out the best way to achieve them within the boundaries of how their education taught them that the economy functions.

The goals and values of economics are assumed

Economics has no mechanism for societies to influence democratically what is deemed to be valuable in economic theory or policy.

174

As we have seen, efficiency is the central value to be maximised in economic theory, where it is framed as a trade-off with equity. At a macroeconomic level, GDP growth, productivity, low and stable inflation, and more recently financial stability, are taken as the goals of economic policy and there is no consideration of how these goals (and the values implicit in them) do or don't reflect broader social priorities and values. Improving the economy, defined in this way, has become an end in itself, not a means for pursuing broader social objectives.

These assumptions are reinforced by the methods of research and decision-making that economics has developed. Accepted methods of economic research don't focus on understanding public priorities and values, or use methods that are likely to uncover them.

Neoclassical economic theories, like 'revealed preference', claim that consumers' preferences can be revealed by what they purchase under different income and price circumstances. If this is accepted, then economists can simply collect data on people's consumption and use this to understand their preferences. They have no need to engage in any conversations with people in which they might hear them explain their views, needs and preferences in their own words.

When economists in government do a cost benefit analysis on whether to build a new public transport route or new housing, they might use revealed preference techniques. For example, they might study how much people pay for other forms of transport or house prices in the area to estimate how much they would be willing to pay for this development and use this to come up with a money value for the total benefit that would be created if it went ahead.

This kind of process is completely technocratic and couldn't be further from any more participatory or deliberative forms of democratic decision-making which could be used to evaluate whether to go ahead with transport and housing developments.

Ignores and discredits collective action

Much of politics is about combining individual preferences or actions into collective choices. In democracies a key element of collective choice is voting.

Neoclassical economics has focused on mathematical modelling of forms of collective choice and the 'rationality' of various possible voting procedures. In general, collective choice is portrayed in the negative, or at least as inferior to individual choice via the market. In recent decades, economics students have learned about the 'collective choice problem', the challenge of aggregating individual preferences into collective choices.

More advanced economics students are taught about Arrow's 'impossibility theorem', a mathematical proof that demonstrates that when voters have three or more options, no ranked voting electoral system can convert the ranked preferences of individuals into a community-wide ranking while adhering to mandatory principles of fair voting procedures.[19]

These approaches misunderstand the actual practice and possibility of collective choice, which is not simply an aggregation of the preferences of individual citizens. If it was, then collective choice would be very difficult to achieve because each citizen will have different wants and aspirations which cannot just be added up.

However, John Alford argues that collective choices

> are necessarily the outcome of political interaction and deliberation, in which citizens or their representatives engage with each other in advocacy, debate, and negotiation. Sometimes these processes manage to reconcile conflicts or identify convergent interests, but often they do not. When they don't the political process follows some procedure, usually enshrined in a constitution, for arriving at authoritative determination.[20]

By failing to recognise this, economic knowledge undermines and discredits the collective action and decision-making necessary for groups to effectively manage their own economic development.

Because many places have been governed as if these ideas were true, and they have become embedded in public narratives and individual psyches, the possibilities of collective action and decision-making are reduced.

There are limitations in viewing social movements such as the independence movements in former colonies, the civil rights movement in the US, Black Lives Matter and the Fridays for Future student climate crisis movement through a neoclassical lens. In seeing these diverse movements simply as the aggregated preferences of individuals who happen to have the same preference for social change, the interpersonal generativity of the group process, where the whole can be more than the sum of its parts, is discounted.

Misunderstands and misrepresents government

Public choice theory applies the tools of rational choice theory to government and democracy, framing politicians, civil servants and voters as individual agents making decisions to optimise some outcome, whether it is political power, size of budget or utility.

While most economists recognise the necessity of government action to address market failures, the general framing is that the role of the state should be limited because government intervention distorts markets, and in the first instance, market rather than government approaches should be used to achieve policy goals such as becoming carbon neutral.

This framing posits markets as naturally arising and governments as intervening, when we highlighted in the last chapter that governments provide the rules, institutions and legal arbitration necessary for markets to function and capital to be accumulated. By underplaying the role of the state, economics obscures both the positive and negative aspects of its important role in modern economies.

One area where neoclassical economics does recognise the role of government is in the provision of public goods. Public goods are goods that are:

- *Non-rivalrous* – consumption of the good by one individual does not reduce availability of the good for consumption by others;
- *Non-excludable* – goods that are difficult or impossible to keep non-payers from consuming.

Typical examples given in economics textbooks are national defence, a lighthouse, or a firework show. Because of these features public goods will often be underprovided in a market system because consumers have an incentive and the ability not to pay to consume them. They therefore represent a market failure that justifies government intervention.

Government taxation may then be necessary to provide these public goods and services or to redistribute resources in pursuit of equity objectives, but all of this relies on drawing resources from the productive economy.

However, neoclassical economics fails to see that governments don't just intervene in markets or redistribute resources; they are also producers. Government is a productive, wealth-creating organisation in the same way as any private business because, to varying extents, it supplies direct utilities such as energy, gas, water and broadband networks, and the building of houses, schools and hospitals.

Governments also provide more intangible services that nevertheless create enormous value such as food and drug safety, basic scientific research and innovation, street lights, stop signs, emergency call services, disaster relief, a legal system, bank deposit insurance and various types of social insurance including unemployment benefits and pension schemes.

Writing in 1939, Paul Studenski described the economic role of government:

> In every type of political organization known in human history, from the most primitive to the most elaborate, government has had to furnish services satisfying important needs of the members of the society, help them to make a living, influence their productive processes and consumption habits, manage economic resources to these several ends, and generally function as the collective economic agent of the people.[21]

Certain common needs can only be met, and some complex problems can only be solved, through collective effort and shared cost. Economics currently fails to study or understand how these goods are produced. Of course, for economics to genuinely understand and improve government it is necessary to engage not just with government as producer of public goods, but also the ways in which government action can be harmful and oppressive to particular groups in society.

Ignores the connection between economic power and political power

Neoclassical economic theory has an extremely limited theoretical understanding of power. It focuses on how market power changes the standard model of perfect competition,[22] but it ignores broader political and legal institutions, such as how the law plays a key role in the accumulation of capital.

The neoclassical framework fails to identify the mechanisms such as lobbying government and funding supportive research through which those with economic wealth are able to translate it into political power, which in turn can be used to influence economic rules and institutions.

This, in combination with its commitment to methodological individualism, means that economics misses the scale of resources that are put into behavioural change in order to sell products or win votes. Commercially, this is achieved through traditional advertising, and in recent years through data analytics and targeted advertising online. These tools have been put into use by political parties to target voters with individual messages via social media using highly detailed psychological profiles built up from their data.[23] This is a clear mechanism by which the economically powerful actively aim to change people's tastes and preferences (which neoclassical economics often assumes are fixed) on a mass scale.

Another example of this trend is the UK's 'Behavioural Insights Team', also known as the 'Nudge Unit'.[24] Inspired by the relatively young field of behavioural economics, the task of this organisation is to 'nudge' people towards certain decisions, or in their words to enable people to 'make better choices for themselves'.[25] After ten years it has offices around the world and its work has been applied in over thirty countries in one year.

Here the economic power of governments and large businesses gives them the resources to encourage large-scale behaviour change in populations, a tool that gives them significant political power, and risks undermining democracy and self-determination.

Up until the late 1970s, the dominant economic paradigm was characterised by nationalised industry, large public sectors and active government economic management. A significant criticism from economics was that this paradigm relied on centralised decision-making by politicians and public sector managers, which led to the ineffective and undemocratic allocation of resources because it had no way of assimilating all of the distributed knowledge and preferences in an economy.

Hayek advocated market price systems as the best way to capture distributed knowledge and preferences in an economy and this argument influenced the increasing use of price and market mechanisms in education, transportation and healthcare, as well as privatisation and outsourcing and reorganisation of government to make it more business-like.

In practice, market systems don't take into account the knowledge or preferences of future generations and other market non-participants. Those with more income have greater power in markets and so it is their knowledge and preferences which shape market based economies. The large structural inequalities and concentrations of economic wealth which characterise modern economies mean that markets don't effectively assimilate all of the distributed knowledge and preferences in an economy. In market-based economies with structural inequalities economic power translates into political power.

In this way, neoclassical economics doesn't adequately recognise how concentrated economic power undermines the use of markets as a legitimate tool for allocating resources.

What connects the post-war consensus paradigm and the dominant economic paradigm that replaced it in the 1980s, is a foundational belief that society can be designed and shaped according to rational, scientific criteria by experts and elites, usually with the backing of the state.

James Scott, in his book *Seeing Like a State*, argues that states built on this belief often cause harm because they don't adequately distribute power or collective decision-making, in ways that allow for particular groups in society to prevent state action that will harm them.[26]

Next we turn to consider three case studies from the US, South Africa and India that show how these tensions between economics and democracy play out in practice.

Two perspectives on economic policy in post-Apartheid South Africa

In this case study, we compare two accounts of the South African government's economic challenges and policy options in the early 2000s not long after the fall of Apartheid and the country's first democratic elections in 1994.

The first is from Dani Rodrik, an economist who was part of a World Bank team invited to advise South Africa in 2005. The second is from the writer and activist Naomi Klein who visited the country in the same year, and wrote about her experience in a book called *The Shock Doctrine: The Rise of Disaster Capitalism*, first published in 2007. The differences in their accounts of the same situation are striking.

Rodrik provides an economic analysis of the South African economy at the time. It 'had not been able to generate enough work at reasonable wages for the large number of job seekers, both new entrants into the labour market and workers released from shrinking sectors (mining and agriculture)'.[27]

He uses the concept of supply and demand to highlight that a slow rise in labour demand and a rapid rise in labour supply would mean that 'either wages would fall to rock-bottom levels or there would be high unemployment'. Of these options the South African government 'had chosen unemployment, but had also instituted a relatively generous system of public financial assistance to prop up the living standards of the poor and unemployed'.

Rodrik suggests that the 'the only way to create well paying jobs for the unemployed was to significantly expand manufacturing production'. This was because 'Agriculture and mining were unlikely to revive, and service industries such as finance (which had been doing reasonably well) employed mostly skilled workers.' The economic goal he prescribes based on this diagnosis is to try and increase the profitability of 'manufacturing in South Africa, which would stimulate private investment in the sector'.

Importantly, Rodrik highlights 'the rules of the game' in which South Africa had to achieve this goal were quite restrictive and that 'China's rise as a low-cost exporter had made competing in manufactures more difficult'.

Policy tools that might allow the government to support manufacturing were not available. Import tariffs, which tax foreign goods brought into the country and make locally produced goods relatively cheaper, 'had been slashed and international agreements made it difficult or impossible to raise them significantly'.

The government was providing subsidies for certain industries, such as automobile manufacturing. This was already in the grey area of laws imposed by the World Trade Organization (WTO), an international organisation that promotes and regulates global trade, to prevent 'trade-distorting subsidies (also known as state-aid)'.

South Africa also had an independent central bank and had liberalised capital flows, which meant that it didn't have regulations that controlled the movement of money in and out of the country. This meant that the government weren't able to 'contemplate a devaluation of the currency (the rand)', which would have made imports to South Africa more expensive and South African exports cheaper for other countries to buy, both of which might have made manufacturing in the country more profitable.[28]

Rodrik's narrative clearly describes the challenges South Africa faced at the time and the limited policy space it had to build its productive capabilities. But, echoing our criticism of economics in the last two chapters, it underplays the broader historical and political context that is so crucial to understanding the South African economy at the time.

As a result, the 'rules of the game' that severely limited the policy options available to the South African government to facilitate the country's economic development are presented as neutral and objective rather than arising from specific economic ideas, designed by policymakers from certain countries and negotiated through international institutions where certain countries had significantly more power than others.

In contrast, Naomi Klein focuses much more on exploring the historical and political context, and how it influenced the challenges faced by the African National Congress (ANC) party when it came into power after the first post-Apartheid elections in 1994.

Klein highlights a pattern we identified in the last chapter of political but not economic decolonisation. There were negotiations between the Apartheid government and the African National Congress party in the years running up to the first democratic elections, and the outcome of these negotiations then constrained the ANC when they formed a government after winning those elections.

Redistributing land, ownership of which was highly unequal along racial lines, was out of the question because 'at the last minute, the negotiators agreed to add a clause to the new constitution that protects all private property, making land reform virtually impossible'.[29]

Producing generic AIDS drugs to provide to the townships – poor racially segregated urban areas, where the disease was spreading rapidly – was not possible because of an intellectual property rights commitment under the WTO, which the ANC joined with no public debate.

The debts of the Apartheid government were passed on quietly to the new government and, as we saw in the last chapter, in the early years of democracy they cost about 30 billion rand annually to service (about \$4.5 billion). Klein asks, what about printing more money, before reminding us that monetary policy was controlled by the Apartheid era head of the central bank.

Capital controls aim to control flows of money in and out of the country through regulations or taxes, in order to limit financial and economic instability. However, for South Africa their imposition would 'violate the \$850 million [International Monetary Fund] deal', which Klein points out was 'signed, conveniently enough, right before the elections'.[30]

Klein highlights that this IMF deal also committed the government to 'wage restraint' in order to manage public finances but that this significantly reduced policy space to address the problem of low wages.

Like Rodrik, Klein highlights the limited ability of the new government to create jobs because of the international agreements it had signed up to. Hundreds of 'factories were actually about to close because the ANC had signed on to the GATT, the precursor to the World Trade Organization, which made it illegal to subsidise the auto plants and textile factories'.[31]

Unlike Rodrik, Klein highlights how much pressure the ANC were under from powerful countries, the finance sector and businesses to conform. In 1955 the Freedom Charter had called for democracy and human rights, land reform, labour rights and nationalisation to address the structural economic inequalities

Apartheid had created between the Black majority and White minority in the country.

As the possibility of Apartheid ending grew, Nelson Mandela and the ANC experienced a taste of the pressure they would come under if they tried to enact demands of the Freedom Charter in government. When Mandela was released from prison 'the South African stock market collapsed in panic; South Africa's currency, the rand, dropped by 10 percent. A few weeks later, De Beers, the diamond corporation, moved its headquarters from South Africa to Switzerland.'

Klein highlights that

> [this] kind of instant punishment from the markets would have been unimaginable three decades earlier, when Mandela was first imprisoned. In the sixties, it was unheard of for multinationals to switch nationalities on a whim and, back then, the world money system was still firmly linked to the gold standard. Now South Africa's currency had been stripped of controls, trade barriers were down, and most trading was short-term speculation.[32]

She vividly describes

> a call-and-response between the ANC leadership and the financial markets – a shock dialogue that trained the party in the new rules of the game. Every time a top party official said something that hinted that the ominous Freedom Charter might still become policy, the market responded with a shock, sending the rand into free fall.[33]

Unlike Rodrik, in whose hands 'the rules of the game' are neutral and objective, for Klein they are clearly created by powerful countries, sectors and businesses, whose interests they are designed to further, at the expense of the national interest of South Africa.

She explains that the 'rules were simple and crude, the electronic equivalent of monosyllabic grunts: justice – expensive, sell; status quo – good, buy'. When, shortly after his release, Mandela once again spoke out in favour of nationalisation at a private lunch with leading businessmen, 'the All-Gold Index plunged by 5 per cent'.[34]

Even statements that had nothing to do with the economic status quo 'but betrayed some latent radicalism seemed to provoke a market jolt. When Trevor Manuel, an ANC minister, called rugby in South Africa a "White minority game" because its team was an all-White one, the rand took another hit.'[35]

For Klein, it was this experience that meant that rather

> than making the centrepiece of its policy the redistribution of wealth that was already in the country – the core of the Freedom Charter on which it had been elected – the ANC, once it became the government, accepted the dominant logic that its only hope was to pursue new foreign investors who would create new wealth, the benefits of which would trickle down to the poor. But for the trickle-down model to have a hope of working, the ANC government had to radically alter its behaviour to make itself appealing to investors.[36]

The difference in the focus of Rodrik and Klein's analysis leads them to very different perspectives on the economic path taken by the ANC. For Rodrik,

> South Africa had undergone a remarkable political and economic transformation since its democratic transition in 1994. Following the end of White minority rule, it had managed to avoid a descent into acrimonious recrimination, endless redistribution, and populism that would have decimated the economy and turned the country into a sham democracy.[37]

Klein quotes Yasmin Sooka, a prominent South African human rights activist, who felt that the transition from Apartheid to democracy was like being told: 'We'll keep everything and you [the ANC] will rule in name ... You can have political power, you can have the façade of governing, but the real governance will take place somewhere else.'[38]

Klein concludes that the journey from Apartheid to democracy was 'not a remarkable political and economic transition' but 'a process of infantilization that is common to so-called transitional countries – new governments are, in effect, given the keys to the house but not the combination to the safe'.[39]

The impact of economics on gender and racialised wealth inequality in the United States

In this case study, we return to consider central banks, which we have seen increasingly being made independent from elected governments on the basis that monetary policy is a technical area of decision-making that shouldn't be politicised. Here Francesca Rhys-Williams details how supposedly technical decisions by experts in the US central bank (the Federal Reserve) had direct effects on racialised and gender wealth inequality and how, on this basis, it is inherently political.

In late 2008, with the US and global economy on the verge of a deep recession, central banks intervened to try to save the global financial system. The key policy the Federal Reserve and other central banks used was quantitative easing (QE), which is a tool to electronically inject money into the economy to boost lending and investment, and stimulate growth. There is clear evidence that QE in the US at that time created a 'wealth effect' for households, which is an increase in the value of their assets and net-wealth.[40]

From December 2008 until October 2014 the Federal Reserve spent a total of US$4.5 trillion on QE programmes to create electronic central bank reserves that were then used to purchase mortgage-backed securities (MBS) and government bonds from private sector portfolios. MBS are a collection of mortgages and loans that are pooled together and then sold on financial markets to investors, while government bonds are a financial asset issued by governments, normally considered the safest type of asset to invest in.

From December 2008 into 2009 the Federal Reserve bought $1,250 billion of MBS. They did this partially to reduce mortgage interest rates to make it more affordable for borrowers to finance and repay a mortgage. This boosted the housing market and eventually house prices rose. Consequently, this would have increased the wealth for households who owned their own home, all other things being equal.

Then, in November 2010 the Federal Reserve purchased $600 billion of long-term government treasury bonds or government debts.[41] As there were fewer government bonds in circulation, investors put their cash into other assets such as stocks, property, and land. This increased the value of these assets, and so the households that owned them had their net-wealth increase, all other things being equal. Stock prices were found to have reacted more strongly and positively to QE than house prices.[42]

There are clear racialised disparities in which households own stocks in the US. Data shows that in 2010, nearly one in five White households owned stocks compared to one in twenty-nine Black American and one in forty Hispanic households. More starkly, in 2007 White households had 1.4 times more wealth in stocks than Black American households. By 2013 this had increased to 4.4 times more wealth in stocks.

As a result, White households will have seen a much bigger increase in their wealth between 2009 and 2013 from the increase in value of their financial assets caused by QE.[43] White households are also more likely than Black and Hispanic households to directly or indirectly own stocks through their pensions. Even White working-class families have on average more assets than people of colour.[44]

In the decade before the financial crisis, the racialised gap in home ownership had widened, with Black Americans 50 per cent more likely than similar White households to lose their home.[45] For the period of QE after the financial crisis, although homeownership fell for all racialised groups, we can calculate the racialised gap in home-ownership between Black and White households, and Hispanic and White households. A ratio of 1 would mean that the racialised groups have the same rates of homeownership. During the six-year period of QE post-financial crisis, the Black to White ratio in homeowner-ship went from 0.65 to 0.59, a 6 per cent gap increase. The Hispanic to White ratio in homeownership went from 0.65 in Q4 2008 to 0.63. Thus, the already significant racialised gaps in home ownership were increasing in the exact period of QE in the US.

QE was not the cause of the increasing racialised gaps in homeown-ership, but this trend will have meant that Hispanic and to a greater extent Black American households had less wealth from a home than White households. Consequently, it was less likely their net wealth increased from the 'wealth effect' created by QE in the housing mar-ket. Women, and Black women particularly, were also less likely to be homeowners and so less likely to see their wealth increase.

Before QE was implemented in the US, how it might impact women and people of colour was overlooked by economists and central bankers. It clearly should have been crucial for them to take an intersectional approach to understand and evaluate the impact this policy would have on different groups, especially in the US where, as we have seen, there are significant racialised wealth ine-qualities.[46] In this case, the intersections of gender and racialised inequalities that already exist in society were reinforced and repro-duced by economic policies.

While intersectional approaches have already been used to study the impacts of policy responses to the global financial crisis, these mainly focused on government fiscal policy such as taxation and government spending, not the actions and monetary policies of central banks.[47]

We suggest this is at least partly explained by the view that central bank policymaking is technical not political which diverts focus from the way in practice it redistributes resources between groups.

Some economists have argued that we should not worry about whether QE increased net wealth inequality between groups because they believed that no household was made worse off as a direct consequence of the policy (in an appeal to the concept of Pareto optimality we explored in Chapter 3).[48]

While QE may not have made certain households directly poorer, it did make them relatively poorer and the money spent on the policy could have been used on another policy that would have actually made them better off. In contributing to widening racialised structural inequalities in the US, it is also likely to contribute to worsening economic and social outcomes for racialised groups and society as a whole.

Although this argument uses US data, the findings can be applicable to other economies. The UK, for example, also has a racialised wealth gap and likely has also seen increases in gender and racialised wealth inequality because of QE. This also applies for gender inequality in the Eurozone. The impact of QE on wealth inequality is still very relevant as QE is being used by central banks again during the Covid pandemic.

Who pays the cost of coal?

In our third case study, Brototi Roy, who we heard from in Chapter 3, takes us to her home country India to explore the economic experiences of farmers and Indigenous Forest People in eastern India.

Brototi's research identifies how the cultures, ideas and needs of income-poor and Indigenous communities are ignored by political decision-makers and corporate leaders in the name of India's economic expansion.

This 'development' imposes costs – displacement, ecological damage, loss of culture and community – on local communities and future generations who have no formal way to influence decisions and so resort to protest and resistance.

In this way, the government and large energy companies in India justify the building of new coal mines using economic narratives of development in ways which bypass and undermine democracy.

Economic production creates externalities or spillover effects on third parties which reduce their freedom. Pollution is the go-to example of a negative spillover: a factory may pollute a nearby river, which damages farmers' crops downstream, the ecosystem and the ability of people to use the river as a resource. If the factory had to pay the costs of cleaning up the river, or compensating the farmer for damaged crops, this would increase the costs of production, forcing it to sell its goods at a higher price, which would lead to demand for its goods to fall. Negative externalities represent the factory shifting the costs of pollution on to others, and society as a whole, which allows it to produce more, at the expense of environmental damage and harm to others.

Neoclassical economics does not recognise the pervasiveness of externalities in modern economic systems and the implications of this. Martinez argues that 'externalising costs, is a form of theft. It is taking something for nothing.'[49] The third parties who bear these costs do not voluntarily consent to them through market exchange and they don't have the economic power to prevent their imposition.

The concept of Ecological Distribution Conflicts (EDCs)[50] describes the social conflicts that arise when groups perceive that the distribution of access to natural resources and the costs of pollution are unfair or unjust in some way.

The number of EDCs increase in societies where there are large structural inequalities in land ownership, income and power because certain groups can decide who can access natural resources and who will bear the costs of pollution while others are excluded from this process.

Structural inequalities in India are significant and as a result one would expect a large number of EDCs. Figures from EJAtlas,[51] an online database of more than 3,000 ecological justice movements around the world, support this. Out of 224 movements against coal extraction, transportation and combustion documented worldwide, 65 are from India.

The case of coal in India

In 2017, India was the second largest producer and importer of coal, the dirtiest fossil fuel in the world, which accounts for a substantial part of its electricity generation and carbon dioxide emissions.[52]

From extraction to transportation and combustion, coal is a contested resource that contributes to India's interlinked socioecological challenges, specifically ecological degradation and climate change. A large area of India is and will be seriously threatened by climate change, from people in low-lying densely populated coastal areas, to agricultural lands, to industrial sites already contaminated by air pollution. The country's poor are disproportionately affected by climate change. Yet the reliance on coal is not expected to decline any time soon.

Figure 5.1 An opencast coal mine in Dhanbad, Jharkhand (picture by Brototi Roy, March 2017)

This growth poses serious threats not only in the shape of climate change but also to local wellbeing. Beyond the carbon dioxide emissions, coal mining and coal-fired power plants have other adverse health impacts. According to a study, there are about 80,000 to 115,000 premature deaths per year in the local population living around coal-fired power plants in India.[53]

Coal-mine workers and communities that surround coal mines face many adverse effects, prominent among them pneumoconiosis (commonly known as black lung disease) due to inhalation of coal dust. There are multiple deaths each year due to mine collapses and accidents.

By describing two specific cases of EDCs involving coal mining and thermal power plants, we can see how power relations form an integral part of the decision-making process. This is because these cases involve different stakeholders whose voices carry different weights due to social and historical inequalities based on class, caste, gender and religion, etc.

A thermal power plant with imported coal for exporting electricity in the coal-rich, electricity-poor district of Godda, Jharkhand

The state of Jharkhand in eastern India is one of the richest in terms of natural resources. It is home to about one third of India's total coal reserve (see Figure 5.1). Consequently, many coal mines and thermal power plants are in various stages of operation in areas with high tribal populations. One such thermal power plant currently being constructed and fraught with protests is located in the district of Godda. Godda is one of the twenty-four districts of the state of Jharkhand, lying in the north-eastern part of the state and with a large tribal presence.

In August 2015, a non-legally binding memorandum of understanding (MoU) was signed between the Bangladesh Power Development Board and India's largest corporate power supplier Adani Power Limited (hereafter Adani), to supply electricity to Bangladesh from Godda.

Adani then proposed to build a new power plant in Godda to produce this electricity. Consequently, in 2016, the government of Jharkhand signed an MoU with Adani to build the power plant. In the initial proposal the coal needed for electricity generation was to be supplied from the Jitpur mines, which are about 20 km away.

However, later in 2016, the company revised the proposal and stated that it would be using imported coal instead, which would be brought in via the Dhamra port in Odisha. This port is 700 km away and owned by a subsidiary of Adani.

The rise of a new ecological distribution conflict began when ten villages became contested territory due to the construction of the power plant in Godda, which required over 2,000 acres of land. Between 2016 and 2019 (and still ongoing) there were multiple cases of crimes including threats and physical violence towards the tribal people who have raised their voices against this project.[54] From destroying crops to preventing entry into the public hearings, from false charges against local activists and journalists to contested claims of compensations being paid, tribal villagers have been continuously attacked by a range of state and corporate actors involved in constructing and operating the new thermal power plant in Godda.

By March 2019, Adani had received formal and in-principle approval to develop hundreds of hectares of land for the project. A few months earlier, this project became India's first standalone power project to get the status of a Special Economic Zone, which gave it additional tax benefits.

The case of the thermal power plant in Godda gives rise to at least three different EDCs – one at the site of the construction of the plant, one at the site of the source of water, and one at the site of source of the construction material (sand from the riverbeds). There are latent conflicts brewing at the site of the water source, which would affect many communities dependent on the rivers from where the power plant has proposed to source its water, as well as the land under which the pipelines would be constructed.

This is coupled with the rampant illegal sand mining that locals point out cannot be easily quantified as it is carried out during the night, and under the influence of a 'sand mafia'. There are also reports that argue that the power purchase agreement puts Bangladesh at great financial risk and will 'deepen' poverty in the country.

There might be economic growth due to the creation of a new plant and revenues from exporting electricity, but it will bring much harm to local communities due to the loss of their homes, identities and way of life caused by forced relocation and the pollution of fertile land and water sources for those who remain. This raises important questions about the parameters that we use to define economic growth and development.

130,721 trees to be felled to make way for a coal mine in Odisha

Odisha, another state in the eastern part of India, is also rich in mineral resources, and with a high presence of Indigenous communities. It is also the state with the second highest coal reserves (after Jharkhand). In March 2019, clearance was given to divert 1,038 hectares of forests for opencast coal-mining projects of the Talabira II and III coal blocks (mines), located in the districts of Sambalpur and Jharsuguda. These two blocks have a combined reserve of 553 million tonnes of coal and have been operated by Neyveli Lignite Corporation (NLC) India Limited since 2016.

In 2018, NLC India Limited appointed Adani Enterprises as mine developer-cum-operator for both the coal blocks. The mines are expected to begin operating from 2021 to supply coal for generating 4,200 MW of electricity for its thermal projects – the 3,200 MW Talabira Thermal Power project in Odisha and the 1,000 MW thermal project at Tuticorin, in the southern state of Tamil Nadu.

By December 2019, villagers and local environmentalists claimed that over 40,000 trees had already been cut down in Sambalpur, whereas the official figures claimed the total was only 17,000. The next round of tree-felling in Jharsuguda is expected to garner further protests.

For the villagers, many of them from the Indigenous groups of Munda and Gond, this has been a deeply saddening and traumatising experience. Not only do the villagers heavily depend on these forests for their livelihoods, they had also actively been conserving the forest for the last four to five decades.

This was done by a tradition called *thengapalli* wherein every family would contribute either money or 3 kg of rice for community members to patrol the forests to ensure that trees are not cut for timber. There are also multiple reports of illegal procedures, including forgeries of documents to get the required clearances.

In a statement, Prafulla Samantara, recipient of the 2017 Goldman Environmental Prize, said:

> In a time when India needs to protect its forests to fight against climate change, forceful destruction of long standing natural forests protected by communities over decades without their consent to mine climate-killer coal is a climate crime. It is especially tragic since this verdant forest nurtured by marginalized forest communities is one of the last forests left in Sambalpur- Jharsuguda industrial belt, an area where climate change fuelled temperatures tend to reach 48 degree Celsius in summer.[55]

According to Ranjan Panda, a local activist based in Sambalpur working on issues of climate change and water:

> It doesn't make any sense to build new coal mines and power plants in an area already suffering from severe water scarcity, heat and pollution due to excessive concentration of mining, power and industrial activities. Chopping off 130,721 full grown natural tree species in this location will further aggravate the multiple stresses of the people and the ecology, making it an [un]inhabitable place.[56]

This case of the coal mines in Talabira depicts the difference of values between the villagers and the mine operators. For the villagers, the forest is more than an economic means; it is a part of their culture and heritage (as well as a source of livelihood). This difference in values fuels a growing conflict, in which local and national activists highlight the threat of the entire region becoming uninhabitable, and term what is happening a climate crime.

The cost of 'development'

Similar conflicts over natural resources are occurring across India and worldwide. They often involve Indigenous People and escalate into violent and dangerous clashes. Conflicts over coal follow a similar pattern and pose additional threats due to the impact of carbon dioxide emissions on climate change.

These patterns include government and businesses invoking the need for economic development as justification for forced displacement and ecological destruction. They often involve marginalised communities, misrepresentation of information and facts, and violence at different levels from direct physical violence, to *structural*, *ecological* and *slow violence* felt over years and generations due to loss of soil fertility, destruction of cultural identities and loss of sense of belonging. This reminds us of our argument in the last chapter, of the need to broaden our understanding of violence, to see its prevalence in our modern economies.

As an example, we can see how Indigenous communities have been disproportionately at the receiving end of the 'cost' of development as a form of structural violence. In the Indian context, the marginalised Indigenous communities, known as *Adivasi*, who at a population of 104 million account for just under 9 per cent of the Indian population, are disproportionately displaced. According to one report, they account for 40 per cent of all the displaced population of the country, often without any compensation, and in many cases waiting years for resettlement.[57]

There is concrete evidence from these two cases that shows the systemic exploitation of nature and oppression of Indigenous communities in the name of economic growth and development. Both these cases show how the claims and rights of Indigenous communities are disregarded by those with power including company officials, forest division members, the police, the local state and national government.

These case studies highlight the importance of questioning our understanding of economic growth and development by delving deeper into the meaning of wellbeing. A coal mine and a thermal power plant might increase the percentage of final goods and services produced in the economy, but does that really lead to more wellbeing when it also results in rising pollution, violent clashes over natural resources, and the further marginalisation of Indigenous communities that have been historically oppressed? We need to evaluate the benefits of "development" projects with broader criteria, and decisions about whether to proceed with them need to be taken through democratic processes which include the voices of all the stakeholders who will be affected. We return in Chapter 7 to consider how economic development can be led from the bottom up.

Part II

Reclaiming economics

Chapter 6

Reforming academia

*With contributions from Ariane Agunsoye,
Michelle Groenewald, Danielle Guizzo
and Kamal Ramburuth-Hurt*

Francesca Rhys-Williams, a contributor to this book, encountered stigma from other students, as they assumed she had chosen economics because she wanted 'to make lots of money'.

Frustrated with this stereotype, Francesca was compelled to carry on studying economics to prove it can be a force for good in society. With this goal, she and many others across the world are working actively to try to change the practice of economics.

In Part II of this book, we turn to explore how economics can be reclaimed to address what has gone wrong and build a healthier discipline. In this chapter, we make the case that it is necessary to diversify, decolonise and democratise academic economics (we call this the three Ds). This is crucial for economics to contribute effectively to creating economies which promote racial justice, gender and social class equality, and stewardship of the planet for future generations.

Diversifying economics is about broadening both the people and knowledge of the discipline. This requires moving from rigid hierarchies where certain groups and countries dominate, towards a more decentralised and egalitarian discipline in which economists better represent the societies they are from, and knowledge production addresses local and specific realities including structural inequality and historical oppression. We suggest that this requires a pluralism of theories and methods and a much more interdisciplinary approach which will require a deep shift in mindset from the current assumption that there is one right way to do economics.

Decolonising economics requires embedding an analysis of history, oppression and power at the foundations of our understanding about how economies operate, which will lead us to new ways of thinking and different economic policies. Decentring knowledge production should include actively seeking and incorporating perspectives from outside of the US and Europe, including from Indigenous communities, which will broaden our collective understanding of how economies can be organised to achieve different goals.

As we have seen throughout this book, neoclassical economics has largely rejected economic policies that structurally address the distribution of resources and power. Part of decolonising is to develop theories and policies which effectively and legitimately reset the distribution of resources, to reduce structural inequalities, which have been created and reproduced as a result of historical oppression.

A democratised economics would put the principles of democracy and self-determination at the core of economic development, setting goals and developing policies that represent the needs, priorities, values and cultures of the communities who will be affected. It requires recognising that if everyone plays multiple roles in the economy including carer, worker, owner, saver, investor, citizen and public service user, then everyone has an expertise that stems from their economic experience.

We end the chapter by exploring how the three Ds can be embedded into economics education so that the next generation of economists will be equipped with the knowledge, skills and values needed to truly transform the discipline and our global economy. This focus reflects our interest in educational reform and our belief that educating the next generation of economists is key to achieving the change we seek.

Diversifying academic economics

'Diversity' is broad in its definitions but can generally be regarded as 'the fact of many different types of things, people, ideas or opinions being included in something'.[1] In this book, we have illustrated the lack of diversity and representativeness of economics students and academic economists (particularly at the top of the profession) and the lack of diverse thinking within mainstream economics.

Diversifying who becomes an economist is necessary for the profession to claim to represent the interests of society rather than particular groups, and to be seen as legitimate and trustworthy by the societies they operate within.

An academic economics that was more diverse, in terms of racialised and gendered identities and socioeconomic background, would also over time develop a more holistic and diverse understanding of economies and economic behaviour, and it would focus on different research questions and policy prescriptions.

Ensuring different identities are represented in academic economics is not enough to ensure that the discipline is better equipped and more interested in addressing issues of racial justice, gender and class equality, but it is a necessary foundation. Without diversifying the people in economics, we either end up with disinterest and lack of focus on these issues, or a well-meaning but ultimately paternalistic approach in which economists apply economics to needy, marginalised, and underrepresented communities.

When attempting to diversify the people in economics it is essential to take an intersectional approach. Intersectionality is the idea that it is necessary to consider the overlap of people's various social identities, such as gendered, racialised identity and social class (or status) rather than a single identity on its own, because this lens helps make visible the interacting ways that individuals experience oppression and discrimination.[2]

When diversity is reduced to a tick-box exercise it becomes about achieving targets for a certain amount of representation of women and people of colour in an economics department, in a way that removes the intersectional focus on power. A deeper focus on diversity asks whether particular groups and communities, such as low-income, Black American women of colour in the US or Muslim women in India, are represented in and have access to becoming an economist.

Likewise, a focus on diversity can't just focus on individuals abstracted away from the knowledge, research agendas, structure and culture of economic departments, universities and the discipline as a whole. Economics is a hierarchical discipline and, for increased diversity of people to translate into changes in how economists think about the economy and practise economics, it must be combined with broader reforms.

One crucial aspect of this transformation that falls under the heading of diversifying economics is around the body of knowledge, methods and research questions that are accepted as legitimate economics. We have explored in depth how economics has become increasingly narrow over the last half century and the negative effects of the policing of what is and isn't economics.

Neoclassical economics rests on the idea of *monism*: the belief that it is both possible and desirable to aim to develop a single unified set of theories and methods to analyse your subject matter, in this case economies.

Pluralism in contrast recognises and teaches a range of different approaches to understanding the economy and its interaction with the wider social and ecological systems in an interactive, reflective and engaging manner.[3]

Economics should turn away from attempting to find abstract, universal laws of the economy, and instead actively develop multiple approaches to studying the economy that attend to the specifics of how economies function in different places at different times.

Here we briefly outline theory, methods and interdisciplinarity as three avenues through which pluralism can be fostered.

Theoretical pluralism

In Chapter 2, we identified a trend of economics becoming a theoretically narrower discipline and in Chapter 3 we explored the core framework of neoclassical economics. Economics is actually much broader than many economics students, economists and the general public realise. There is a long, rich and diverse tradition of research in different economic perspectives.

Table 2.1 (p. 62) illustrated ten different coherent economic perspectives that highlight the true diversity of economic theory, which is currently actively restricted and discouraged.

These perspectives provide fundamentally different ways of thinking about the economy from the ground up. They have different assumptions about human behaviour and the role of institutions, and how the two interact. Their different foci and priorities represent value judgements about what is important; this means they ask different questions. They have different tools and approaches that lead them to different answers to economic questions. They are diverse and not all of equal validity, but they all hold valuable insights.

Our interviews with students and academics from under-represented backgrounds highlighted that identity-based discrimination was often entangled with theoretical and methodological discrimination. This finding is confirmed by other research including the American Economic Association's survey of economists. Demanding respect and tolerance of different ideas and theories in economics is clearly intertwined in some way with seeking racialised, gendered, and social class equality in the discipline.

Pluralism of methods

In Chapter 2, we heard about the struggle some economists went through to get their research funded and published when it explored topics using methods not considered valuable in neoclassical economics. *Fortune* recently released a list of nineteen Black economists to watch and it is striking how much of their research is qualitative in comparison to the articles which appear in the top ranked economics journals.[4]

A classic response from mainstream economists is that reliance on qualitative methods is a sign of failure to master difficult maths, but a key finding of our interviews was that the choice to use qualitative methods was a considered response to how best to approach the research question, taken despite the fact that interviewees knew this would make it harder to fund and publish.

In many cases we heard that this experience of one's research being devalued and discredited created a hostile environment for economists from backgrounds underrepresented in the discipline. This highlights the way that narrow accepted research topics and methods can serve to homogenise the identity and background of the people who feel welcome and able to flourish in economics.

Recognising the legitimacy and value of qualitative (and non-standard quantitative) research methods in economics is important for other reasons beyond creating a more inclusive environment for economists. It might be that the requirement for quantitative approaches in economics actually prevents the discipline from adequately addressing topics like racism. A field historically dominated by White people is less likely to gather quantitative data on issues that affect people of colour, and this absence will render their experience invisible in quantitative research. Even if data is captured, it is widely recognised that quantitative approaches are less suited to answering certain questions.

For example, qualitative data and/or mixed methods can explore how meanings, values and relations are interrelated and establish a connection with the people being studied. Rachel, a Black African economics lecturer in the US, explains that

> interviews I did both with migrant women as well as with family and community members and what I learnt has really shaped my own thinking about development, about what development is, about what development should mean, about who benefits and who loses, and the kind of knowledge that we choose to privilege.

Qualitative fieldwork requires more time spent with the subjects of the research and opens more possibilities for a deeper understanding of people's culture and reasoning. From experience, extended qualitative fieldwork research helps the researcher to assimilate the wider history and politics of a location that is simply not possible to do from the confines of a library, or analysing numerical data about a place and its population. Speaking or learning the language of who you want to conduct research with is essential, and the latter should be incorporated into research budgets and timeframes.

In development economics, advocates of the Randomised Control Trials we discussed in Chapter 5 argue that they allow them to get closer to interact with people and their customs, but we've argued that in practice they are delivered in a top-down way which takes little account of people's experiences and priorities.

If economics accepted the legitimacy of qualitative methods, it could explore and develop the role of participatory and peer research methods. This could provide ways for research questions and methods to be led by the communities who have previously had economics done to them and have been seen as passive subjects, particularly in the context of development economics. This in turn would begin to build relationships and legitimacy where economics is seen to represent the public interest, and not particular government or private interests.

Pluralism of methods opens up the possibility of mixed research designs that include qualitative data in the form of primary data such as interviews and quantitative data in the form of economic statistics.

For instance, Professors Jamie Morgan and Wendy Olsen note the detrimental effects of micro-finance on economically deprived groups in rural India.[5] By combining questionnaires to collect quantitative data, with semi-structured interviews, the authors find that instead of empowering women and low-income households, micro-finance often reinforced inequalities based on gender and caste. Integrating qualitative research into quantitative economic analysis, allows the exploration of intra-group relationships, power imbalances and everyday life, which gives a more complex and realistic understanding of the world.

In this sense, economics could learn from other disciplines like sociology, which conducts statistical analysis with large sample sizes; observes organisations, neighbourhoods and villages to better understand how they operate; runs laboratory and field experiments where a hypothesis can be tested under controlled conditions; and examines historical documents through close reading to better understand the broader contexts which shape the present. Economics should embrace this methodological diversity.

Interdisciplinary

Neoclassical economics is a closed standalone framework that can be applied to a whole range of topics outside the core focus of the economy including addiction, marriage and crime. A suggested strength of mainstream economics is that it can incorporate new insights into this flexible framework and in this way adapt to criticism and accomodate broader developments.

However, critics have argued that the process of integration into the neoclassical framework often strips the theory being integrated of the content which made it valuable in the first place. For example, behavioural psychology has highlighted the prevalence of biases and imperfections in human reasoning, thus potentially undermining the economic concept of rationality and the foundations of microeconomics. Over time, this has been incorporated into the neoclassical framework as adjustments to the utility-maximising approach, through a bias or some other form of bounded rationality being added into the model of consumer behaviour, without ever questioning the underlying assumptions.

For us, an interdisciplinary approach is most valuable when it highlights difference in perspective which is not compatible with a neoclassical framework because we are challenging both the possibility and desirability of any single framework to describe the economy. For example, one of our interviewees, Bea, found courses in feminist theory within International Political Economy were 'eye opening' as they 'talked about the unpaid sector of the economy that's not included in GDP and all the unpaid care work that women do'. While this helped her to see why women generally earn less than men, it also made Bea realise how gender inequalities in economics were inadequately discussed.

A deep shift

Economics requires a deep mindset and culture shift to embrace theoretical, methodological and interdisciplinary pluralism. The idea that 'there is no such thing as different schools of economics, there is only good economics and bad economics'[6] is deeply ingrained. Some economists argue against pluralism, claiming that there are simply too many uncertainties or contradictions about what exactly this would entail.

Economics needs to be more open to complexity, uncertainty and multiplicity. A single framework is more limited and requires actively suppressing certain ideas and methods, as well as clearly delineating economics from other social sciences. In the context of unequal power relationships between different identity groups and countries, this suppression takes on a racialised, gendered and social class or status dimension. The single dominant framework in economics represents a particular worldview and not others.

Decolonising academic economics

Decolonising refers to the thought and action needed to redress forms of systemic disadvantage associated with racism and colonialism. In this section, we begin by exploring what it would mean to decolonise knowledge and practice within academic economics, before considering what role the discipline should play in the broader process of decolonising economies.

Decolonising economic knowledge

Michelle Groenewald, a contributor to this book, remembers sitting in her first economics class in South Africa, starting with the very first chapter of her economics undergraduate textbook. She was introduced to the great thinkers in the field; the lecturer explained with enthusiasm the contributions of Adam Smith, John Maynard Keynes and Karl Marx. She found their contributions fascinating and valuable. However, as she paged through the rest of her textbook, she found only graphs, equations and assumptions. There was no mention of any women economists nor a single African economist, never mind an African woman economist! Michelle remembers looking around her first-year class wondering whether this meant that great economists couldn't be people in her country, or that valuable contributions couldn't be made by women in the field of economics?

Nearly a decade later, Michelle would return to that same undergraduate economics class as a lecturer. She has been privileged to be introduced to critical, economic scholarship, both at home (the African Programme on Rethinking Development Economics), and abroad (at the School of Oriental and African Studies, London). At the beginning of term Michelle asks her students to name even a single economist who is not a White, Western, man. Not a single hand is raised. Now she takes the semester to ensure that all her students know about great Black African and women economists, and the valuable contributions they have made. Does Michelle think diversifying who, what and how she teaches is enough to solve all the problems in economics? No. But it is one part of starting to address the structural problems our discipline faces, so that every student in Michelle's class knows that they can make great and valuable contributions to economics.

Echoing Michelle's views, a background assumption for us is that global histories of European and later US domination have had the effect of limiting what counts as 'authoritative' knowledge, whose knowledge is recognised, what economists are taught, and how they are taught it.[7] Decolonising is a call to recognise the colonial history of economics and how it has shaped the modern discipline, and for economics to utilise ideas developed by people in former colonies.

Problems highlighted by students underscore the necessity of decolonising the curriculum – and economics more generally. But what does that mean for economics in particular? During the Rethinking Economics For Africa (REFA) student conference workshops in 2019, one of REFA's founders and contributor to this book, Kamal Ramburuth-Hurt, recorded that students defined the 'decolonisation' of the economics curriculum as ultimately rejecting the 'one-size-fits-all' approaches that characterises the economic status quo. They wanted the removal of barriers that prevent the freedom to pursue economic ideas and practices that are suited to unique contexts. This would involve unlearning and relearning a new economics, thereby reclaiming the discipline. Students also voiced that:

> a decolonised economics curriculum is one that is pluralist, relevant and constructed to solve African problems in order to improve human development and the wellbeing of Africans. It offers positive freedom through the empowerment of students to have access to quality

education. It has negative freedom through an international approach
to theories and applications that place Africa at the centre. This is a
freedom from Eurocentricism. It is a curriculum that is enforced by
institutions of education that are anti-racist; with these institutions
playing a role in affirming African identities.

Pluralism is clearly necessary to decolonise economic knowledge.
History and hierarchy ensures that the neoclassical economic
framework provides a thoroughly US and Western Europe centred
view of the world. Even if things were different, or in the future,
the balance of power within economics shifts, we wouldn't want to
replace one single framework for another.

However, it is important to be clear that it is perfectly possible to have pluralism without decolonisation, and most of the perspectives in Table 2.1 (p. 62) have developed mainly in the US and
Western Europe to address specific experiences, needs and priorities in these regions.

We see decolonisation not as critique but fundamentally as a
process of construction, of developing new ways of understanding and explaining economic realities and solving problems. While
there are many starting points for this rebuilding, we see the rein-
tegration of history, power and oppression as key steps to begin to
decolonise economic knowledge and practice.

History

It is vital that economics recognises its roots in colonial history
and how this is continuously relevant and deeply embedded in current economic practice, in terms of the approaches and people that
are most 'valued' within the discipline. This is about remembering
and understanding what actually happened and how it has shaped
the present, not about passing moral judgement. We in economics

should start by accepting our collective ignorance of parts of our history and embark on a process of collective learning.

Oppression

We have seen that mainstream economic approaches to studying discrimination have focused on individual and not structural explanations. Economics should incorporate frameworks such as the four 'I's of oppression to better conceptualise how oppression operates in economies.

- *Ideological* – Any oppressive system is based on the notion that one group is somehow superior to another, and hence has the right to govern the latter. More intellectual, harder working, stronger, more capable, more noble, more deserving, more advanced, chosen, normal, superior and so on are all variations on this theme. This is how the dominating group sees itself. Of course, the other group is labelled as ignorant, lazy, weak, inept, useless, undeserving, backward, aberrant, inferior and so on.

- *Institutional* – The belief that one group is superior to another and has the right to govern the other is ingrained in society's institutions, including laws, the legal system, and police practice, education, hiring rules, public policies, housing development, media images, political power and so on. It is not necessary for institutional injustice to be intentional.

- *Interpersonal* – Individual members of the dominant group are given licence and reinforcement to disregard or mistreat individuals in the oppressed group as a result of institutional oppression. Interpersonal racism refers to what individuals of one racialised identity do to those of other identities on a personal level, such as racial jokes, name-calling, stereotyping, beatings and harassment, threats and so on. Men's sexual abuse and harassment, violence directed at women, ridiculing, dismissing women's thoughts and sexist jokes are examples of interpersonal sexism.

- *Internalised* – The fourth method of oppression can be within some individuals from groups who are the most victimised. Oppressed individuals can internalise inferiority ideology when they see it represented in institutions or they encounter interpersonal disrespect from members of the dominant group, and as a result, they gradually internalise negative messages about themselves. It's not strange that we believe it if we've been taught we're stupid, useless, and abnormal our whole lives and have been treated as if we are. This can make us unhappy within ourselves.[8]

Power

Neoclassical economics focuses on choice and voluntary exchange and only considers power in a narrow way as market power. In the real world, an individual's gendered, racialised and class identities shape how they experience the economy and individuals enter it with structurally unequal resources and power that fundamentally shape the choice sets available to them. We would like to see economics focus much more on how power is distributed and operates in modern economies as a necessary step to effectively addressing imbalances that stem from patriarchal, colonial and elitist histories.

Decentring knowledge production

We have seen how centralised the production of legitimate high-status economic knowledge is through the top five economics journals based in the US and a broader ring of US and Western European journals.

A crucial part of decolonising economics is consciously reorganising so that there are multiple centres of knowledge production without extreme hierarchies in status between them. Supporting countries and regions as well as different groups within countries to generate economic knowledge relevant to their experience, needs and priorities is an important foundation of democracy and national self-determination we explore further in the next chapter.[9]

Earlier we heard from Kamal that REFA student groups called for decolonised economics to promote and support the development of economic knowledge and practices from outside the US and Western Europe. As an example, he writes about '*Umuntu ngumuntu ngabantu*', a Zulu phrase that could be translated into English as 'a person is a person through other persons' or 'I am because we are'. Kamal describes how this concept, which has an important cultural role for many South African economics students, grates with the description of human behaviour as atomised and utility maximising that they are taught in their economics classes. Decentring economic knowledge production would mean that South African economists have the freedom and resources to develop theory and methods from values and behaviours which are more relevant to their cultural experience.

In parts of Latin America, the concepts of *Buen Vivir* ('Living Well') and *Pachamama* (the rights of nature) have been used as a basis to develop different economic perspectives, and governments have legally recognised Indigenous community lands. This innovation in land rights is a significant departure from US and Western European developed neoclassical economics, which strongly asserts the centrality of private property to a well-functioning economy.[10]

The First Nations-Canadian economist Carol Anne Hilton has been developing a decolonised 'Indigenomics'. It 'draws on ancient principles that have supported Indigenous economies for thousands of years ... Indigenomics is about honoring the powerful thinking of Indigenous wisdom of local economy, relationships and human values.'[11] It has led to the creation of an Indigenomics Institute, which provides information, support, guidance and expertise in economic frameworks, practice, community development (plus the barriers and challenges to it and their solutions), from an Indigenous worldview.

The exchange of economic thinking between equal parties has the potential to bring mutual gains and broaden our collective understanding of how economies can be organised to achieve different goals. The Indigenous Australian writer Tyson Yunkaporta, sees the strength of non-Indigenous thinking in examining things intensively in isolation, but suggests that Indigenous thought is highly contextualised and situated in dynamic relationships with people and landscape, considering many variables at once.[12]

Throughout this book we have returned to the need for more holistic, diversified, and interrelated forms of knowing in order to better engage with the complexity and growth of modern economies, as well as their interactions with other systems such as the living world.

To do this, economics must go beyond the deeply embedded dualisms of modern/primitive and developed/underdeveloped which structure our thinking about the global economic system and what is legitimate economic knowledge, but in fact are products of our colonial histories.

A note on decolonisation

Decolonisation is a process which will require patience. Appleton warns that we should use the word decolonisation with extreme caution and perhaps speak initially of our attempts to 'diversify the syllabus and curriculum, digress from the canon, decentre knowledge and knowledge production, devalue hierarchies, disinvest from citational power structures, and diminish some voices and opinions in meetings, while magnifying others'.[13]

In fact, a lot of the work we may be doing is almost certainly smaller steps in a larger decolonising process. It will require an understanding that decolonising curricula necessitates also decolonising the university, and universities are in turn embedded in an economy that also requires decolonising. It is to the task of decolonising the economy that we turn to next.

We use the word decolonising here as a recognition of the power that such a word holds as a rallying cry for students, as a call to action within universities and as a challenge for those outside academia to get involved in something that affects us all. In order to not be reductionist in our approach to decolonising economics, we take seriously the need to diversify, digress, decentre, devalue, disinvest and diminish, as we join other scholars in a larger decolonising process.

Decolonising economies

For some people, the decolonisation of knowledge we described above is a distraction. Instead, the primary purpose of decolonisation is the task of connecting contemporary racialised inequality with wider historical processes of colonialism, seeking to expose and transform inequalities through forms of collective reflection and action such as reparations.[14]

While we have argued that decolonising economic knowledge, culture, institutions, and practice is important, we recognise that without this wider effort, it becomes a metaphor or performance that doesn't meaningfully address the issues. Here is Kamal Ramburuth-Hurt again clearly making the link between decolonising economics and the broader process of decolonising in South Africa and the African continent more broadly:

> Why do we use the word decolonisation – and not 'transformation', or 'justice'? I argue that this is because the word 'decolonisation' explains where the power lies currently. It reflects the persistence of the legacy of colonisation on knowledge systems, and on economic systems. Decolonisation explains that the power imbalances that we are experiencing stem from Apartheid and the colonial project. Decolonisation explains that the rainbow nation has not worked out as evidenced by persistent racialised inequality.

> We use the word decolonisation because it contextualises the racial power dynamics experienced between racialised groups within a given country as well as between countries [connected through histories of colonisation]. It offers a history of the reasons for these power dynamics. And it serves as a reality check of how little has changed in post-colonial Africa as a reflection of the frustration that 'we still have not decolonised!'

Globally, decolonisation is about rebalancing power, land, resources, status and agency to those who have been dispossessed through historical oppression. A decolonised academic economics could support this process through exploring how to reset the distribution of resources and power in economies. We introduce this idea now, before developing this argument further in Chapter 8.

Resetting distribution

Our major criticism of mainstream neoclassical economics in this book is that through its failure to focus on broader systems and historical context, it makes invisible in its analysis the structural inequalities that fundamentally influence how individuals with different identities experience the economy.

We saw how development economics has turned away from structural interventions which aimed to shift a country's economic trajectory towards micro- and behaviour change interventions. Development economics obscures the root causes of poverty by ignoring power relations and historical oppression. This is consistent with a broader shift in economics that has seen many attempts to close the racialised wealth gap in the US, for example, through greater educational attainment, better financial decisions, and other changes in habits and practices on the part of people of colour.

This approach too often tacitly supports victim blaming where the cause of a country's poverty is corrupt or inept governments and poor economic outcomes for Black Americans are explained by their culture. Economics fails to recognise how colonial power relations are embedded in the rules of the global economy on one hand, and how ideological and institutional racism and White supremacy has been baked into the US economy on the other.

As part of its journey to decolonising, economics must recognise that while interventions and policies to address the symptoms of poverty and economic deprivation are part of the picture, on their own they are wholly inadequate to address the scale of economic inequality created through hundreds of years of oppression.

A decolonised economics would develop the thinking behind and argue publicly for policies that would redistribute economic resources within and between countries to address systemic inequalities caused by historical oppression.

Within countries structural policies might address ownership of land, property, business, financial assets; accumulated wealth; incomes; and access to essential goods and services like housing, food, education and health. Internationally structural policies might address debt, technology transfer, suspension of intellectual

property rights, access to markets and guaranteed prices for strategic resources.

Language is important here. The ideas of debt forgiveness, which
is often discussed internationally, and redistribution within a country, both reinforce a framing where the successful are giving to the
unsuccessful for some reason. However, where the original distribution was not determined in a way that was just (even if it was legal),
then debt can be cancelled, and resources distributed differently in a
way that seeks to repair and rectify that historical injustice.

This call for thinking and policy which addresses the structure
of national and global economies does not mean returning to an
earlier time of top-down government management of the economy.
In the next chapter, we set out an approach to economic planning
that is led by and centres individuals and communities, particularly
those currently furthest from power.

Rebalancing power

Is an economy organised in such a way where those with economic resources can translate them into other forms of political
and social power and use this to accumulate further resources?
Or does it effectively separate control of economic resources from
other forms of power and prevent the wealthy from reorganising
the economy to benefit themselves?

A notable feature of our global economic system and many
national economies is the growth of wealth among the wealthiest
in society. Much of this wealth is intergenerational and, in the case
of nations, is linked to historical oppression of other countries.

The second task of decolonising economies is to rebalance
power more equally between different groups within countries and

between countries internationally. This will involve utilising policies that mainstream economics has deemed unacceptable.

At a national level, a sample of these policies might include rent controls and increasing the rights of tenants to rebalance power between renters and landlords, promoting unions, and developing sectoral bargaining particularly in low-wage sectors to rebalance power between workers and employers. They can also include developing wealth and inheritance taxes to prevent economic power accumulating over generations.

Internationally, policies might include supporting countries to impose exchange and capital controls that rebalance power between national governments and international financial markets, and implementing tariffs and subsidies that give nations tools to rebalance power between national and international producers in specific strategic sectors.

These are all legitimate tools of economic policy. They all have risks and downsides like any other policy and are not always appropriate. Design that engages local specifics is important and experimental approaches that are small scale, responsive and adaptable can help identify what works to achieve different goals when we don't have all of the answers.

At a deeper level, a decolonised economics would consider how the legal rules which underpin modern global economies could be rewritten to balance power better between owners of wealth, workers, savers, future generations, and the living world.[15]

Democratising economics

Democratising economics is about who gets to make decisions and how they are made. It refers to decision-making within the discipline and in broader economies. We explore each in turn here before returning to develop this argument in the next chapter.

We have seen that academic economics is undiverse and hierarchical. The higher up the discipline you go, the less diversity there is but the more power individuals have to shape the knowledge, culture, institutions and practices of economics. Reforming the discipline so that there is greater collective ability for economists globally to shape the future of academic economics is a precondition to addressing many of the issues we have highlighted in this book.

Democratising academic economics is also about broadening the purpose of the discipline. We have seen in Chapters 4 and 5 how economics has in practice often contributed to undermining national sovereignty and democracy.

Because we are all part of the economy and it plays an important role in shaping the environment we live in; how it functions, its purpose and the values embedded in it should be collectively agreed through democratic debate and decision-making. If this view is accepted, then the role of academic economics is to support communities to reorganise their economies and contribute to developing different forms of economics that people can participate in.

Democratising economics involves exploring how economic knowledge is produced and communicated outside universities in households, communities, workplaces and political systems. If everyone plays multiple roles in the economy including carer, worker, owner, saver, investor, citizen, and public service user, then everyone has an expertise which stems from their experience of these roles. Later in this chapter we provide ideas about how the process of learning economics can include two-way dialogue between non-economists in these varied roles and university economics students, through a range of teaching methods.

In this way, democratised economic knowledge and practice would be more responsive to the expressed needs, priorities and experiences of different groups in society.

Democratising economies

In the next chapter we explore how economics could be reclaimed as everyday practice to support communities to shape their economies from the bottom up. One measure of success of a democratised economics is the extent to which it is useful in supporting a community or social group's ability to shape its environment to secure its needs and flourish (in the way it defines).

This task connects with democratising and decolonising economies because communities, particularly Indigenous Peoples, and countries which were colonised, must be free to organise their economies in ways which reflect their localities, histories, knowledges and cultures, rather than being forced to use economic frameworks and policies imposed on them by others.[16]

To democratise economics, we need a new type of public-interest economist who recognises that collective decision-making is a social not technical process and therefore must be done 'with, not to or for' citizens. We need a new social contract between experts, politicians and citizens that sets out these shared commitments.

We also need a deep and nuanced concept of public interest that clearly sets out who the academic discipline of economics is accountable to. While much funding for economics will come from government and private business, being accountable to a broader public interest is key to rebuilding the legitimacy and effectiveness of economics in the twenty-first century.

Here it is important to consider power relations and historical oppression so that public interest can engage with, represent, and advocate for groups with less power. In this way, they could become an important democratic institution that checks and redistributes economic and other forms of power.

At an individual and community level, having access to public-interest economics (and economists) in particular situations, such as the proposed redevelopment of an area, could come to be seen as a right in the same way people have the right to a lawyer if accused of a crime. This would establish the idea that everyone had a right to independent economic expertise and support to represent them around particular events or decisions that would have a big impact on their life.

The message this would send is that the discipline of economics actually does represent public and not private interests. Public-interest economists would serve those who aren't powerful. They would stand with those people and represent them. They would build relationships with them over time, not be isolated in their universities, and they would learn about the economy from them.

Change in academic economics

Going deeper

We believe that economics needs to go through a deeper process of how its knowledge, people, culture and institutions have been shaped by historical oppression and continue to reproduce systemic inequalities.

This process begins internally with consideration of the history of economics and its current institutions and culture, but then widens to question how the discipline can contribute and not impede wider attempts to decolonise universities, societies and economies.

This involves reflecting on economic knowledge and understanding how it embeds certain ideas and excludes others.

This reflection might take the form of commissions, reviews and enquiries organised by national and international economic associations, but it should also take place at university department level as an important part of academic life for economists and be integrated into economics education. Economists have a responsibility to reflect individually on these questions in the context of their life, career and research, while considering what role they have to play in diversifying, decolonising and democratising economics.

We look at economics today and don't see that it is ready to embark on this process of deep reflection. Until it is, we won't achieve the kind of transformative change that is needed.

Embedding the three Ds into economics education

Let us then conclude this chapter by suggesting the following eight questions that economists and students can ask as we begin the journey of diversifying, decolonising and democratising economics education.

Who are we teaching?

What message are we sending to our students if we only refer to White, male US and European economists like Marx, Smith, Keynes, Ricardo and Hayek? Students need to be made explicitly aware that economists come from all corners of the globe and from many different walks of life. They need to, and indeed want to, see themselves reflected in their curriculum.

The complex social phenomena we engage with as economists can be better understood when we draw on a wider array of economic thinkers. We are actually training better policymakers, academics and civil servants, when we also teach the likes of Ibn Khaldun, Joan Robinson, Elinor Ostrom, Samir Amin, Kwame Nkrumah, Julius Nyerere and Thandika Mkandawire, to name but a few!

It can be really difficult, especially as a young academic, to know where to begin looking for the work of more diverse authors. This is compounded when, in most instances, we ourselves will not have been taught any of what we are now endeavouring to add to our curricula. In this instance, we cannot emphasise enough the importance of reaching out to networks of other scholars. Using social media, such as #econtwitter and #academictwitter, can be potentially useful in this regard.

The good news is that often, once one finds a starting point, there are many avenues for further exploration. As an example, the *Handbook of Alternative Theories of Economic Development*[17] has a brilliant chapter written by Yash Tandon. This gives a brief overview of the work of Nyerere, Nabudere and Amin. Once you know what to look for, it becomes much easier to start reading outside the established canon.

It will likely be very useful to consider incorporating content from other disciplines such as sociology, anthropology, psychology and political science, although the inward-looking nature of economics highlighted in Chapter 2 may make this harder. As we seek to incorporate more diverse authors and content in our curricula, we may find ourselves having to defend against those who would claim that a decolonised curriculum doesn't teach 'real economics'. The key here is to not relegate content from other disciplines to the 'additional resources' section of the curriculum but to set this as core content that will be engaged with in lectures, class discussion and tutorials.

This type of work might be challenging for economics students who have often become so comfortable with mathematical problems that an article published in a sociology journal may be really difficult to grapple with. Nevertheless, it is important that teachers should encourage students to develop the ability to think critically and to be more reflective in their practice.

Teachers should also ask who are our students? What are their lived experiences? What are their socioeconomic backgrounds? Do they have specific expertise based on their own research or previous work experience that might be particularly useful for us to bring into the classroom? Are we taking the time to get to know students and for them to get to know us? How can we let that inform the topics we might teach and who might do the lecturing on some weeks? How can assessment practice change, based on a better understanding of students?

What are we teaching?

Economics students must be exposed to various schools of economic thought, because this is a critical part of a diversified and decolonised curriculum. We have also touched on the importance of economic history, and history of economic thought, being integrated into compulsory modules from first-year economics courses. Economics curricula must explore how colonialism and neo-colonialism has (and importantly in some instances has not) influenced our economies today.

What is taught should also depend on the specific country and context. Economics education in South Africa, for example, should incorporate the variety of cultural frameworks that exist in the country, and while the study of other countries is absolutely crucial, they must be studied in a way that places Africa at the centre.

In South Africa, one way of doing this, is moving away from teaching economics solely in English, and integrating one or more of the ten official languages of the country into courses.

There should also be courses available that delve into the specifics of the economy the students live in (if it is underrepresented currently in courses), as well as the history of economic thought and economic history in different countries and continents. These topics are under-taught and under-researched and therefore unlikely to be considered in textbooks written in Europe and the US. For example, in South Africa it would be useful to include topics such as the informal economy and stokvels (invitation-only saving schemes).

A decolonised economics would place areas of the world colonised by European powers at the centre of discussions, analysis and research. This is a decolonised approach because students in these countries would be learning about their own country, not just Europe or the US. Students in Europe and the US should also engage with subject knowledge from the perspectives of colonised peoples and countries, and how this links to their countries' economic histories and development.

This will make students and teachers more aware of the power imbalances that continue to foster inequality that is experienced between people of colour and White people, as well as the inequality that exists between different countries (and between men and women, and other different identities). When we learn about these inequalities, we are able to start thinking from a young age about how to deal with them constructively, and most importantly, how not to reproduce them.

Currently we know there's a heavy focus on quantitative methods in economics and we recognise that it is important for students to have strong quantitative skills. However, to allow students the freedom to be able to ask broader research questions, they also need to be taught and to practise qualitative methods, such as the interview training economics students took to conduct peer-to-peer research for this book – training that is often sorely lacking in economics curricula.

We would highly recommend, if at all possible, not using a single textbook at undergraduate level. Teachers send a strong message to our students when they do not set students coursework from just a single source of knowledge. Students are likely to have become so used to a single textbook (at least at undergraduate level) so teachers should be explicit when explaining to them the decision to draw on multiple sources of economic knowledge, which might in turn start important discussions about knowledge production and dissemination.

This also gives teachers the freedom to draw on various sources that students might not have thought could be legitimate forms of economic knowledge. As an example, we would point to a Twitter thread[18] by Ingrid H. Kvangraven, who we cited in Chapter 5. In this thread she collates insightful pieces of work critiquing Randomised Control Trials, which she then follows up with her own insights on the topic. This provides a succinct and engaging way for students to further explore a relevant and highly topical debate that they would almost certainly never have been exposed to in the pages of a textbook.

We would also encourage students to interrogate the idea that economic knowledge only exists if it has been codified in written form, and to consider, the value of verbal and visual communication, as important sources of economic knowledge. This might take the more conventional form of assigning videos as part of the curriculum. But might teachers also encourage students to think of the discussions they have with their family and friends, about their own lived economic experiences and views, as a means to understand that the knowledge is not confined to bullet points on a reading list? We encourage students to see their understanding of the economy come alive, outside of the confines of the classroom.

Additionally, economics students should do a compulsory semester of 'community service' or 'compulsory internships' as part of the curriculum, the same way that medical students have placements in community health services. Students should have an opportunity to intern as economists in an accredited institution that functions to the benefit of society. This could be within civil society, state or business organisations. The purpose of this would be to both ensure that students leave university with work experience and have developed the motivations and skills which will underpin any democratised public-interest economics.

To develop an education that is sensitive to issues of justice, freedom, democracy and self-determination, universities would be well advised to establish a compulsory ethics class, like those offered in both law and medicine. An ethics class is necessary because economists are practitioners in economies that are full of ethical dilemmas, in the everyday functioning of individuals, firms and the state.

How do we teach?

In our classrooms are we implicitly adhering to the notion of the 'superiority of economists', where we as lecturers present ourselves as founts of knowledge, and assume that this knowledge will simply diffuse through to our students? Or do we see our students (who by most formal standards would not yet be considered economists) as equal partners? Are they partners, who we recognise as being able to teach us and their fellow peers concepts based on their lived experiences – or indeed from their own independent research?

As economists are we open to the idea of different knowledges? It is possible to have our students become active co-creators in their journey of learning by leaving space in the curriculum for them to choose a topic they are interested in and exploring it further from the perspective of their economic realities?

It is far too easy to forget that students play an integral role in the diversifying, decolonising and democratising process. It would be doing them a disservice to not value students as essential partners in this movement.

Our recommendations relate here as to how to approach teaching various schools of thought or a topic relating to a specific country context. This can often be intimidating and time consuming, and students may feel that this plurality of perspectives is confusing. Using schools of thought as an example (see Table 2.1, p. 62), we would recommend providing just one different school of thought to the mainstream perspective, per theme or topic. So as an educator you may decide to structure your curriculum as follows.

When covering unemployment, you may want to teach the mainstream understanding of this topic and then contrast it with the Marxist concept of the reserve army of labour. When approaching economic growth theory, you can introduce students to the mainstream literature on this and then juxtapose it with Feminist Growth Theory. Finally, you might teach Real Business Cycle Theory and then compare this to the Austrian Business Cycle. The key here is to be explicit in showing your students that there are competing and alternative ways of knowing and that they are then able to make up their own minds, by ensuring that you are encouraging critical thinking. This will enable students to decide when they might want to draw on different schools of thought to answer a specific question.

Including real-world examples and engaging with the lived experience of economic deprivation is important. Not only will this help to educate students about the complex socioeconomic barriers people outside their own social networks have faced in life, but it will help students who have faced such barriers to see that economics does reflect their realities and that they too can become economists.

Disaggregated and intersectional data should be used when teaching and learning about identity-based economic inequalities. This will strengthen students' data analysis and transferable skills and provide them with a more complex understanding of how to approach such topics.

It is also important to explore ways of including reflections about White Privilege[19] in the classroom, and to promote deep learning about racialised relations and the damaging subtleties of racism through reflections about our personal experiences in a learning environment.

Similarly, our interviews showed that students of economics who identified as women experience the dominance of men in group discussions, while some perceived that their ideas garnered greater criticism than the men in their cohort. These experiences must be surfaced, discussed and addressed.

How do we assess?

Research presented in *The Econocracy*[20] shows the ubiquity of multiple-choice questions in economics education. How can we ensure that students are given more opportunities to write essays to develop their critical thinking skills and to build the confidence to share their opinions?

Beyond even that, what options are there for students who may not test well in the written form? While we certainly think that it is important to develop clear and coherent writing skills, is it not equally important that we encourage students to develop their verbal skills too? This is especially important when we think about how crucial it is for economists to be able to communicate complex economic concepts in a compelling yet accurate way to the general public.

In terms of assessment methods, we would encourage economics curricula to diversify, decolonise and democratise by thinking about the importance of 'devaluing hierarchies'.[21] Teachers would do well to recognise that students are likely to be interested in topics far beyond the scope of what can be taught in a single course, or for that matter in a single undergraduate degree.

Teachers could try using book reviews and blogs as a way to promote reflective learning, and challenge the common perception students have, that their lecturer is the fount of all economic knowledge. Students should be encouraged to find any non-fictional piece of work that they are interested in learning more about. Teachers should be explicit in explaining to students that this is an active exercise in devaluing hierarchies that often place textbooks or lecturers at the pinnacle of knowledge dissemination. Students should then be asked to create a blog/podcast, where they post weekly reviews (either in written or verbal form) on the chapter they read that week and try to find links to the work being done in class. Reviews should be encouraged to be short (to practise the ability to synthesise), to be critical of what they have read that week (to practise deconstructing), and reflective on what they would have done differently if they were writing the chapter (to practise constructing).

Some of the contributors to this book have tried this with their students and received really positive feedback. Students report feeling empowered to seek knowledge on topics they may have been interested in, but didn't think were possible to link with their perceptions of what counted as 'real economics'. They discussed how valuable it is to be encouraged to have their own opinion on the work of scholars they would previously have seen as impossible to critique. They also explained the importance of using reflection over an extended period of time to construct and create their own ideas about a topic, instead of only memorising work from a textbook.

Who does the teaching?

This relates to the importance of diversifying and decolonising not just the curriculum, but the university in which that curriculum is embedded. When we are in positions to do so, how can we ensure that women, minoritised ethnicities, people who have been economically marginalised and scholars from outside of Europe and North America, are given opportunities within academia? How do we ensure that those positions are not exploitative nor tokenistic and offer a real chance at success? Related to this, are we willing to acknowledge our own privileges and our own biases, so that we can question how this might reflect in our teaching?

So, too, we might ask ourselves who we invite as guest lecturers into our classrooms? Are we giving opportunities as an example to Black, Brown or Indigenous People of colour, women economists and economists from low-income backgrounds to share their knowledge with us and students? Linked to this, we might ask questions about who we see as a 'qualified' guest speaker in our classrooms. Do we strive to invite people into this space who must have at least completed a PhD at an elite university in Europe or the US? Again, this type of knowledge and expertise would certainly play an important role in shaping our curricula. But would it not also be important for us to invite an informal trader into the classroom if we are discussing the informal economy?

We would encourage economists to leave space for students to co-create their curricula. Part of diversifying, decolonising, and democratising economics is to see our students as true partners in the learning process. At the beginning of the semester, explain to students that there will be a week or two or three (as much as you think is feasible in your curriculum) close to the end of the semester, in which they get to choose whichever topic they are interested in learning more about. Of course, you can limit them to making sure that it broadly relates to microeconomics, macroeconomics, development economics, ecological economics, etc.

One can then set a group project, with submission dates throughout the semester, where students are responsible for collecting, synthesising and using their lived experiences to contextualise the content. In those open weeks of class, students are encouraged to present their work on the topic to the rest of their peers, giving students an opportunity to show that their lived experiences are an intrinsic part of this course. The resources and presentations can then be uploaded for all the students to access. As a lecturer you can draw from what the students have gathered and presented, to create a lecture that pushes you to investigate new topics and ideas.

Also, as you lecture throughout the semester, you can invite students to share, with you and their fellow classmates, resources beyond those you have provided to them. This allows students the opportunity to co-create throughout the entire semester and to engage in opportunities to shape their curriculum.

How does research influence our teaching?

What we research will invariably influence our teaching and how we design economics curricula. When we are conducting our own research, do we push ourselves to read outside the established canon? With the 'publish or perish' culture of economics so stark, are we willing to devote time and energy to diversify, decolonise and democratise our curricula, when it is likely to take time away from our research?

When reading these recommendations, many academics will invariably feel that there simply isn't the time for any of this, given the already long working hours and the need to publish research in order to get hired and promoted. We would certainly acknowledge that this is a major challenge in starting the process of transforming economics education.

In response, we think it is important to emphasise again that starting to develop the three Ds is a process. One that is rich and layered and constantly evolving. One that has numerous starting points. But start we must. Take some time to reflect and decide step-by-step what is feasible to begin with given the time constraints you face.

We would recommend that economists see this as a unique opportunity to incorporate the three Ds into their own research. This should be approached with humility and a genuine willingness to learn and engage by checking your position of power and privilege. This is likely to open you up to new ideas, areas of research you may not have been familiar with, a wider array of tools to apply in your own research and new networks of people to collaborate with.

We would encourage everyone to remember that there is a whole community of people who are enthusiastic about seeing change in economics specifically and society more broadly. It might be useful to reach out to academic networks and to broaden the pool of people we ask for help. Getting in touch with networks like D-Econ, Rethinking Economics, The Black Economists Network or The Sadie Collective might be a useful starting point. So, too, reaching out to other academics even just via email, especially those outside Europe and the US, and asking them to share their teaching practices and reading lists might be really helpful in starting to gather resources beyond those you might be using right now.

Asking for help, swapping ideas, sharing resources and experiences are all likely to make you feel that you are not in this alone, and will save you time in not having to do everything yourself. We would urge that a key part of the three Ds is to approach this work with the help and support of a broader community.

What challenges do we face, and what opportunities exist?

These challenges will undoubtedly be different in different countries and likely quite dependent on the specific courses and the particular department we teach in. A '3D' curriculum will not come in neatly packaged textbooks with convenient supplementary materials all laid out. In most instances we will have to teach ourselves the content that, in just a few weeks' time, we will be teaching to our students.

While it may seem that there can be a lot of challenges to take in as one starts the process of transforming economics education, it might be helpful to actively ask ourselves what are the opportunities that this presents? As we engage more deeply with students, what opportunities do their contributions provide us with?

Does this transformation allow us to rethink unjust practices and dismantle powerful hierarchies in and outside of the classroom that can lead to a fairer and more equitable society? Who are the researchers, teachers, activists, and artists who we can reach out to as we embark on this journey?

Ultimately, we hope that you are excited by this process. This is an opportunity for change, for innovation, for discovery, for a diversity of people, ideas, and an interdisciplinary approach in economics. There are enormous challenges. But therein also lies the opportunity, to have more of the lived experiences of a more diverse group of people, reflected back at us in a way that encourages us to build and to construct anew.

Chapter 7

Everyday democracy

With contributions from Kamal Ramburuth-Hurt

In this chapter, we argue that it is necessary to reclaim economics as everyday democracy and we set out steps to achieve this goal. The aim is to build the democratic institutions, skills and practices that are necessary to enable everyone to participate in decisions about how the economy they live in is organised.

This must be accompanied by decentralisation and redistribution of economic power and resources to ensure nobody is excluded from participating because they are struggling to survive, and to prevent some from buying political power and unduly influencing economic rules and institutions.

A greater ability to come together at different levels and collectively decide how to organise our economies will increase our sense of agency and connectedness, both of which are foundations of good health and wellbeing. In this sense, it should be seen as a goal in its own right.

Importantly, this work will also lead to better economic outcomes. This is because these outcomes will be more closely linked to what actually matters to people. Increasing democracy in economic decision-making also provides an answer to the challenge posed by the economist Friedrich Hayek, which we highlighted in Chapter 5, of how decentralised knowledge and priorities can be combined to inform economic activity and planning.

The power to shape the economy

One of the first barriers which prevents more people playing an active role in shaping how economies are organised is a deep sense of inevitability and powerlessness. In this section, we explore how implicit understandings of what the economy is, and how it works, contribute to this feeling of powerlessness.

Mental models of the economy

There is a small but growing body of research about how non-economists think about the economy.[1] As might be expected, there is no 'one size fits all' model and most research has found that people tend to view the economy in many different and sometimes contradictory ways, both as a personal economy and as a regional, national or international economy. People's views about the economy may be strongly held but they can also be internally contradictory as well as fleeting and unstable.

Researchers have explored people's mental models of the economy. A mental model is a representation of the surrounding world, the relationships between its various parts and a person's intuitive perception about his or her own acts and their consequences.

One of the main findings is that these models often centre on money, understood through the metaphor of circulation around a space. Here the economy is another way of talking about money such as how much things cost.[2]

One implication of this understanding is that people, geographical areas, or activities where there isn't any or much money being held or exchanged are viewed as not part of the economy. In interviews in the UK, some people expressed the idea that the economy was physically located in London because that is where it is perceived money is circulating.[3]

243

Another common metaphor is the idea of the economy as functioning like a national pot with people putting into the pot (contributing) and taking out of it (draining). Here the economy is a fixed amount of resources, often thought about as money, and the government has a fixed budget, often thought about in the same way as a household budget. According to this view, the economy is a constraint on what we are able to do as individuals and a society, so attention is focused on balancing budgets and reducing debt.

The pot model can lead older people to feel 'out of the economy' and younger people to feel like they are 'not yet in the economy' if they have not started to work. This image underpins political narratives in some countries that seek to differentiate between people who are productive and contribute to the economy and people who don't and drain from it. People also use the model of a container to talk about the balance between imports and exports, and about national self-reliance.[4]

When interviewees explained economic phenomena, many tended to focus on observable individual motivations and actions, looking for people responsible for a particular state of affairs. Structural or systemic explanations where particular outcomes arise from the interplay of lots of different factors, sometimes without any obvious cause, were less common.

People's mental models of the economy were shaped in complex ways by their economic experience – childhood, education, health, work and security – which in turn is shaped by their racialised identity, gender and socioeconomic status. Anna Killick suggests that people in the UK with higher incomes understand 'the economy' as a neutral term for largely impersonal forces, while people on lower incomes understand it to be rigged by elites.[5]

Disconnection from economics

There have been two approaches to research looking at how non-economists understand and relate to economics.

The first, what we might call the top-down approach, explores how people understand economics as defined by economists in the way we've outlined in this book.[6] This research finds that non-economists (that is, the vast majority of people) have very little understanding of economic knowledge and concepts, and people fail to employ rational economic reasoning. The basic assumption is that public misunderstanding is the outcome of biases, fallacies or ignorance and lack of education.

One of the strongest findings in this research is that knowledge of mainstream academic economics varies by demographics such as age, ethnicity, gender, socioeconomic class and education. Women, younger, less educated and lower income people are shown to have less economic knowledge. This top-down approach has been criticised as offering a restricted and distorted window into the economic understanding, views and experiences of non-economists.[7]

Top-down studies tend to ask questions about core economic concepts such as inflation, GDP and quantitative easing, but much less about questions such as social security, payday loans, the cost of essential goods and services or minimum wages, which are much more immediate economic issues for many people. Maybe these implicit judgements about which areas of the economy are important are shared by White, male, high-income and highly educated survey respondents who then appear more knowledgeable and confident.[8]

In contrast, a bottom-up approach attempts to design research which, as far as possible, doesn't take the mainstream academic economic view of the world as the starting point, instead asking open-ended questions that explore how people articulate their economic views and understanding in their own words.[9]

This approach recognises that we all have an in-depth understanding of many aspects of economics that relate to the lived experiences we gain through the different economic roles we play. It finds that often economic terms and concepts like 'consumption', 'unemployment' and 'economic crisis' take on everyday meanings which are different from how they are used in mainstream academic economics. In this way multiple parallel understandings of the economy often exist in a society at any one time.[10]

All this research has highlighted several areas where most people think about the economy differently to neoclassical economists. The pot of money and fixed pie mental models highlighted earlier are often combined with a sense that if one person or country gains, there must be a loser (reflecting a belief that the economy is a zero-sum game).

Non-economists tend to focus much more on distribution, fairness, power and struggle, which as we have seen in Chapter 3 is often made invisible in the theoretical world of voluntary exchange and mutual benefit presented by the neoclassical framework.

These mental models underpin a wide range of political views, from a condemnation of powerful businesses exploiting workers and suppliers, to a resentment of groups such as migrants or unemployed people, who are perceived to be draining resources from 'the economy'.

In all of this, non-economists tend to evaluate and view economics drawing on psychological, social and moral reasoning, whereas neoclassical economists tend to focus more on efficiency considerations when making economic judgements.

When you broaden academic economics to include different perspectives beyond the mainstream neoclassical framework, you see that some of the views of non-economists, on say power and struggle in the economy, are closely aligned with some of these alternative perspectives.

This is important because it validates the lived experience of people who experience power and struggle in the economy, and other perspectives that are able to describe aspects of people's economic realities which neoclassical economics can't.

Reframing the economy

While more research is needed, particularly bottom-up approaches in a wider range of countries, it is clear that over time, certain mental models of the economy and ideas about what economics is, and who it is for, have become deeply rooted in our societies.

Overall, there is a widespread sense that only certain people have the knowledge and power to influence the economy. While the relationship between mental models and people's experience is complex, the sense of powerlessness and inevitability many people feel about the economy can be better understood in the context of our economic history. Ever since our modern idea of 'the economy' took shape in the 1920s and 1930s, the dominant mode of organising our economies has been through top-down and technocratic decision-making and this is profoundly disempowering for those who are excluded.[11]

For more people to have a role in reorganising economies from the ground up and to effectively build democratic institutions for collective economic decision-making, we must reframe how we all think about the economy. Here we sketch out some key points of this reframing.

Economies are complex systems organising the production, distribution and consumption of resources such as money, jobs, housing and food in a geographical area. They are about much more than money. For example, without the vast amounts of unpaid care work, mainly done by women in all societies, economies would very quickly break down. Economies are also not standalone; they are embedded in and dependent on the natural world, drawing resources from it for economic production, and releasing waste back into it. Economist Kate Raworth uses the metaphor of a doughnut to highlight how our use of ecological resources must not overshoot our planetary boundaries.[12]

National economies are not a singular entity but multiple distinct economies which operate in different ways. Local, regional and national economies overlap and intersect with each other and are shaped by particular geographies, cultures and histories which inform how they are organised.

Different sectors of the economy also operate in fundamentally different ways. For example, the production of some goods and services can be outsourced to wherever production costs are the cheapest in the world and then transported to their market. Others, such as house building, or food retailing, utility supply (gas, water, electricity, broadband and phone networks), health and education, must take place in the area that is being supplied. As a result of this difference these sectors will operate in different ways and have different potential to be reorganised democratically.[13]

For all of these reasons, it is important to reject a rigid, top-down monolithic view of the economy as a single entity (machine, organism, system) that has universal rules, levers, logic, behaviours and design principles.

Instead, we recognise a pluralist approach to economics and a diversity about how economies operate across households, communities, businesses, sectors, regions, countries and different social groups. This view creates space for the diversity of lived experience people have of the economy.

It requires us to develop specific analysis of how different economies operate, which we cannot easily understand through a top-down lens. It also underscores the value of incorporating lived experience and people's expressed needs and priorities into research and policy.

Finally, we assert that economies can and should be organised through collective, democratic processes and decision-making. The organisation of economies affects all of us, we are all active participants, and we all have a responsibility of stewardship for our children and future generations.

In doing this we explicitly recognise that economic reasoning is never separable from moral, political, social, and ecological considerations. Many societies and communities place a higher value on consumption of goods and services which are essential to survive and/or groups such as children, which have particular needs. All of this highlights how the foundations of economies might be thought about and organised differently if we reintegrate broader reasoning and considerations through greater democratic participation.

Believing a different economics is possible

The other side of reframing the economy is thinking differently about agency – the capacity of individuals to act independently and to make their own free choices. Feeling a sense, or at least the possibility of agency, in the economy, is a necessary precondition for people to take part in efforts to re-shape it from the ground up.

To make visible how people can have agency in the economy, it is important to combine individual-level analysis, which explores how identity shapes one's economic outcomes and our ability to 'do economics', with a structural analysis of how cultures, institutions, norms and beliefs reproduce or challenge systemic inequalities.

Identity and economic structures are important, but too often they are seen as opposing and viewed separately. It is, after all, vital to remember that the personal is political and the political is personal.

The recognition of the effects of multiple intersecting identities, and how these foster states of privilege – or lack of privilege – within systems which reproduce structural inequality, is vital in recognising how individuals experience the economy based on their personal identities.

Popular economic and political narratives often encourage us to think of ourselves and others as making choices and taking actions that determine our path in life. Success or failure is perceived to be of our own making.

This is a story that particularly suits those who are privileged, that their position in the world, that their success is caused by their own hard work. More than that, it is crucial to the idea of fairness and justice that underpins our societies and economies.

What the focus on the individual misses is that we are all part of economies and they significantly shape our life chances. While we are part of systems and are influenced by them, in turn we can also shape them through community organising, speaking up, campaigning, pooling economic resources, identifying and developing economic assets, etc.

Our position in the economy influences what resources we have access to, our standing in society, our caring responsibilities, and our relationships with others.

Combining individual and structural analysis in this way allows us to recognise that we live in a world of hugely imbalanced power and an economic system which has been constructed under these conditions. This system produces structural oppression and exploitation, and we must see this outcome is a result of a particular historical trajectory and not inevitable or natural.

For example, housing and urban development outcomes might be influenced by government rules, regulations and planning decisions, private developers or local communities. The agency of different actors to influence the course of urban development is shaped by the distribution of economic resources and power in a mutually constitutive process. The question to ask is not whether it is possible to reorganise the economy, but who has the power to do it and whether that power is being wielded according to democratic and public or narrow sectional interests?

It is absolutely possible to construct a system in which economic power is distributed equally. It is absolutely possible to change the relationship that communities furthest from economic power have with their economy so that they can build the power and resources needed to reorganise it from the ground up. This is a foundational belief it is necessary to hold before even considering how one might build the power to shape how the economy is organised.

Rethinking the economy and its relationship to the individual is about developing new framing, narratives and language as well as consciously engaging with economics. It is only through seeing people democratically decide how to organise the economy, with our own eyes, that we can begin to believe it is possible. This is the task of reclaiming economics as everyday democracy and we now turn to how it can be achieved.

Reorganising the economy from the ground up

In this section we explore how more people might build the power, resources and practices needed to be able to reorganise the economies they live in from the ground up.

Our starting point is that people without significant economic resources or power need to organise collectively to influence more effectively how broader economies are organised.

Groups that might come together to attempt to reorganise their economy could include communities of identity and their intersections (women, racialised or religious groups, people with disabilities, or LGBTQI people for example), geographical communities (residents of a social/public housing estate, informal settlement or rural area) or communities of interest (social care workers, other employee groups, market traders or small business owners).

This is a challenge because resources, skills and leadership are required to bring together groups to operate collectively. In many places globally, there is a long history of organisations like trade unions, which have attempted to collectively organise workers, being undermined and suppressed by government and businesses.

More generally, people are often encouraged to enter the economy as an individual rather than as a group with a shared set of interests, which results in less of a culture of collective identity and action.

In places where there are significant everyday struggles to survive, resources such as money and time, which help people mobilise, are scarcer, and the sense of powerlessness is often stronger. On the other hand, the urgent need to reorganise the economy is often that much clearer.[14]

Here we believe an organising approach can be valuable as part of the process of groups forming and then working together to reorganise the economy. A group might work together to:

1. identify and agree their economic needs and priorities;
2. analyse their position within the broader economy including strengths, weaknesses, opportunities and threats;
3. identify what resources they might be able to access;
4. develop and run a campaign for change or a programme of economic activity;
5. build alliances across civil society.

Activities that might aid this process include:

4. organising community conversation about needs and priorities in the context of how broader economies are organised;
5. creative and artistic approaches to developing imaginative new ideas, language and narratives for economics that are rooted in everyday life and which open up alternative futures;
6. community-led education and training to build a shared analysis of their economy, learn from other communities working on similar issues, and develop collective capabilities and leadership.

These activities can help facilitate the journey of a community developing a shared understanding, vision and programme of activity.

Across the world, communities are actively engaged in social and political struggles and often much of the mobilising and organising work outlined above is already happening. While each struggle is unique, some common themes include identity-based exclusion and discrimination, oppression of workers, ecological degradation and exploitation, and widening access to the basic essentials necessary to survive. Another recent example of communities organising, are the Covid mutual aid groups that have come together across the world to help communities support each other through the pandemic.[15]

A root cause of the grievances which spark many of these struggles lies in how broader economies are organised, how resources are distributed, what and who is valued and who is able to influence the rules of the economy. This provides an opportunity for communities to connect their struggle to broader struggles about how the economy is organised. This might form a set of demands to government or business in the area, or a programme of economic activity led by and for the community.

One of the challenges will be identifying points of intervention where economies can be reorganised from the ground up. One initial focus might be on renewing or developing the parts of the economy that are most essential to meeting human needs, which in turn are the foundation of health, wellbeing and security. This might include food production and retail, childcare, housing, healthcare, adult care, primary and secondary education, high street banking, housing and utilities.

The objectives of reorganising these parts of the economy will vary across countries, regions and communities. For many, the task is to secure universal, reliable and affordable access to these goods and services. In other places, it will be about ensuring that the people working in these sectors are valued through their pay and terms and conditions of work, investing in outdated and decaying infrastructure, or finding new ways of organising services to improve quality. Many of these activities, such as food production, distribution and consumption, need to be reorganised to reduce their planetary burden in terms of carbon emissions, resource use, and impact on biodiversity.[16]

This everyday focus provides a gateway for more people to begin engaging with how broader economies are organised. Through doing so, people will inevitably become more aware of how broader systemic economic issues influence their lives.

Across the world there are many examples of different groups and communities effectively mobilising to shape the economy around them, whether that is directly through specific economic activity or indirectly through influencing governments and business. While none of this can be simply transplanted wholesale to another place, it can and should provide inspiration and learning that can be drawn on by others addressing similar challenges.

This networking between different communities trying to reorganise economies from the ground up is essential to turning isolated efforts into systemic change.

The process of developing and spreading a ground-up democratic approach to organising economies is ultimately a task of practical doing not writing. It is a difficult and gradual process of decentralising and distributing economic power and resources, through communities taking action.

Civil society groups – NGOs and charities, voluntary and community organisations, trade unions, campaign groups, artistic and cultural organisations – have an important role to play in supporting communities to reorganise their economies from the ground up.

In many countries civil society organisations will play a role in their local economies, even if they don't think of themselves as economic actors. They employ people, purchase goods and services and provide important community assets and services. They might also have finance, funding and business planning capabilities.

Some of these organisations will be able to support the communities in which they operate. They can do this by reorganising their own activities or supporting community-led economic development through providing access to resources and expertise.

It is crucial that this is support offered without strings attached or attempts to control agendas. Currently, too many civil society organisations like charities and NGOs think of their role as simply

255

providing services to 'clients' or 'service users' from 'low-income' or 'hard to reach' communities. But this top-down approach towards people who are deemed to be in need undermines the possibility of communities reorganising economies from the ground up. Engagement by civil society organisations with grassroots communities should be very clear about building capacity and providing a supportive infrastructure.

This goes with a reframing of 'low-income' or 'hard to reach' communities as 'historically excluded', which recognises how power and oppression has affected their place in our societies and economies. It recognises that these communities have always exhibited enormous amounts of creativity and commitment to survive and that these strengths can be the basis for them to build economic power.

Generating different knowledge and new narratives

We suggest that reorganising the economy from the ground up will generate different economic knowledge and new narratives, which will change how we think and act as societies.[17]

Knowledge can be divided into categories. There is *practical knowledge* that comes through doing.[18] This kind of knowledge is implicit, not codified, and is rooted in and adapted to the specifics of the environment it takes place in. Farming, cooking, riding a bike, driving vehicles, diplomacy and politics all require this kind of *practical knowledge* and can't be learned through theory alone or following a set of instructions. Practical usefulness is the test of this type of knowledge.

In contrast, *technical knowledge* is precise, codifiable and universal. It can be broken down into small, explicit and logical steps that can be verified and taught theoretically. It is often represented by closed forms of reasoning like mathematics – or in neoclassical economics – where the findings may be logically derived from the initial assumptions. The test of this kind of knowledge lies in its capacity for explanation and verification.[19]

Our lives and circumstances are transient, shifting, disconcerting and ambiguous and as a result they do not lend themselves to the precise measurement, exact calculation and rigorous logic of *technical knowledge*. Many practical choices cannot even in principle be adequately and completely captured in a system of universal rules.

Across the world, throughout the twentieth century, governments have attempted to reorganise societies and economies based on *technical knowledge*.

In these initiatives local, *practical knowledge* is often ignored and seen as threatening because it is dispersed and autonomous and can't be systematised or controlled from the centre. Governments rely on *technical knowledge* gained from censuses, surveys and maps to give them the information they need to have administrative control, for example, to be able to collect taxes effectively.

A similar tendency can be seen in large capitalist businesses. Where neoclassical economics simply focuses on efficiency, others have argued that control is needed in order to allow firms to realise profits, as illustrated by the following example.[20]

Before the development of factories in nineteenth-century Britain, textile production took place in people's homes and workers could dictate the pace of the work, control the usage of raw materials used and employ various strategies to increase their returns.

From the point of view of the owner, the major advantage of factories was that it made it possible to control the intensity of work and hours and control the raw materials. From that point on, and increasingly as mass production developed, there have been ongoing attempts to make factories into archetypal sites of central-ised *technical knowledge* where only the factory manager had the knowledge of the whole process and workers were reduced to the execution of small, repetitive tasks.

Even in this space, researchers have argued that practical knowl-edge plays an important role in keeping production going, and workers, even when deemed unskilled, fix and adjust processes according to accumulated tacit *practical knowledge* that couldn't be codified in a manual.[21]

A concerted shift by more communities to reorganise their econ-omies from the ground up will inevitably require dispersing existing *practical knowledge* and creating more, in ways which will erode the deeply hierarchical nature of economic knowledge. In this way, eco-nomics will change, becoming as much about the *practical knowl-edge* of how to navigate and reorganise economies, as it is about the *technical knowledge* of economic theory, although at its best, the two will inform each other.

We must create economies that primarily work for us and the living world. This shift highlights the role of experts by experience in different sectors and regions of the economy, or by virtue of their identity and background.

It reorients academic economics in ways we argued for in the last chapter, emphasising the importance of developing participatory, peer and community-led action research methods including surveys asking what matters to communities, workshops, and citizens' panels.

This work will resurface how much historical, contextual and local knowledge economics has excluded, and continues to exclude, in order to narrow the field of inquiry enough to achieve the logical consistency of *technical knowledge*.

As we have argued in this book, the claimed objectivity, pre-cision and universality of neoclassical economic knowledge is illusory and when we recognise this we are forced to value more highly the everyday, *practical knowledge* that communities use to understand, navigate and survive in their economy.

We realise we have less knowledge than we thought because our neoclassical economic *technical knowledge* is not what it claims to be. But we also have access to a huge source of *practical knowledge* about the economy distributed in people across society, that we have long ignored and devalued.

This then leads to different methods of economic development and policymaking. We recognise that we will often start by not knowing what to do when attempting to reorganise specific economies as the context will always be unique.

Therefore, economic development and policymaking should be explicitly experimental and about finding out what works through collective discussion about needs, priorities and choices. Building democratic dialogue and decision-making into the process is a mechanism to surface practical knowledge about how economies are functioning.

All of this is about finding ways to integrate local, distributed practical and technical knowledge in ways which help us solve problems, which themselves have been identified collectively and publicly rather than by experts or elites.

Everyday democracy and collective decision-making

The work of reorganising economies from the ground up rests, we have argued, on collective dialogue, decision-making and action. This clearly then provides a way to think differently about democracy, going beyond the dominant idea of representative democracy – consisting of professional political parties and periodic voting – to more everyday, participatory and deliberative forms.

This could have broader benefits. There is deep dissatisfaction about democracy, particularly among young people in the UK and US. Across the world, there is a rise in popular authoritarian leaders, who are not committed to democracy as a political system, and in many places including China and the Gulf states, democracy does not exist in any meaningful way.

Efforts to reorganise economies from the ground up are about rebalancing power in the economy through extending democracy as a counterweight to the great concentrations of wealth and power that continue to exert influence on our economic, social, cultural, and political lives.

It also challenges a trend where large areas of economic decision-making from monetary policy to corporate governance, trade policy and the credit rating of countries are being taken out of the political sphere of elected government and run by 'independent' technocratic, quasi-governmental or private sector organisations. By challenging these trends, we can contribute to the development of democratic skills and culture across society, and rebuild trust and legitimacy in the promise of democracy as self-rule by the people.

A related development in many societies is a sense of increasing polarisation and fragmentation between different groups. The kind of everyday democracy involved in communities reorganising economies from the ground up is built on dialogue about needs, priorities, problems, goals and trade-offs.

The focus on local, practical knowledge emphasises the need to highlight people's lived experiences of powerlessness and inequity, and incorporate them into a shared conversation about community, moral values and collective action that cuts across lines of racialised, gendered and socioeconomic background. Surfacing grievances and oppression in order to work through and effectively address them is the only way to build a sustainable social cohesion and solidarity that is the bedrock of peace and security.

Finally, the everyday democracy practised through communities coming together to reorganise their economies is an essential part of societies achieving the rapid transition to operating within planetary boundaries in a legitimate and equitable way. The changes required to reduce carbon emissions, resource use, biodiversity loss and waste are systemic and individual, technical and behavioural. It will require communities to develop different patterns of living and working as well as reimagining their relationships with each other and the living world.

In summary, everyday democracy in the economy is necessary to rebuild the trust and legitimacy of democracy as a political system, rebalance power and resources to effectively meet everyone's basic needs and address historical oppression, transition to operate within planetary boundaries in a way that is just, and improve our economic knowledge. In the next section, we go on to explore how we might build and reshape democratic institutions to support participatory economies.

Building participatory economies

We believe that a bottom-up approach to reorganising economies must be combined with top-down efforts by local and national government and economic institutions. Their goal should be to build the democratic institutions and practices that allow everyday collective decision-making about how to organise economies.

In this section we explore how this might be achieved in local and national government, the media, corporate governance, new economy movements, international economic institutions and international NGOs in turn.

Government

The two main approaches to economic policy in the twentieth century have been state-led planning and nationalised industry on one hand, and the construction of markets, privatised industry and outsourced public services on the other.

Both have required a strong central state to either directly plan parts of the economy or to construct and regulate markets and manage outsourced services. Centrally created strategies and command, either directly or through policy, funding and regulation, have been the hallmark of government economic management.

The first step is for governments to recognise that they need to take on the role of enabler in the economy. The role of government as an enabler is to listen to and respond to the expressed economic needs and priorities of its citizens; develop goals and measures of economic performance that reflect democratically agreed priorities; connect businesses, communities and civil society institutions working on sector- and place-based economic development; resource and coordinate activity and facilitate learning and the transfer of successful approaches.

This is a relational approach that requires governments to let go of control. However, it is vital that this approach recognises how deeply unequal the distribution of economic resources and power are in most societies and how these inequalities often operate along racialised, gendered and social class-based lines.

The role of government power here is to create spaces where different groups are meaningfully able to contribute to collective discussion, decision-making and action around how local, regional and national economies are organised.

That involves explicitly recognising the historical oppression and structural inequities faced by certain groups in society and committing to reorganise economies so that these groups have the economic security and power to meaningfully contribute to these collective processes. This imperative provides a strong rationale for governments to consider structural economic policies and interventions such as reparations and the redistribution of land and capital.

In doing this, governments would recognise that the health of democracy and economies are deeply interconnected. Economies that reproduce deep inequalities of wealth and power increase the ability of wealthy and powerful actors to reshape systems to benefit their interests. This destabilises democracy by undermining social cohesion, trust and legitimacy. The existence of inclusive and healthy democracy relies on economies that widely distribute power, opportunity and wealth.

Governments can then use participatory and deliberative methods and processes to set the goals of economic policy and planning. A citizens' assembly is a group of people who are brought together to discuss one or more issues and reach conclusions about what they think should happen. The people who take part are chosen so they reflect the wider population – in terms of demographics (e.g. age, gender, ethnicity, social class) and sometimes relevant attitudes (e.g. preferences for a small or large state). They typically comprise 50–160 people.

Citizens' juries (typically 12–25 participants) are another similar but smaller (and therefore cheaper) approach, which may be more manageable for some local governance systems. Citizens' juries have varied widely in their design and implementation but typically follow a uniform procedure. Members of the general public (the 'jurors') participate in a process of dialogue under the guidance of a chair or 'facilitator' and are selected to reflect the community and act as independent citizens rather than experts or representatives. They interrogate expert commentators (sometimes called witnesses) chosen because of their knowledge of a particular subject. Unlike legal juries, it is an issue, rather than an individual, that is 'on trial'. Jurors then draw up and publish their conclusions through deliberations informed by evidence provided by experts.

Both tools can be combined with participatory budgeting, a democratic process in which community members directly decide how to spend all or part of a public budget.

These approaches can be integrated into the negotiations which central governments have with local governments and around any devolution of power to regional or local bodies. Central banks should run citizen assemblies and other forms of engagement to aid decision-making and communication of their role and policies.

Central government departments, particularly finance and treasury departments, should commission citizen assemblies and juries for major economic decisions and reviews, and commit to implementing their decisions, or at the least, giving clear reasons if they are not able to.

Governments should also fund civil society organisations to provide accessible independent analysis of economic policy, including from outside of the traditional economic sphere, and provide open and online data tools to allow public scrutiny of economic data.[22]

Democratic dialogue should go beyond economic measurements like Gross Domestic Product (GDP). A range of proposals have been made for other headline indicators, that could be used to measure the overall success of economies and societies, based on key outcomes such as health, equality, wellbeing and environmental sustainability.

Corporate governance

Corporations depend on governments to create and uphold the legal frameworks that enable them to operate, as well as to provide educated workers and a functioning infrastructure, and on workers to produce goods and services, and consumers to purchase them, while the decisions they make have knock-on costs and benefits for all of these groups.

Just 100 companies have been responsible for more than 70 per cent of the world's greenhouse gas emissions since 1988.[23] Many of the largest have annual revenues bigger than the GDP of countries. In 2017, Alphabet's (Google's parent company) revenues were bigger than Puerto Rico's GDP, Amazon's revenues bigger than Kuwait's, Apple's revenues bigger than Portugal's, Volkswagen's bigger than Chile's and Walmart's bigger than Belgium's.[24]

The way these corporations are managed affects everybody and the future of human life on earth. But they are controlled by a very small group of owners (shareholders in public limited companies and governments in state-owned companies) and professional managers.

Core democratic principles of accountability, transparency and collective decision-making are absent from the governance arrangements of the world's most powerful companies. Most people in the world have no say in how these companies are run or what investments they make.[25]

For large parts of the twentieth century the professed intent was that corporations should be accountable to a range of stakeholders and interests; that they needed to balance a range of goals such as to promote national strategic interests, create employment, support networks of suppliers and develop new technology, as well as create an adequate return for their shareholders.

In the late 1970s and early 1980s, a new approach gained traction through teaching in US economics departments and business schools before spreading worldwide to become dominant in many places. It argued that the corporation had to pursue one single goal – the maximisation of shareholder value (MSV) – and that managers should be incentivised to respond to (financial) market forces, because this would ensure that scarce resources were being allocated most efficiently.[26]

Reclaiming economics as everyday practice requires exploring with how these corporations can be brought into the democratic space through increased accountability, transparency, and collective decision-making input from different stakeholders including workers, communities, governments, and future generations.

The first challenge is to reframe how we think about these companies, their activities, and the wealth they create. The idea that these are private businesses refers to their legal ownership, but in practice most of their activities are deeply social. They rely on physical infrastructure to transport goods and services, and on an educated workforce provided by governments and funded by taxpayers.

There is a strong public interest in how these companies are managed and, in the same way that society requires people to get a licence to drive or practise medicine, we should make the social licence of corporations to operate dependent on meeting certain democratically agreed conditions.[27]

Corporations often play a central role within communities they operate in, providing employment that brings income, and often a sense of identity. For some groups, this is secure, high-wage, high-status work, though for others it is insecure, dangerous, low wage and low status.

While the conditions imposed would be different for different companies and countries, here are a few areas they might cover. They might be negotiated with individual companies, in sectors of the economy, or at a national level covering all large businesses.

A key issue social licences might address is taxation. Financial engineering, accounting practices and tax havens allow large companies to run rings around national tax systems choosing low tax, low transparency jurisdictions to register profits in, and constructing group accounts to show low profits or losses in places with higher taxation.

They may also address governance, requiring a shift towards engaging a broader range of stakeholders in decision-making, pursuing a wider range of goals, and crucially bringing some invested groups, such as workers, into governance structures.

Other requirements for social licences could include certain ecological and labour standards, commitments to diversity and inclusion, local purchasing, or good treatment of suppliers.[28]

A final area might be around the transparency and communication of reporting. Companies above a certain size are required to have their annual financial accounts audited by an independent third party. These accounts have a written narrative and a set of numbers that report a company's financials including its revenue (what it's earned), costs, profits (revenue minus costs), cash flow (how much cash is coming in and out), assets (what it owns) and liabilities (what it owes).

The rules that govern how these numbers are reported and the ability of different groups to engage critically with them are crucial. For example, one key question is, does the valuation of a company's assets take into account future climate change and ecological damage?

In the last thirty years these audited accounts have swelled from thirty to three hundred pages on average and this makes it much harder to understand or scrutinise them. Social licences for corporations, might require them to publish certain information in their audit accounts in ways that are clearer and more accessible. This would make it easier for workers, communities and governments to understand them, which in turn is a precondition for rebalancing power between large corporations and the rest of society.

Of course, the challenge here is power. We have seen that many of the largest companies are bigger than countries and that will make it harder for many countries to impose meaningful social licences on these companies. Likewise, the international reach of these companies in the globalised economy, means that governments and campaign groups need to act collectively to be able to challenge corporate power.

The opportunity is that many governments and businesses recognise that corporate governance is in urgent need of reform. When looking for different approaches we must be wary of proposed changes which are superficial and presentational.

Here reclaiming economics as everyday practice involves supporting different groups in society to contribute to these ongoing debates to ensure that reform is structural, and genuinely rebalances who has the power to influence how the world's largest companies are managed.

The media

Returning to governments, another role for them is to resource the infrastructure necessary for societies to have an inclusive dialogue about how to organise economies. Here national, local, and social media have significant influence setting the terms of public conversation about economies as well as determining who has a voice.

Media coverage globally is dominated by academic and professional economists, public policy experts and politicians, who, as we have seen in this book, are often highly unrepresentative of broader society. This reinforces the perception economics is a technical and complex subject that is best left to experts.

As a result, media coverage amplifies the voices of certain groups in society and silences others, reproducing the dominance of *technical knowledge* of the economy derived from higher education against *practical knowledge* derived from lived experience.

Globally, media businesses have been struggling to adapt to a world in which advertising revenues have moved into the digital space, and been monopolised by the tech giants, Facebook and Google.[29] This has led to media organisations reducing their economics coverage, and contributed to the decline of local media, meaning they are less able to engage with specific economic realities for different people in different places.

Similarly an increasing focus on national macro indicators like GDP growth and inflation fails to reflect the diversity of people's lived experience of the economy according to region, identity and background.

We need innovation in media coverage of the economy to promote a culture of democratic dialogue that surfaces different perspectives, evaluates evidence and argument, holds economic-decision makers accountable, identifies difference and creates possibilities for compromise.

For this to be inclusive, and effectively capture dispersed practical economic knowledge, it needs to be combined with investment to create local media infrastructures which can engage with the specifics of people and place.

Reformed media landscapes can improve the quality and inclusiveness of society's dialogue providing a better picture of people's needs and priorities as well as the strengths, weakness, opportunities and challenges their economies face.

New economy movements

Across the world there are think tanks, academics, NGOs and campaigns advocating to different extents for 'systems change' to our economies in response to varied challenges and opportunities including the ecological crisis, poverty and inequality, and development. These new economy movements have different motivations, goals, and theories of change.

There is a significant risk that these movements unintentionally reproduce the problems of economics we have explored in this book and by extension reproduce the very systems they are trying to change. First, because academic economics is so undiverse, it is often the case that the people in these organisations who have economic expertise are not representative of the broader societies they live in.

In the UK, looking through the 'meet the team' pages of some of the leading new economy think tanks you can see the overrepresentation of White people and men in economics roles very clearly. Globally, economic expertise in think tanks and civil society organisations is more likely to represent the professional, university educated, economically privileged sections of society.

In the UK, the new economy movement has been criticised from within for failing to address the need to decolonise economics and the organisations within it. An organisation called Decolonising Economics has been set up to address this gap and build a new economy movement rooted in racial justice principles.[30]

These movements also often reproduce the top-down, techno-cratic and expert-led approach to economic research and practice. Theories of change are often premised on convincing governments, businesses, the media and other powerful stakeholders of the need to shift to a new economy because that is where power currently lies.

While many organisations might seek to mobilise public support at times or conduct participatory research with people affected by the issues they are addressing, there isn't enough consistent focus on how to support citizens generally, and marginalised groups particularly, to build economic power over time. The governance and funding of these organisations is often not democratic nor accountable to broader groups in whose names they are trying to build new economies.

All of this undermines the collective ability of new economy movements to develop effective and popular alternatives, build broader social alliances and legitimately advocate for change.

Economic system transitions are unlikely to be possible, effective, fair or legitimate unless a broader and more stable social alliance is built and there is inclusive public participation and deliberation around the goals, design and implementation of the transition.

To reclaim economics as everyday practice these organisations and movements must go through a deep process of reflection and reform and see this as part of the core work rather than a separate and less immediate issue of diversity and inclusion. Questions to be asked include: Where might the colonial mindset impact the way we think about our work? How is the values filter of 'racial justice' embodied in our project? How are we shifting economic control to communities with this work? What is the culture of this work, and who does it speak to? How do we practise self-governance and accountability? Organisations and funders of this work need to consider how they can decentralise power and resources further to the communities who they claim to work for, stepping back and creating space for others.

New economy organisations need to consider the role of democracy in their governance and do more to build strong relationships with existing membership organisations such as trade and tenant unions, faith groups, and sectoral groups representing community organisations and small businesses.

To build new economies in a way that is legitimate requires a mass movement like the independence movements in former colonies, or the civil rights movement in the US. A mass movement working on different aspects of economic systems change might look and feel similar to the breadth of social responses to Covid-19, but would need to be maintained over a longer period.

International development

In Chapter 5, we saw how development economics has failed to do enough to prioritise the self-determination of lower-income and less powerful countries to chart their own course of development or decide how far they integrate with the global economic system.

In recent years there has been a trend among international non-governmental organisations (INGOs) to localise their development programmes. However, there has been criticism from grassroots organisations in countries these organisations operate in.

The critique is that this is just another passing fashion which fails in its stated aim because it doesn't rebalance the highly unequal distribution of power and resources. These inequalities are the product of historical oppression and have become embedded in a global economic system that gives INGOs access to resources and denies them from grassroots organisations.

On 5 March 2020, an open letter was published on *Open Democracy* by 204 individuals and organisations worldwide claiming that localisation and shifting power had just become forms of branding, which don't actually rebalance economic power or resources at all.[31] While appreciating the services INGOs provided and the platform they had given to issues such as debt relief, gender and the climate crisis, the letter amplified criticisms of the whiteness of INGOs and that funding for their projects benefiting their head offices in North America and Europe more than the regions for which funding was originally granted.

This, in effect, sidelined local civil society groups from developing and implementing their local agendas as they had to 'compete with a multi-million-dollar INGO, with an entire marketing, communications and fundraising team, whose project budget for this endeavour probably outstrips that of most of our national organisations for a year, then comes into the South to raise money "domestically"'.[32] In turn, the signatories decried: '[This] keeps us in a master/servant relationship continuously begging for grants from your institutions, while we remain bereft of core funding ourselves … Our plea is that you work with us, not against us. We need to be supported, not competed with, and certainly not replaced.'[33]

Alongside this letter, the #shiftthepower movement drafted a manifesto for change consisting of nine demands that have inspired our ideas about reorganising the economy from the ground up:

If we want to create a genuine alternative to existing ways of deciding and doing, we need to:

1. Embrace a vision of a 'good society' built around core values of equality, democracy and sustainability and a set of organizing principles based on global solidarity and distributed leadership.
2. Cast off the restrictive framework of 'international development,' which is defined by money and power and which creates

artificial barriers between communities and movements [in different parts of the world].

3. Move away from a system that is preoccupied with quick 'solutions,' and is premised on and organized around the transfer of funds. Change how we approach, and seek to measure, the notion of success.

4. Creatively find ways to unlock the inherent power of communities in determining their own development course – however they define it – and let the language of 'beneficiaries' and 'recipients' be a thing of the past.

5. Move away from 'building capacity' as defined by external actors and requirements, towards community organizing and movement building, where 'capacity' equates to relevance, rootedness and constituency.

6. Ensure that external funding recognizes, respects and builds on local resources and assets, rather than over looks, undermines or displaces.

7. Expand our horizons beyond money as the central driver of change, and place greater value on other kinds of infinite non-financial assets and resources (knowledge, trust, networks etc.).

8. Change the language we use so that it enables new ways of working and thinking, rather than constrains them. And challenge the dominance of English.

9. Change ourselves. We need both humility and boldness, and to be ready to challenge our own power and to listen to and work with others.[34]

The role of reclaiming economics as everyday practice is to reform 'development economics' so that it aligns with the values articulated in this manifesto, and engages meaningfully with histories of oppression and how they have shaped economies today.

A key shift here, which we highlighted in the last chapter, is from charity to reparations. This can be in the form of money, but it might also be debt write-offs, suspending patents, providing cheap finance, and supporting import tariffs and exchange controls as measures to increase domestic policy space. As Arundhati Roy states, 'Charity douses anger with pity … Charity keeps the structures in place'.[35] Roy underscores the need to reject any framings that draw on concepts of charity, as we work to dismantle unjust structural inequalities and address historical oppression.

Economics education for everyone

Reclaiming economics as everyday practice rests upon a principle of economics education for everyone extending across school, university, adult education, public service broadcasting and local media.

This requires accessible public education opportunities that could take the form of organised workshops, community spaces, provision of economic news or facilitation of social media discussions to name a few. A goal of all of this is to make economics feel accessible, engaging and relevant – not, as we've already seen is currently the case, this big complex hierarchical entity that is only able to be understood by university-educated people.

It is also important that schools teach economics to students. This will help prepare all young people, not just those with existing contacts in economics, to be able to navigate and shape the economies that they inherit. It will provide an understanding of the subject so more students have an opportunity to access further education.

In this way, teaching economics at schools is an important part of diversifying who becomes an economist and democratising access to economic education.

It would also include developing democratic skills such as listening, learning, compromising, synthesising, summarising and facilitating as well as different models of leadership. Facilitators, teachers and schools will need resources and support to do this effectively.

It is important that economics within schools and communities is not simply a basic version of the neoclassical theories we outlined earlier in this book and is both broader and more relevant. Public economics education could aim to promote economic literacy and citizenship, defined as:

- *Economic literacy*: The knowledge, skills and confidence to understand, question, and critique the many different ways of thinking about the economy, and to develop independent judgements and ideas about how it could be organised.[36]
- *Economic citizenship*: Being able to use economics to have a voice in society and secure what you need from the economy. In a society that promotes economic citizenship, citizens meaningfully take part in economic discussion, decision-making and problem-solving.

Here it is important to make a clear distinction between economic and financial literacy, the latter of which is much more common across the world. Financial literacy aims to provide people with the knowledge and skills to manage their personal finances and might include budgeting, opening bank accounts and understanding compound interest rates.

These are all important skills but importantly they do not identify or question the broader economic structures that financial decisions are taken within. This often has the effect of focusing attention on the individual and narratives of individual success or failure to explain one's financial position, rather than a more holistic explanation that also considers structural factors such as, for example, historical and current racialised or gender oppression.

Economic literacy, in contrast, situates the individual within their broader economic environment, exploring how resources are distributed, banks operate and interest rates are set, and combining individual analysis with a broader focus on power, history and ideas.

Crucially, economic citizenship makes the learning process active, focusing attention on what we can do individually and collectively to be able to influence how the economies we are part of are organised, which provides a complementary activity to managing our individual finances as best we can.

Chapter 8

For future generations

In this final chapter, we turn to the future. It is quite clear to us, as it was to Joelle Gamble whose story we heard at the start of this book, that we are living in a world of multiple and inter-related crises – whether it's the wildfires, rising sea levels, ocean acidification and droughts of the climate crisis, or the Covid pandemic.

Everywhere we look, deep-rooted structural inequalities shape who lives and who dies, who thrives and who struggles. In the pandemic, low-income people in Asia, the Middle East, Africa, Latin America and the Caribbean, and communities of colour in the UK and US, are at greater risk of dying or being made destitute.

There is even a crisis in the mundane. The young people who are jobless in massive numbers across the world who are just waiting for something to happen. The mindless work many people endure; with low pay, low status and little possibility of progression, feeling like they have no purpose or value.

In this chapter, we explore how the organisation of our mod-ern economies has driven two of the biggest global crises the world faces: pandemics, and climate and ecological breakdown.

We then demonstrate that structural economic inequalities play a significant role in determining who lives and who dies in these crises.

While Covid-19 and the ecological crisis are the direct causes of harm to women, people of colour, and people who are economically marginalised, it is the structural inequalities in wealth, power and health produced by our economies that makes them more vulnerable to this harm than other groups in society.

Transformational change is necessary to address the ecological crisis and structural inequality, both of which are tearing our world apart. It is necessary for our generation to survive and flourish and to have a world to pass on to our children and grandchildren.

The economic roots of pandemics

In recent decades we have witnessed an increase in zoonotic outbreaks of infectious diseases, that is from animal pathogens infecting humans. This century has seen waves of Severe Acute Respiratory Syndrome (SARS, 2002–2004), Swine Flu (2009–2010), the Middle East Respiratory Syndrome (MERS, 2012 to present), the Ebola Virus Disease (2014–2016), and Covid-19 (2019 to present).

The encroachment of human activity into natural ecosystems is a major risk factor. Our economies are driving increases in activities such as logging, mining, road building, intensive agriculture and urbanisation, which have led to widespread habitat destruction, bringing people into ever-closer contact with animal species. As the United Nations' environment chief, Inger Andersen, put it: 'Never before have so many opportunities existed for pathogens to pass from wild and domestic animals to people.'[1]

According to the US Centers for Disease Control and Prevention, three-quarters of new or emerging diseases that infect humans originate in animals.[2] In the case of Covid-19, it is believed that the virus originated in China's bat population and was then transmitted into humans via another mammal host. On our current trajectory, while Covid-19 might be the first pandemic many of us have experienced, it will almost certainly not be the last.

Recent research has highlighted the links between intensive farming and disease outbreaks. It finds that more than two-thirds of the biggest meat, fish and dairy producers globally are in danger of fostering future zoonotic pandemics owing to lax safety standards, closely confined animals and the overuse of antibiotics.[3]

Deepening existing structural inequalities

Covid-19 has spread across a world characterised by the deep structural inequalities between countries, and different groups within them, that we highlighted in Chapter 3.

This is a major factor explaining why Covid-19 has caused disproportionate economic harm in certain countries and in certain groups with marginalised identities, particularly women, people of colour and those on low-incomes.

Closed borders, markets and shops, as well as restricted travel were more likely to result in job losses or decreased income for women, who also make up much of the informal labour sector worldwide.[4] Women working in this sector were not entitled to paid benefits such as sick pay and were more likely to work in sectors harder hit by the pandemic such as hospitality and tourism.[5]

A global snapshot of the impacts of Covid interventions upon women a few months after lockdowns begun in 2020, looks like this:[6]

- In Palestine, half of women lost all their income because of Covid-19, compared to a third of men.

- As three out of four women in East Africa worked in the informal economy, they immediately experienced a loss of livelihood.
- Likewise did the 126 million women who worked in the informal economy in Latin America and the Caribbean, with 40 per cent working in the service sector.
- In Asia, 24.5 million women were at risk of losing their jobs in the tourism industry.

The pandemic's effects upon women's lives stretch beyond their incomes. This is because, as we have seen before, women are more likely to be the primary carers of dependants in their families and responsible for household budgeting such as buying food, both of which become more difficult and time-consuming in a pandemic. There has been a lack of foresight about the harmful effects of Covid lockdowns specifically felt by women due to existing structural inequalities.

For example, in India, economist Bina Argawal assessed the direct effects of livelihood loss upon women, as well as its indirect effects.[7] These effects included: food insecurity, poverty, indebtedness, asset loss (including livestock to earn money for other necessities), isolation (such as the inability to access community support during lockdown), more care and domestic work (from family members returning home and children not in education), hunger and domestic violence (by men returning home due to lost employment elsewhere).[8]

In the UK, over three in four of the 3.2 million workers in 'high risk' roles with higher exposure to Covid-19 were women. These roles included those which 'paid poverty wages' and women carried out 98 per cent of such jobs. People of colour were also over-represented in high-risk roles.[9]

The Fawcett Society[10] highlighted that women bore the brunt of unpaid care work at home in the UK when nurseries and schools were closed, which meant some gave up their paid work or reduced their work hours as a result. In the long term, reducing paid work would also mean a reduction in pension payments when these women retire, adding further to the inequalities in pension savings that women experience, previously highlighted in Chapter 3.

Of course, it is not just a lack of resources that engenders this vulnerability. As we have already seen during the global financial crisis in 2008, historically oppressed groups did not have the economic, social or political power to ensure that their needs and interests were prioritised in government decision-making about how to respond. The same pattern can be seen globally during the Covid pandemic.

The UN found that of the 206 countries and territories that have taken 2,517 measures in response to Covid-19, only 117 measures directly strengthened women's economic security and 111 addressed unpaid care work.[11] Examples that increased women's protection when Covid began to impact societies do exist, such as Ecuador and Peru's public awareness drives and changed labour laws to protect domestic workers' rights, and in Uzbekistan, where one of the working parents was given full paid leave during school and kindergarten closures.[12] However, UN Women concluded that most government responses to Covid failed to support women who weren't able to work, and failed to support women returning to work when public health restrictions were lifted.[13]

While at the national level vaccines are mainly being distributed according to need with the most vulnerable being offered vaccines first,[14] on a global level distribution to date has been dominated by wealthier countries. As we write, in early 2021, the pandemic has been worsening in several areas of the world including Latin America, South Asia, and Sub-Saharan Africa. Even though nearly a billion vaccine doses have been administered, access remains inequitable as the United States, Europe, China, and India account for more than 70 per cent of all vaccinations.[15] Jayati Ghosh refers to this inequitable distribution as 'vaccine apartheid'.[16]

This situation was compounded by two things: first, bilateral trade agreements between individual countries (or regional trading blocs such as the EU) and pharmaceutical companies for vaccine orders worth billions;[17] second, these companies' ownership of intellectual property rights[18] for Covid-19 related products, which help them to protect and maintain their control over who uses them and at what cost. The latter led to a letter signed by nearly 400 civil society groups worldwide, and in principle supported by the World Health Organization, to call for a waiver on international patent law on vaccines and their production processes. This would enable greater access to vaccines for all countries through greater international collaboration and increased production.[19]

While proponents of patents argue that they provide incentives for private investment in research and development of new products, in the case of Covid-19, public investment to develop vaccines was crucial.

Until we address structural inequality both between and within countries, crises like the pandemic will harm those groups in society at the bottom of the economic hierarchy, deepening inequalities further in a vicious cycle.

The way our economies are organised is a root cause of this pandemic, and is increasing the likelihood of further pandemics, the cost of which will be counted in human lives, particularly those who are already on the receiving end of structural inequalities. Unfortunately, pandemics are only one outcome of a fundamental unsustainability at the heart of our economies.

The economic roots of the ecological crisis

The global economy has developed in such a way as to be fundamentally unsustainable. Overall production and consumption levels and the waste by-products from this are causing devastating global heating, biodiversity loss, ocean acidification and increased extreme weather events.

Academic neoclassical economics is fundamentally unable to grapple with this crisis because it fails to recognise that infinite growth of economic activity on a finite planet is an impossibility. The economist Kate Raworth recalls that as a student at Oxford University she and her peers: 'did not stop to ask whether GDP growth was needed, always desirable, or indeed, always possible'.[20] Recently, upon a return to Oxford, while observing a core first-year economics lecture, she found that students were still not encouraged to consider the economy's purpose.[21] The dominance of the neoclassical framework in government, business and society has facilitated the vast damage to our planet to an extent that threatens our very existence.

Least responsibility and most harm

If we take global heating and explore which groups in the world have emitted the most carbon from their economic activity, as well as which groups will be most negatively affected by the consequences, such as rising sea levels and increased droughts, a by now familiar story emerges.

As illustrated in Figure 8.1, Oxfam found that between 1990 and 2015, 46 per cent of the growth in carbon emissions were caused by the richest 10 per cent of the global population.[22] The wealthiest 1 per cent produced three times more growth in carbon emissions

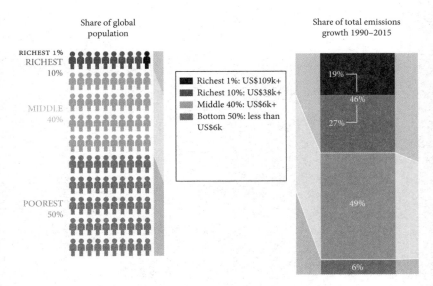

Figure 8.1 Share of global population and their share of total carbon emissions growth 1990–2015 by global income groups

than the poorest 50 per cent of people in the world (who are responsible for just 6% of total emissions growth in this period).

Through global economies, high-income countries in North America and Europe benefit economically far more from the raw materials, energy, land and labour from low-income countries than the countries which they are extracted from. This process was termed ecologically unequal exchange in the 1970s by Egyptian economist Samir Amin,[23] a pioneer of Dependency Theory, an economic perspective we highlighted in Chapter 2.[24]

The map in Figure 8.2 shows areas in the world most responsible for cumulative (or historical) carbon emissions from 1850 to 2011.[25] When understanding responsibility, it is important to account for

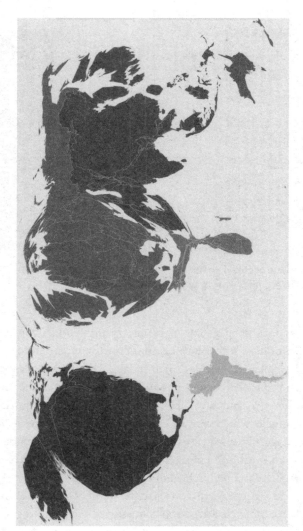

Figure 8.2 CO$_2$ emissions from energy use 1850–2011, countries by size according to the amounts of emissions

cumulative emissions, as about half of emissions ever released come from Europe and the US.

In direct contrast, the map in Figure 8.3 illustrates where in the world people are currently at most risk from the negative impacts of climate change including personal injury, being left homeless and being displaced.[26]

These maps demonstrate that those groups and countries who have the least historical responsibility for emitting carbon and driving global heating will be worst affected. People in areas with the biggest historical carbon emissions will be less at risk from the effects of global heating.

These unequal impacts are being felt now. For instance, following unprecedented cyclones in 2019, Mozambique, the world's sixth lowest income country, now shoulders the burden of $3.2 billion in loss and damage. Nonetheless, the International Monetary Fund (IMF) concluded that the damage was not serious enough to qualify for debt relief, and some of the reconstruction funds came from new IMF loans,[27] thus increasing Mozambique's national debt. The impacts of the climate crisis are far from isolated cases; it is estimated that by 2030 the annual costs of climate-related damages worldwide will reach $300–700 billion.[28]

In the Caribbean, home to about half of the world's small island nations, the effects of climate change include: rising sea levels and coastal erosion particularly in areas of coastal development; climate variability, which includes prolonged droughts and unseasonal flooding, as well as more frequent and extreme tropical storms; coral bleaching and ocean acidification because of warming waters, as well as the negative impacts on ocean life forms; and new disease trajectories.[29]

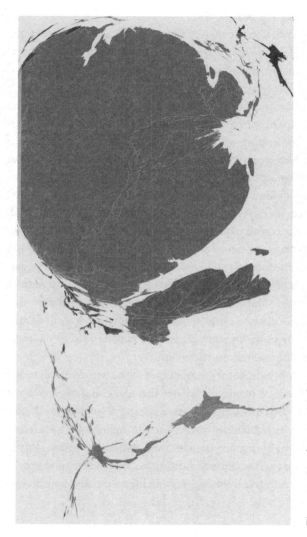

Figure 8.3 People injured, left homeless, displaced or requiring emergency assistance due to floods, droughts or extreme temperatures in a typical year, countries by size according to the levels of risk they face

Leon Sealey-Huggins, a specialist in global sustainable development, emphasises that to comprehend these existential challenges we must acknowledge Caribbean countries are among the world's most indebted, an indebtedness that can be traced back to colonialism and imperialism.[30] He makes us aware that as a result of the economic debt crisis experienced by many former colonies, Caribbean countries were forced to restructure their economies around now climate-compromised export sectors such as tourism, agriculture and fishing.[31] This indebtedness was exacerbated by these countries' post-independence integration into the vastly unequal global economic system, which we have explored in earlier chapters.

The effects of climate breakdown, including increased drought and increased extreme weather events, are already directly driving global flows of migration and causing conflicts that in turn cause migration. When climate migrants trek to the southern border of the United States or try to cross the Mediterranean to get to Europe, it must be remembered that many are fleeing damage caused by the action and inaction of countries in Europe and North America, and only much more recently countries like China.

The disproportionate impact of the climate crisis on countries with no historical responsibility for it will only become more important. It is estimated that by 2050 there will be 1.2 billion people at risk of displacement from ecological threats, particularly in Sub-Saharan Africa, South Asia, the Middle East and North Africa. Already, ecological disasters on average displace 24 million people each year.[32] To provide some context, that's just under two and half times the population of Mexico City or Greater London, and five and half times the population of Johannesburg.[33,34,35]

The fact that the people who have had least responsibility for the ecological crisis are being most harmed by it strikingly illustrates how our modern economies are unjust and illegitimate.

Climate crisis and gender

As with Covid, climate change has a larger economic impact on women and girls because it exacerbates the effects of existing gender inequalities. Action Aid[36] highlights that in some low-income countries, climate-related disasters such as floods or drought cause household livelihood insecurity, which in many cases lead to girls dropping out of school to seek work to help their families.

The effects of natural disasters, such as those linked to climate change, are known to increase the risk of gender-based violence as, with their subsequent displacement, this increases the vulnerability of women and girls to underage marriage, adolescent pregnancy, sexual assault and trafficking.[37]

Using the example of the 2004 Asian tsunami, the UN Development Program[38] highlights that women made up 70 per cent of its victims because, in comparison to men, many more women and children were inside their homes when it struck and were unable to escape from them.

In Asia and Sub-Saharan Africa, women are more likely than men to rely on land and natural resources for food and income, both of which are threatened by the climate crisis. For example, in Nigeria, where agriculture accounts for over 40 per cent of GDP, Chidiebere Onwutuebe finds that women are more vulnerable to climate-related problems than men as their work is concentrated in traditionally gendered occupations such as small-scale and rain-fed agriculture.[39]

Consequently, when climate change disrupts agricultural activities and threatens these women's livelihoods, their independence is reduced and as they become more dependent upon men in their household.

In Arctic communities, Indigenous People, older people, women and children are considered especially vulnerable when climate change alters the region's biodiversity, which in turn endangers people's food security.[40]

Tahnee Lisa Prior and Leena Heinämäki argue that there is a lack of recognition in climate policy-related circles of the distinct challenges brought by the climate crisis for Indigenous women, and that the gender component of Indigenous self-determination receives less consideration.[41]

They add that this is problematic since calls for Indigenous self-determination often obscure patriarchal structures and power dynamics in Indigenous cultures, resulting in tiered and unequal access to assets such as land, political power, and a voice that is heard.

The disenfranchisement of women through structural systems of patriarchy shapes how the impacts of the climate crisis will be felt by communities worldwide.

Deep transformation or technical fixes?

The current dominant approach globally to 'fixing' climate change is to frame it as a narrow technical challenge. In Paris, in 2015, the world committed to trying to hold the increase in global temperature to as close as possible to 1.5°C above pre-industrial levels.

Reaching net zero emissions globally by 2050 is estimated to give a 50 per cent chance of limiting warming to 1.5°C, a target now widely understood as necessary to mitigate the most catastrophic impacts of climate change. A growing number of countries are making legal commitments to achieve this goal.

According to the dominant view globally, the best way to achieve net zero emissions is through driving down the cost of renewable energy, realigning incentives in financial markets and reducing energy use by retrofitting houses, moving to electric cars and decarbonising economic production. We call this the technical approach.

In recent years the cost of solar and wind power and the batteries required to store it have been driven down much more rapidly than forecast. This is a major achievement, which opens new possibilities for rapid and mass scale transition, for example, to electric cars.

Despite this success, as of 2020, fossil fuels still made up 85 per cent of global energy production.[42] Research suggests that the production of coal, oil and gas must fall each year until 2030 to keep global heating under the 1.5°C target, but many countries are planning yearly production increases and G20 countries have, at the time of writing, given 50 per cent more Covid-19 recovery funding to fossil fuels than to clean energy.[43]

This is because for hundreds of years our economies have been set up to finance and support resource extraction and economic production in ways that fundamentally undermine the attempt to reach net zero emissions by 2050.

Take finance, for example. From 2016 to 2020, sixty commercial/investment banks from Canada, China, Europe, Japan and the US collectively invested US$3.8 trillion into fossil fuels, up US$1.1 trillion from figures reported in the previous year.[44]

Before the pandemic, US$300 billion of fossil fuel investments were held by the world's three largest asset managers which invest money from people's private savings and pension contributions.[45]

Greenpeace argues that the finance sector, which includes banks, insurers and pension funds, is 'as culpable for the climate emergency as the fossil fuel industry'.[46] Another report called *Bankrolling Extinction* found that in 2019 the world's largest banks financed US$2.6 trillion in sectors that drive biodiversity loss, which is inextricably linked to the climate crisis.[47]

Late in 2020 the World Meteorological Organization said that the current rise *already* stands at 1.2°C, with at least a one-in-five chance that we will see an annual average above 1.5°C before 2024.[48]

Given this context, seeking to realign incentives in the finance sector is like fiddling while Rome burns or rearranging deck chairs on the sinking *Titanic*. Without reforming economic sectors like finance in a much more fundamental way, targets to limit global heating to 1.5 degrees will not be met.

Given the high likelihood that global heating above 1.5 degrees is now baked in from carbon already in the air, it is vital to allocate resources to climate adaptation. Adaptation involves behaviour and systems change to protect people, the living world and economies from the impacts of climate change. Specific examples might include investments in flood defence systems and skills provision to enable farmers to adopt climate-resilient food production techniques including agroforestry.

Currently investment in adaptation is being neglected in favour of attempts to 'fix' climate change. The Green Climate Fund is part of the United Nations framework to help low-income countries respond to the threats brought by the climate crisis.[49] Data shows that 93 per cent of global climate finance for 2016/2017 went to climate mitigation (avoiding and reducing carbon emissions through the uptake of renewable energy for example), compared to just 5 per cent for adaptation.[50] As a result, funding for adaptation that helps to foster the long-term resilience of countries is well below what is required by the international legally binding Paris Agreement made in 2015.

The technical approach to reaching net zero obscures the broader economic drivers and racialised outcomes of the ecological crisis. It presents an idealised world without the vast structural inequalities of wealth and power we have explored in this book.

Rathin Roy, the Managing Director of Research and Policy at the UK's Overseas Development Institute, has branded the focus on reducing carbon emissions as 'a profoundly colonial framework'.[51] Roy highlights that there is another, older approach that clearly locates the root cause of the ecological and climate crisis in the unprecedented acceleration in human consumption and production.

This older approach, focuses attention on the extreme inequalities in current and historical global consumption, both within and between countries. It highlights the necessity of reducing some people's consumption, while increasing the consumption of others, as we rapidly work to reduce the planetary impact of total human production and consumption.[52]

The rise to dominance of the net zero carbon emissions agenda has shifted the global objective away 'from equitable consumption'. It is replaced by the narrower more technical objective of achieving a drastic reduction 'in carbon emissions, secured by developing commercially viable carbon reducing technologies that permitted existing high consumers to maintain their consumption levels'.[53] According to this view, climate action is about switching from one type of energy consumption to another.

Roy explains that this narrative leaves intact three core principles of economic development. 'First, "development" continues
to be about all nations and peoples aspiring to attain the levels of
consumption and comfort that rich people and nations enjoy.' The
technical approach does not question whether the lifestyles of the
rich are sustainable for everyone to attain.

Second, it continues not to differentiate between consumption
to meet needs versus luxuries, a point that we highlighted stems
directly from neoclassical economics in Chapter 3. As a result,
whether 'a unit of energy lights a poor Indian household, or keeps
a rich Indian in air-conditioned comfort, is irrelevant ... as long as
the energy is produced using low carbon technologies.'

Third, it does not make visible, much less address, the structural
inequalities that mean that the accumulation of wealth from this
fundamentally unsustainable economic production and consumption disproportionately goes to richer people and countries. Roy
points out that research 'focuses on how to make clean technologies for private consumption – cars, central heating, air travel –
commercially viable. Yesterday's fossil fuel tycoons are today's low
carbon billionaires.'

For Roy, this context means that, 'Shrill cries about the dangers
facing "our common planet", and about "planetary boundaries" are
advocacy tools to force those geographies that have yet to complete
their development transition to do so without recourse to fossil
fuels.'[54]

Guppi Bola summarises the findings of the 2015 Lancet
Commission on Health and Climate Change. Any 'progress on
health at a global level will easily be reversed by the catastrophic
direct and indirect impacts of climate breakdown. The direct effects
of climate breakdown, including increased floods, heat stress,

drought and storm intensity are estimated to cause up to a quarter of a million deaths per year between 2030 to 2050.'[55]

Many of the pathways by which climate change will indirectly impact health are socioeconomic and 'often rooted in a community's "adaptive capacity" to respond to radical and abrupt changes to their living conditions'. For Bola, it 'is overwhelming to articulate just how severe air pollution, food insecurity, greater spread of infectious disease, displacement, conflict and the mental trauma associated with these events will be on human health'.[56] This cannot be the inheritance we leave for our children and grandchildren.

The legal commitments governments are making to reach net zero are crucial, and civil societies must ensure that they are held to account on delivering them. However, transition to economies that are genuinely sustainable and just requires much more than finding technological solutions to lower carbon emissions; it requires fundamental change.

The case for a new economic system

Transformational change is necessary to address the ecological crisis that is tearing our world apart. We need a new economic system to be able to address unjust historical oppression, which has contributed to economies characterised by extreme structural inequalities that dictate who is most vulnerable to climate and ecological breakdown.

We need a new economic system that ensures that the groups that currently have least resources and power are represented in decision-making, as our economies go through this process of ecological transition and adaptation. We need a new economic system based on a fundamental social, economic and ethical transformation of societies.[57]

In sum, we need a new economic system because our economies are unjust, illegitimate, and destructive, particularly for the most historically excluded but ultimately for all of us and for future generations. This is not to imply that the global economy is run by evil, racist, sexist and classist people. That would be to make the mistake of focusing on individuals not systems.

Ideologies of White male supremacy have over the last fifty years become increasingly socially unacceptable (although there are signs that this trend could be reversing). But White male supremacy is embedded in our economies through how it has shaped structural economic inequality.

Treating everyone the same way when there are structural inequalities within and between countries, is not equal as it reproduces inequality. This is why reparations to address historical oppression are necessary, along with policies that redistribute wealth and power, such as land reform.[58]

When our economies are rooted in histories that value whiteness, maleness and wealth, we should not be surprised by the inequalities that show up. Structural inequalities need systemic change, change that filters through every level of the system, otherwise we risk reproducing and deepening them. White and male supremacy are not the only hierarchies embedded in our economies, many of which are stratified along lines which include caste, religion, tribe or nationality.

This structural focus does not absolve us of individual responsibility. It is not the case that everything bad in the world is the fault of 'the evil system'. We need a more nuanced understanding of how individual actions are both shaped by and in turn shape broader systems. We must go beyond the dichotomy of *either* free individual choice in a contextless vacuum *or* individual choice as completely determined by the broader system. It is clear we need *both* system change, such as in the distribution of economic resources and power, *as well as* individual change, such as eating less meat, gender equality and anti-racism training.

Another way to think about this is as needing both top-down change, through collective decision-making which changes how governments, businesses and populations operate at international, national and regional levels, and ground-up change through individual and small group decision-making that changes how specific individuals and communities operate.

It is important to recognise that these approaches to change are mutually constitutive and reinforcing. Individual change can influence others and scale up into systems change, while systems change shapes the range of choices and actions available to individuals.

Economies built on moral equality and freedom

One of this book's contributors, Kamal Ramburuth-Hurt, undertook his undergraduate education in Johannesburg, where he participated in a number of student movements. In his first year of university, South Africa saw a massive student movement for free education that compelled him to start a Rethinking Economics for Africa group.

> From unequal access to education, to huge poverty and industrialisation, it was absolutely clear that we had economic problems to solve. Our economics textbooks held no answers to these problems. We needed different knowledge to solve these problems. We needed Rethinking Economics for Africa and that's why I got involved.

As someone 'born-free' after South Africa became a democracy, Kamal is driven by the need to create the social and economic conditions for freedom.

We believe that the case for a new economic system should be supported by people with a range of political beliefs as long as they include a commitment to moral equality – the idea that all human beings, as such and without exception, are entitled to certain rights, respect, dignity, and to be treated as having intrinsic value that is separate from any usefulness to other people or the economy.

Some people define fairness as equality of outcome, which focuses on the equal distribution of economic resources, while others define it as equality of opportunity, which focuses on the equal opportunity to own or consume these resources.[59]

Another aspect of this question is the overall structure of the economic system. Some might define fairness as equality of opportunity *only if* the overall gap between the 'winners' and 'losers' is not too big *or* that the losers could still meet their basic needs and participate in society. We will call this definition of fairness *the qualified commitment to equality of opportunity*.

The presence of structural inequalities between and within countries, which can be directly and indirectly attributed to historical oppression, and continues to shape who has power, who is healthy and who is most affected by crises, means that our modern economies do not meet any of these tests of fairness.

The philosophy of libertarianism seeks to maximise autonomy and political freedom, highlighting the importance of free association, freedom of choice, individualism and voluntary association, and on this basis we might assume that it would oppose coordinated collective action to achieve economic systems change.

However, some libertarians do recognise that where the historical acquisition of private property has been unjust and this influences economic outcomes today, then justice requires a return to the distribution that would have occurred had the injustice not taken place; and recognise that there can be a role for government in doing this.[60] Unjust historical acquisition of property and its continued effects on the present have been central to the history we have traced, and on this basis there is a libertarian case for economic systems change to rectify past injustices.

What then about freedom? The classical liberal idea of freedom is that a person has negative freedom if their actions are not restrained by anyone else (freedom from), and positive freedom if they are able to do the things they want (freedom to). Another idea is that a person should have maximum freedom to pursue happiness consistent with the freedom of everyone else.[61]

It is clear on the evidence presented that our modern economies undermine the negative and positive freedoms of many groups across the world today and that ecological breakdown will further reduce the freedom that future generations have. It is also apparent that the freedom of some today to consume natural resources, and emit carbon and other waste resources, undermines the freedom of other groups and future generations through driving ecological breakdown, thus violating the maximum freedom principle.

In the political and economic debates of the twentieth century, freedom and equality were pitted against each other as opposites, with societies able to choose one but not the other. This dichotomy rests on a narrow ahistorical conception of freedom and equality in which you can promote increased equality through government redistribution of economic resources, but this relies on the threat of coercion and therefore undermines freedom, or you can promote freedom, but then we must accept significant economic inequality as its price.

If, as we and many others are now advocating, you view our modern economies in the light of the historical oppression that has significantly shaped structural inequalities within and between

300

countries today, then it becomes clear that freedom and equality are necessary for each other.

In a narrow sense, collective action to change the distribution of resources and how economies are organised to reduce unjust structural inequalities, will come with the threat of coercion and thus limit some people's freedom.

However, we widely recognise that people shouldn't have the freedom to own or do things that are unjust or illegitimate or reduce other people's freedom. As we have seen, power and the threat of coercion is an ever present feature of our modern economies. The reproduction of the existing distribution of wealth, which is structurally unequal, depends on legal systems protecting wealth, in the form of assets, against other people's claims to use those resources. This protection is given weight by the State's threat to use coercion and force on people who don't follow its laws.

There is no world where power and its corollary coercion are not present. The challenge is to balance economic and other forms of power more equally within and between countries, as reparations for the historical oppression that makes our current economies unjust and illegitimate. This will prevent continued exploitation and injustice and create the conditions in which greater freedom can be enjoyed by all.

Reclaiming economics for racial justice, gender equality and future generations

To imagine other forms of human existence is exactly the challenge that is posed by the climate crisis: for if there is any one thing that global warming has made perfectly clear it is that to think about the world only as it is amounts to a formula for suicide. We need, rather to envision what it might be.

Amitav Ghosh[62]

301

In recent years, there has been an upswell of books, articles and programmes on the future of our modern economies. Economists and others have looked for ways to hold the centre and protect the status quo, suggesting reforms of varying ambition to address the many crises of the early twenty-first century.[63]

From our position, it is patently clear that the current economic paradigm is unravelling and that ecological crisis will force economic system change on us. For a long time, we have been told that there is no alternative to the way our economies are organised. Now we know there is no alternative but to change our economies. Even if there was an option to continue business as usual, the necessity and urgency for economic systems change is common sense when the status quo is so clearly unjust and illegitimate. The greatest task faced by humanity is working out how to build these new societies and economies.

The next generation are leading the way. Since 2019, young people and other climate activists across generations worldwide have taken part in the Fridays for Future school climate strikes.[64] They call for climate justice for those who have been the most affected by climate change, and clearly identify unequal and racialised dimensions of this both within and between countries. They also highlight the importance of 'centring the voices of Black, Brown and Indigenous people, who for centuries have been resisting the systems that eventually led us to this situation today'.[65]

These themes are developed in a speech given by the Wretched of the Earth collective, a coalition of climate justice groups led by people of colour, at the London Climate Strike on 20 September 2019.[66]

On a sunny afternoon in Central London they told the protesters: 'You've all heard that "our house is on fire". But for many of us, our house has been on fire for over 500 years. And it did not set itself on fire.'[67] This 500-year fire symbolises the long histories of colonialism, racism, sexism and elitism which are embedded in our modern economies.

They set out a vision that a 'climate just future will not be one of extraction but of regeneration and care' in which we collectively move beyond 'the extractivist mindset that decides whose lives and existences matter. Whose rivers, forests and mountains are up for grabs. Whose people's resources can be exploited, and their lands taken. And, of course, whose lives can be taken when they resist'.[68]

That day they quoted the Black American writer and activist Audre Lorde reminding us that: 'Sometimes we are blessed with being able to choose the time, and the arena, and the manner of our revolution, but more usually we must do battle where we are standing.'[69]

We wholeheartedly support this call to create economies that are built on regeneration and care, not extraction from people or the planet. To achieve this, we must do battle where we are standing to reclaim economics for racial justice, gender equality and future generations.

Appendices

Appendix I: Interviews

To gain an understanding of how different students and professionals experience economics, we conducted semi-structured, mostly peer-to-peer interviews with forty-four undergraduate and postgraduate students, as well as interviews with eighteen professionals and academics. Most interviewees had identities and backgrounds that are less represented in economics.

Students identified as: thirty-one women and thirteen men; women accounted for seventeen out of the eighteen professional interviews. Of the student interviews, five identified as working class out of thirty-three who identified their social class background. Interviewees were from: Australia, Austria, Brazil, Canada, Chile, Colombia, Denmark, Finland, Germany, Greece, Hong Kong, India, Italy, Japan, Kuwait, Malaysia, Mexico, Nigeria, South Korea, Sudan, Taiwan, United Kingdom, United States, Vietnam and Zambia. We did reach out to a mix of women and men working in economics for interviews but received a better response rate from women. Our research also included two focus groups with twenty students (equally split between girls and boys) aged 13–17 in diversely populated non-fee-paying schools in London.

The global lack of data[1] about the underrepresentation of different groups within economics highlighted to us the importance of interviews which could capture people's experiences, journeys and any barriers they faced in the discipline. Quotes from these interviews are interspersed throughout the book to better understand the everyday challenges they have faced because of their identity to access or become part of the field of economics. To begin to address a lack of diversity in economics, the need to decolonise and democratise it, and to dismantle patriarchy, racism and elitism within the discipline, we need to hear more from those who are negatively affected by this state of affairs.

Appendix II: Focus groups conducted in London, UK, in October 2019

High-school students, age 13–14, where GCSE and A Level Economics is taught	Students age 16–17 studying an A Level in Economics	
Anita	Ahmad	Leo
Beth	Ali	Lyn
Cara	Barbara	Mark
Danielle	Ben	Marco
Eva	Carlo	Mick
	Daniel	Nina
	Emmanuel	Olivia
	Fiona	

Appendix III: University students/recent graduates of economics – backgrounds gained from interview data

Interviews conducted between March and August 2019.
Information has been withheld to maintain anonymity.

Alejandra	Colombian, woman, undergraduate student of economics in Colombia
Alex	North American, woman, low-income background, undergraduate and postgraduate student of economics in North America
Amit	Indian, man, upper class, undergraduate student in economics and politics in the UK
Andrés	Colombian, European/Indigenous descent, man, working class, undergraduate student of economics in Colombia
Andrew	South African, White, man, middle class, undergraduate student of economics in South Africa
Anna	Danish, Brown, woman, undergraduate student in economics, postgraduate student of politics and economics
Anila	African, Sudanese woman, postgraduate development economics student in the UK
Arianna	Greek, White, woman, studied economics as part of their undergraduate degree in Greece
Bea	British, White, middle-class woman, studied undergraduate economics in the UK and postgraduate economics elsewhere in Europe
Carlos	Colombian, man, upper middle class, undergraduate student of economics but transferred to a different degree subject mid-way in Colombia
Catherine	Canadian, woman, working class, studied undergraduate economics in Canada

Appendices

Chanda	Zambian, man, from a non-privileged background, undergraduate and postgraduate student of economics in Zambia, PhD student of economics in Europe
Charlotte	European-Nigerian, woman, privileged background, undergraduate student in economics and politics, postgraduate student of economics in Europe
Chen	Taiwanese, woman, undergraduate in economics, postgraduate student of economics in Europe
Chiara	Italian, White, woman, middle class, studied undergraduate economics in the UK
Daniela	Chilean, woman, European heritage, privileged background, undergraduate and postgraduate student in economics, PhD student in economics in the UK
Elena	Greek, woman, studied economics as part of their undergraduate degree in Greece
Emma	Danish, White, woman, middle class, postgraduate student of economics in the UK
Emmanuel	Nigerian, Black, man, middle class, studied undergraduate economics in Nigeria
Emilia	Finnish, woman, upper middle class, undergraduate student in politics, philosophy and economics in the UK
Erika	Japanese American, woman, middle–working class, undergraduate student of economics in the US
Esther	Nigerian, Black African, woman, middle class, undergraduate of economics in Nigeria and postgraduate student of economics in the UK
Felicia	Sudanese, woman, postgraduate development economics student in Sudan
Gina	British, Black, woman, middle class, undergraduate student of politics and economics in the UK

Appendices

Hiba	Sudanese, Black, woman, middle-class background, studied undergraduate economics in Sudan, postgraduate economics in the UK
Ibrahim	British Pakistani, man, middle–lower class, undergraduate student in politics, philosophy and economics in the UK
James	Australian, White, man, middle class, undergraduate student of economics and marketing in Australia
Jessica	Canadian, woman, middle class, undergraduate of economics in Canada
Jose	Colombian, man, undergraduate student of economics in Colombia
Juliana	Brazilian, White, woman, high–middle class, undergraduate student of economics in Brazil, postgraduate student of economics in Europe
Kim	South East Asian, woman, middle class–upper middle class, undergraduate economics student in the US
Laura	Austrian, woman, middle class, studied undergraduate economics in Austria and postgraduate student of economics in different European countries
Lee	South East Asian, man, middle class–upper middle class, undergraduate student of economics in the US
Luis	Mexican, man, privileged background, undergraduate student of economics in the US
Maria	Russian, White, woman, postgraduate student of economics in the UK
Nathan	Canadian, man, White, privileged background, undergraduate student in economics in the US
Nguyen	Vietnamese, woman, privileged background, undergraduate economics student in the US
Noor	Kuwaiti, woman, middle class, undergraduate of economics in the UK

Nurul	Malaysian, woman, middle class, postgraduate of economics in the UK
Petra	Austrian, White, woman, undergraduate and postgraduate of economics in the UK
Priya	Indian, woman, privileged middle-class background, undergraduate and postgraduate student in economics in India, and PhD student in economics in the US
Rahul	Indian, man, upper middle class, undergraduate student in politics, philosophy and economics in the UK
Ruba	African, Muslim, woman, undergraduate student in economics and postgraduate student in statistics in Sudan
Taylor	American, White, woman, undergraduate student of economics in the US

Appendix IV: Professionals working in economics – backgrounds gained from interview data

Interviews conducted between September and December 2019. Information has been withheld to maintain anonymity.

Aditi	Indian, woman, middle now upper class, professor of economics in Europe
Advika	Indian, woman, middle class, professor of economics in North America
Amy	American, White, woman, middle class, professor of economics in Europe
Carmella	Italian, White, woman, middle class, professor of economics in Europe
Ellen	British, woman, originally working class, now middle class, professor of economics, UK based
Faiza	British Pakistani, woman, academic researcher in economics, UK based

Appendices

Fatima	Indian, woman, middle class, professor of economics in Europe
Frauke	German, White, woman, lower middle class, senior lecturer in economics in Europe
Isabel	Black American, woman, working class, academic economist, US based
Janet	Black American, woman, upper middle class, economist including university lecturer, US based
Mary	American, woman, middle-class lecturer in economics, UK based
Michaela	Black British African, woman, working-class background, UK civil service economist
Noel	British Nigerian, Black man, working class, assistant economist, UK based
Rachel	Black African, woman, working class/middle class, lecturer in economics, US based
Rebecca	White, woman, middle class, chief economist at a research organisation, UK based
Roopa	Indian, woman, upper middle class, professor of economics in Europe
Sofia	German, woman, middle class, professor of economics in Europe
Zara	White, woman, middle class, advisor on economics and equality issues, UK based

List of figures and tables

Figures

311

Tables

Notes

Introduction

1   Throughout the book we use the term Black American, apart from in quotes, based on guidance by the DC Fiscal Policy Institute that states 'this is how most Black people identify – when referring to cultures, ethnicities, and groups of people, names are often capitalized to reflect reality and respect.' DC Fiscal Policy Institute, 'DCFPI style guide for inclusive language', 2017, p. 4. Available at: www.dcfpi.org/wp-content/uploads/2017/12/Style-Guide-for-Inclusive-Language_Dec-2017.pdf (accessed 14 June 2021).

2   Jonathan Van Dyke, 'Alumna Joelle Gamble goes from Westwood to the White House', *UCLA Newsroom*, 4 February 2021. Available at: https://newsroom.ucla.edu/stories/UCLA-alumna-joelle-gamble-biden-administration (accessed 7 June 2021).

3   Joelle Gamble, '@joelle_gamble' [Twitter], 4 June 2020. Available at: https://twitter.com/joelle_gamble/status/1268603092012015617 (accessed 7 June 2021).

4   Natalie Gontcharova, 'Meet 6 young women who will be keeping the White House running', *Refinery 29*, 27 January 2021. Available at: www.refinery29.com/en-us/2021/01/10272968/biden-white-house-communications-policy-team (accessed 7 June 2021).

5   Throughout we use the term 'White' apart from in quotes based on a view in an article by the US Center for the Study of Social Policy 'To not name "White" as a race is, in fact, an anti-Black act which frames Whiteness as both neutral and the standard … Moreover, the detachment of "White" as a proper noun allows White people to sit

out of conversations about race and removes accountability from White people's and White institutions' involvement in racism.' While the capitalisation of 'White' is associated with far-right groups and a social construct used to reinforce power structures, using it in a different context, such as this book, helps to reclaim the term and dispel the idea that 'white' is the norm. See Brittany Wong, 'Here's why it's a big deal to capitalize the word "Black"', *Huffington Post*, 9 September 2020 [online] www.huffingtonpost.co.uk/entry/why-capitalize-word-black_l_5f342ca1c5b6960c066faea5 (accessed 14 June 2021).

6   Paul Samuelson, 'Foreword' in Phillip Saunders and William Walstad (eds) *The Principles of Economics Course: A Handbook for Instructors* (New York: McGraw-Hill Publishing, 1990), pp. ix–x.

7   We use the term racialised identity rather than race throughout this book apart from in quotes and when reporting the findings of research on race. This decision aims to highlight that race is socially constructed through particular histories which racialise groups in different ways. Race is not a biological category with any basis in genes; it is a racialised identity, which can vary across different countries, cultures and times. For example, someone considered Black in the US, might be considered White in Brazil or Jamaica.

8   We use women/woman and men/man rather than female and male in this throughout this book, apart from in quotes and when reporting the findings of research, as we believe this is more inclusive of transgender women and men. An exception to this is our use of 'male dominance' (patriarchy) in discussing the history and culture of academic economics and wider society.

9   GDP is the total monetary value of goods and services produced by a country during a particular timeframe, i.e. quarterly or yearly.

10   The CORE Team describe this curriculum as 'accessible, relevant, real-world economics teaching, available and free to everyone' and believes 'a radically transformed economics education can contribute to a more just, sustainable, and democratic world in which future citizens are empowered by a new economics to understand and debate how best to address pressing societal problems'. In *The Economy: Economics for a Changing World* (Oxford: Oxford

University Press, 2017). Available at: www.core-econ.org/about/ (accessed 2 June 2021).

11 Rosanna Wiseman, 'Colonialism + capitalism = climate crisis', *Global Justice Now*, 7 October 2019. Available at: www.globaljustice.org.uk/blog/2019/oct/7/colonialism-capitalism-climate-crisis (accessed 22 May 2021).

Chapter 1 Undiverse and uninclusive

1 IDEAS, 'Female representation in economics as of May 2021', IDEAS, 2021. Available at: https://ideas.repec.org/top/female.html (accessed 13 June 2021).

2 Danae Kyriakopoulou and Kat Usita (eds), *Banking on Balance: Diversity in Central Banks and Public Investment* (London: Official Monetary and Financial Institutions Forum, 2019), p. 12. Available at: www.omfif.org/gender-balance-index-2019/ (accessed 17 May 2021).

3 Ginther and Khan (2014), cited in Amanda Bayer and Celia Rouse, 'Diversity in the economics profession: a new attack on an old problem', *Journal of Economic Perspectives*, 30:4 (2016), 221–242. doi: 10.1257/jep. 30.4.221, p. 223.

4 Tim Gill, *Provision of GCE A Level Subjects 2017*, Statistics Report Series No. 123 (Cambridge, UK: Cambridge Assessment, 2018), p. 6. Available at: www.cambridgeassessment.org.uk/Images/520413-provision-of-gce-a-level-subjects-2017.pdf (accessed 17 May 2021).

5 A Level or Advanced Level courses are those that most university students of Economics in the UK study to gain a place at university.

6 Arun Advani, Sonkurt Sen and Ross Warwick, *Ethnic Diversity in UK Economics*, IFS Briefing Note BN307 (London: Institute of Fiscal Studies, 2020), p. 19. Available at: www.ifs.org.uk/publications/15133 (accessed 17 May 2021).

7 Gill, *Provision of GCE A Level Subjects 2017*, p. 6.

8 Interviewees include Priya and Amit, India; Daniela, Chile; Emilia, Finland; Lee, SE Asia; Andrew, South Africa; Gina, UK; Juliana, Brazil; Nurul, Malaysia.

9 Claire Crawford, Neil M. Davies and Sarah Smith, 'Why do so few women study economics? Evidence from England' (London:

Women's Committee of the Royal Economic Society, 2018). Available at: www.res.org.uk/uploads/assets/uploaded/6c3fd338-88d6-47ea-bf2f 302dfee7f37e.pdf (accessed 17 May 2021).

10 Research has found that girls in England who studied maths at age 16–17 were less likely to study economics at university compared to their peers who were boys, while women in US universities were more likely to obtain a degree in maths than in economics. This suggests that the mathematical nature of economics is probably not a hugely significant factor in the low number of girls choosing to study economics. See Crawford, Davies and Smith, 'Why do so few women study economics?' and Martha Starr and Cynthia Bansak, 'Gender differences in predispositions towards economics', *Eastern Economic Journal*, 36:1 (2010), 33–57. doi: 10.1057/eej.2008.50.

11 Committee on the Status of Minority Groups in the Economics Profession, *Report of the Committee on the Status of Minority Groups in the Economics Profession* (Pittsburgh: CSMGEP, December 2020), pp. 12–13. Available at: www.aeaweb.org/content/file?id=13728 (accessed 17 May 2021).

12 *Ibid.*, p. 3.

13 *Ibid.*, p. 3 and p. 6.

14 Ministry of Human Resource Development, *All India Survey on Higher Education 2018–2019* (New Delhi: Government of India, Department of Higher Education, 2019), p. 12 and T-13. Available at: https://ruralindiaonline.org/en/library/resource/all-india-survey-on-higher-education-2018-19/ (accessed 18 May 2021).

15 Joshi and Malghan (2017), cited in Anirudh Tagat, Mihir Parekh, Aditi Priya, Jasmin Naur Hafiz, Arvind Kumar, Srishti Pal, Apilang Apum, Amrita Sharma, Trisha Chandra and Raashid Shah, *Diversity and Representation in Economics in India* (India: Rethinking Economics India Network, 2021), Monk Prayogshala-Bahujan Economists Policy Brief, p. 10. Available at: https://tinyurl.com/yszrwwmz (accessed 17 May 2021).

16 Advani, Sen and Warwick, *Ethnic Diversity in UK Economics*, p. 27.

17 Black Female Professors Forum. Available at: https://blackfemale professorsforum.org/category/subject-areas/economics/ (accessed 17 May 2021).

18   Nicola Rollock, *Staying Power: The Career Experiences and Strategies of UK Black Female Professors* (London: UCU, 2019). Available at: www.ucu.org.uk/media/10075/Staying-Power/pdf/UCU_Rollock_February_2019.pdf (accessed 18 May 2021).

19   In the UK, statistics provide sobering evidence of the discipline's lack of diversity, as highlighted in the IFS's report on ethnic minority student/staff representation in UK university economics (see Advani, Sen and Warwick, *Ethnic Diversity in UK Economics*, 2020). We build on their findings through data we requested from economics departments at the country's leading Russell Group universities at which about half of the country's economics students study the subject. Information requested from them included the gender identity, ethnicity and socioeconomic background of their undergraduates, postgraduates and academic staff in their economics departments in the academic years 2014/2015 and 2018/2019. We also asked if they were UK or non-UK domiciled (if individuals are from the UK or overseas). As data was largely unchanged, we focused on the most relevant data from 2018/2019. This information allowed us to track the representation of different social groups in economics across the academic ladder and to comment on the existence of a leaky pipeline. Of all the Russell Group universities contacted, twenty-one out of the twenty-four of them provided data in response to our requests.

20   Findings based on Freedom of Information data requested from Russell Group universities and received in 2019.

21   Economics is far behind all other disciplines. In the case of the humanities, social sciences and STEM, women now account for nearly 60 per cent of the bachelor's degrees awarded. See Bayer and Rouse, *Diversity in the Economics Profession*, p. 224.

22   Sam Allgood, Lee Badgett, Amanda Bayer, Marianne Bertrand, Sandra E. Black, Nick Bloom and Lisa D. Cook, *AEA Professional Climate Survey: Final Report: September 15, 2019* (Pittsburgh: Committee on Equity, Diversity and Professional Conduct, 2019), p. 2. Available at: www.aeaweb.org/resources/member-docs/final-climate-survey-results-sept-2019 (accessed 18 May 2021).

23   *Ibid.*, p. 15.

24   *Ibid.*, p. 9.

Notes

25 Claudia Sahm, 'Economics is a disgrace', *macromom blog*, 29 July 2020. Available at: https://macromomblog.com/2020/07/29/economics-is-a-disgrace/ (accessed 3 June 2021).

26 Olivier Blanchard, Ben Bernanke and Janet Yellen, 'A message from the AEA leadership on the professional climate in economics'. Available at: www.aeaweb.org/news/member-announcements-mar-18-2019 (accessed 18 May 2021).

27 Claudia Sahm, 'Economics is a disgrace'.

28 Dania Francis and Anna Gifty Opoku-Agyeman, 'Economists' silence on racism is 100 years in the making', *Newsweek* [Online], 11 June 2020. Available at: https://tinyurl.com/pps7vb8q (accessed 18 May 2021).

29 Allgood *et al.*, *AEA Professional Climate Survey*, p. 13.

30 *Ibid.*, p. 14.

31 *Ibid.*, p. 14.

32 Harald Uhlig, '@haraldduhlig' [Twitter], 9 June 2020. Available at https://twitter.com/haraldduhlig/status/1270199700071821312?lang=en (accessed 3 June 2021).

33 K. Thor Jensen and Dan Avery, 'A top economist compared Black Lives Matter leaders to "flat-earthers," saying "sensible adults" need to take over the conversation', *Insider*, 10 June 2020. Available at: www.businessinsider.com/top-economist-compares-blm-leaders-to-flat-earthers-and-creationists-2020-6?r=US&IR=T (accessed 28 May 2021).

34 University of Chicago, 'University of Chicago Policy on Harassment, Discrimination, and Sexual Misconduct', 14 August 2020. Available at: https://harassmentpolicy.uchicago.edu/policy/ (accessed 3 June 2021).

35 Allgood *et al.*, *AEA Professional Climate Survey*, p. 10.

36 We use data provided by the ONS on households' weekly *expenditures* by social classification as our measure of the relative wealth of family households.

37 Advani, Sen and Warwick, *Ethnic Diversity in UK Economics*, p. 3.

38 *Ibid.*, p. 24.

39 This department has produced Nobel Prize winners for their contributions to economics.

40 Claire Alexander and Jason Arday (eds), *Aiming Higher: Race, Inequality and Diversity in the Academy* (London: Runnymede Trust,

2015). Available at: www.runnymedetrust.org/uploads/Aiming%20 Higher.pdf (accessed 18 May 2021).

41 Analytical Services also include the Government Social Research Service, Government Operational Research Service and Government Statistical Service.

42 Civil Service HR, *Civil Service Fast Stream: Annual Report 2017 and 2018*, Table 15, p. 56. Available at: https://assets.publishing.service.gov.uk/ government/uploads/system/uploads/attachment_data/file/767789/ Civil_Service_Fast_Stream_Annual_Report_2017_-_2018.pdf (accessed 18 May 2021). Percentages based on authors' calculations of successful applicants to the Analytical Services of the Fast Stream Civil Service programme.

43 Civil Service HR, *Civil Service Fast Stream*, p. 56.

44 Government Economic Service, *Government Economic Service 2020 Strategy* (London: GES, 2016), p. 10. Available at: https:// assets.publishing.service.gov.uk/government/uploads/system/ uploads/attachment_data/file/550821/GES_2020_Strategy.pdf (accessed 18 May 2021).

45 Advani, Sen and Warwick, *Ethnic Diversity in UK Economics*, p. 34.

Chapter 2 Harmful hierarchies

1 There is some debate about what neoclassical economics is and how it should it be defined. See for example: Jamie Morgan (ed.), *What Is Neoclassical Economics? Debating the Origins, Meaning and Significance* (London: Routledge, 2015).

2 Carlo D'Ippoliti, *Democratizing the Economics Debate: Pluralism and Research Evaluation*, [VitalSource Bookshelf e-book version] (Routledge, 2020). Available from: vbk://9781000066203 (accessed 13 June 2021).

3 See, for example, the curriculum review of all nine universities that teach economics in the Netherlands. Joris Tieleman, Sam De Muijnck, Maarten Kavelaars and Francis Ostermeijer, 'Thinking like an economist: a quantitative analysis of economics bachelor curricula in the Netherlands', *Rethinking Economics Netherlands*, 2017. Available at: www.economicseducation.org/bsc-overview (accessed 13 June 2021).

4   Lionel Robbins, *An Essay on the Nature and Significance of Economic Science*, second edition (London: Macmillan, 1935), p. 15.

5   Robert Cooter and Peter Rappoport, 'Were the ordinalists wrong about welfare economics?', *Journal of Economic Literature*, 22:2 (June 1984), 507–530.

6   Stephen J. Dubner and Steven D. Levitt, *Superfreakonomics: Global Cooling, Patriotic Prostitutes and Why Suicide Bombers Should Buy Life Insurance* (London: Penguin, 2010), p. 16.

7   Roncaglia labels this the 'cumulative view' of the history of economics in Alessandro Roncaglia, *The Wealth of Ideas: A History of Economic Thought* (Cambridge: Cambridge University Press, 2005).

8   Michael Raey, 'The flexible unity of economics', *American Journal of Sociology* 118: 1 (July 2012), 65–67.

9   Marion Fourcade, 'Economics: the view from below', *Swiss Journal of Economics and Statistics* 154: 5 (2018), 5. Available at: https://doi.org/10.1186/s41937-017-0019-2.

10 Sam Allgood, Lee Badgett, Amanda Bayer, Marianne Bertrand, Sandra E. Black, Nick Bloom and Lisa D. Cook, *AEA Professional Climate Survey: Final Report: September 15, 2019* (Pittsburgh: Committee on Equity, Diversity and Professional Conduct, 2019), p. 4. Available at: www.aeaweb.org/resources/member-docs/final-climate-survey-results-sept-2019 (accessed 18 May 2021).

11 University of Nottingham, *Academic Journals* (n.d.). Available at: www.nottingham.ac.uk/nursing/sonet/rlos/ebp/journals/what_are_journals/page_four.html (accessed 19 May 2021).

12 Marion Fourcade, Ollion Etienne and Algan Yann, 'The superiority of economists', *Journal of Economic Perspectives*, 29:1 (2015), 89–114, 94. doi: 10.1257/jep. 29.1.89.

13 *Ibid.*, p. 93.

14 D'Ippoliti, *Democratising the Economics Debate*, p. 56.

15 Dania Francis and Anna Gifty Opoku-Agyeman, 'Economists' silence on racism is 100 years in the making', *Newsweek* [Online], 11 June 2020. Available at: https://tinyurl.com/pps7vb8q (accessed 18 May 2021).

16 Patrick Mason, Samuel Myers Jr and William Darity, 'Is there racism in economic research?', *European Journal of Political Economy*, 21:3 (2005), 755–761. doi: 10.1016/j.ejpoleco.2004.07.005.

Notes

17 *Ibid.*, p. 755.

18 Ann Mari May, Mary G. McGarvey and David Kucera, 'Gender and European economic policy: a survey of the views of European economists on contemporary economic policy', *KYKLOS*, 71:1 (2018), 2–183. doi: 10.1111/kykl.12166.

19 Amanda Bayer and Celia Rouse, 'Diversity in the economics profession: a new attack on an old problem', *Journal of Economic Perspectives*, 30:4 (2016), 221–242, 232.

20 Robert E. Lucas Jr, *The Industrial Revolution: Past and Future,* 2003 Annual Report, Federal Reserve Bank of Minneapolis, Volume 18 (May 2004), pp. 5–20. Available at: www.minneapolisfed.org/article/2004/the-industrial-revolution-past-and-future (accessed 18 May 2021).

21 For example, see Nancy Folbre's work, available at: https://people.umass.edu/folbre/folbre/books.html (accessed 18 May 2021).

22 Ingrid Harvold Kvangraven and Surbhi Kesar, 'Why do economists have trouble understanding racialized inequalities?', Institute for New Economic Thinking, 3 August 2020. Available at: www.ineteconomics.org/perspectives/blog/why-do-economists-have-trouble-understanding-racialized-inequalities (accessed 18 May 2021).

23 Kvangraven and Kesar, 'Why do economists have trouble understanding racialized inequalities?'.

24 Bayer and Rouse, 'Diversity in the economics profession', pp. 221–242.

25 IDEAS, 'Female representation in economics as of May 2021', IDEAS, 2021. Available at: https://ideas.repec.org/top/female.html (accessed 13 June 2021).

26 Ministry of Human Resource Development, *All India Survey on Higher Education 2018–2019* (New Delhi: Government of India, Department of Higher Education, 2019), p. 12 and T-13. Available at: https://ruralindiaonline.org/en/library/resource/all-india-survey-on-higher-education-2018-19/ (accessed 18 May 2021).

27 IDEAS, 'Female representation in economics as of May 2021'.

28 Sam Allgood, Lee Badgett, Amanda Bayer, Marianne Bertrand, Sandra E. Black, Nick Bloom and Lisa D. Cook, *AEA Professional Climate Survey: Final Report: September 15, 2019*, p. 29.

29 Fourcade *et al.*, 'The superiority of economists', p. 98.

30 *Ibid.*, p. 100.

31 Marion Fourcade, 'The construction of a global profession: the transnationalization of economics', *American Journal of Sociology*, 112:1 (July 2006), 145–194, 172.

32 *Ibid.*

33 *Ibid.*, 168.

34 *Ibid.*, 168–169.

35 Joe Earle, Cahal Moran and Zach Ward-Perkins, *The Econocracy: The Perils of Leaving Economics to the Experts* (Manchester: Manchester University Press, 2017), pp. 14–16.

36 Nicola Viegi, 'The economics of decolonisation: institutions, education and elite formation', *Theoria*, 147(63):2 (2016), 61–79. doi: 10.3167/th.2016.6314705.

37 Marion Fourcade, 'The construction of a global profession, 169.

38 Edward Berman, *The Influence of the Carnegie, Ford, and Rockefeller Foundations on American Foreign Policy: The Ideology of Philanthropy* (Albany: State University of New York Press, 1983), pp. 79–80 cited in Marion Fourcade, 'The construction of a global profession, 170.

39 Maria Loureiro, 'The professional and political impacts of the internationalization of economics in Brazil', in A.W. Bob Coats (ed.) *The Post-1945 Internationalization of Economics* (Durham, NC: Duke University Press, 1996), p. 192. Cited in Marion Fourcade, 'The construction of a global profession, 174.

40 Young Back Choi, 'The Americanization of economics in Korea', in A. W. Bob Coats (ed.) *The Post-1945 Internationalization of Economics* (Durham, NC: Duke University Press, 1996), pp. 97–122. Cited in Marion Fourcade, 'The construction of a global profession, 174.

41 *The Region*. 'Interview with Arnold Harberger, Dean of the Chicago Economists', March 1999. Published by the Federal Reserve Bank of Minneapolis. Cited in Marion Fourcade, 'The construction of a global profession, 180–181.

42 Table constructed from the Wikipedia, 'List of Nobel Memorial Prize laureates in Economics'. Available at: https://en.wikipedia.org/wiki/List_of_Nobel_Memorial_Prize_laureates_in_Economics (accessed 13 June 2021).

43 Jishnu Das, Quy-Toan Do, Karen Shaines, Sowmya Srikant, 'US and them: the geography of academic research', *Journal of Development Economics*, 105 (November 2013), 112–130. doi: https://doi.org/10.1016/j.jdeveco.2013.07.010.

44 Marion Fourcade, 'The construction of a global profession', 160.

45 Angus Deaton, *Randomization in the Tropics Revisited: A Theme and Eleven Variations*, Working Paper 27600. Working Paper Series (National Bureau of Economic Research, 2020), p. 3. doi: doi.org/10.3386/w27600.

46 Sabelo J. Ndlovu-Gatsheni, 'The dynamics of epistemological decolonisation in the 21st century: towards epistemic freedom', *Strategic Review for Southern Africa*, 40:1 (2018), 20. Available at: www.up.ac.za/media/shared/85/Strategic%20Review/vol%2040(1)/Ndlovu-Gatsheni.pdf (accessed 13 June 2021).

47 Richard Ely, *Studies in the Evolution of Industrial Society* (New York: Chautauqua Press, 1903), p. 139. Available at: https://ia800304.us.archive.org/31/items/studiesinevolutooelygoog/studiesinevolutooelygoog.pdf (accessed 13 June 2021).

48 Richard Ely, 'Fraternalism vs. paternalism in government', *Century*, 55:5 (1898), 781. Available at: www.unz.com/print/Century-1898mar-00780 (accessed 13 June 2021).

49 George Stigler, 'The problem of the negro', *New Guard* (December 1965). Reproduced online: https://digressionsnimpressions.typepad.com/digressionsimpressions/2020/06/stiglerracism.html (accessed 13 June 2021).

Chapter 3 Blind to structural inequality

1 Victoria Tauli-Corpuz, *Report of the Special Rapporteur on the Rights of Indigenous Peoples on Her Visit to Guatemala*, United Nations General Assembly, A/HRC/39/17/Add.3, September 2018, p. 3. Available at: https://undocs.org/A/HRC/39/17/Add.3 (accessed 18 May 2021).

2 Javier Urizar Montes De Oca, 'The heirs of colonial suffering in Guatemala', *Open Democracy*, 21 September 2020. Available at: www.opendemocracy.net/en/democraciaabierta/heirs-colonial-suffering-guatemala/ (accessed 18 May 2021).

Notes

3 Yael Schacher and Rachel Schmidtke, *Harmful Returns: The Compounded Vulnerabilities of Returned Guatemalans in the Time of Covid-19*, Refugees International, June 2020, p. 18. Available at: https://reliefweb.int/sites/reliefweb.int/files/resources/Yael%2BRachel%2B-%2BGuatemala%2B-%2BJun.%2B2020.pdf (accessed 18 May 2021).

4 Tauli-Corpuz, *Report of the Special Rapporteur*, p. 15.

5 *Ibid.*, p. 16.

6 US Census Bureau, 'Figure 8: Poverty rate and percentage point change by selected characteristics: people', *Annual Social and Economic Supplement of the Current Population Survey*. Available at: www.census.gov/content/dam/Census/library/visualizations/2020/demo/p60-270/Figure8.pdf (accessed 18 May 2021).

7 Oxfam International, 'India: extreme inequality in numbers' (n.d.). Available at: www.oxfam.org/en/india-extreme-inequality-numbers (accessed 1 June 2021).

8 Oxfam International, 'India'.

9 Omar Khan, 'The colour of money: how racial inequalities obstruct a fair and resilient economy', Runnymede Trust, April 2020, p. 8. Available at: www.runnymedetrust.org/uploads/publications/pdfs/2020%20reports/The%20Colour%20of%20Money%20Report.pdf (accessed 13 June 2021).

10 Fashion Revolution, '80% – the women who make our clothes', n.d. Available at: www.fashionrevolution.org/asia-vietnam-80-percent-exhibition/ (accessed 18 May 2021).

11 Based on figures by Labour Behind the Label, 'A living wage is a human right', related to the minimum wage in Sri Lanka of 10,000 Rps', n.d. Available at: https://labourbehindthelabel.org/campaigns/living-wage/ (accessed 18 May 2021).

12 UN Women, 'SDG 2: End hunger, achieve food security and improved nutrition and promote sustainable agriculture', n.d. Available at: www.unwomen.org/en/news/in-focus/women-and-the-sdgs/sdg-2-zero-hunger (accessed 18 May 2021).

13 United Nations Department of Economic and Social Affairs, *World Social Report 2020: Inequality in a Rapidly Changing World*, UN, 2020, p. 39. Available at: www.un.org/development/desa/dspd/wp-content/uploads/sites/22/2020/01/World-Social-Report-2020-FullReport.pdf (accessed 2 June 2021).

14   UN Women, *Gender Equality Rights in Review* (New York: UN, 2020), p. 7. Available at: www.unwomen.org/-/media/headquarters/attachments/ sections/library/publications/2020/gender-equality-womens-rights- in-review-en.pdf?la=en&vs=934 (accessed 18 May 2021).

15   Commission on a Gender Equal Economy/Women's Budget Group, *Creating a Caring Economy: A Call to Action*. Available at: https:// wbg.org.uk/wp-content/uploads/2020/10/WBG-Report-v10.pdf (accessed 18 May 2021).

16   UN Women, *Gender Equality Rights in Review*, p. 7.

17   Daniella Jenkins, 'Constructing gender equality in British pensions policy', paper presented at the *1st Annual Women's Budget Group Early Careers Network Conference*, University of Liverpool, 11 November 2019.

18   United Nations Department of Economic and Social Affairs, *World Social Report 2020*, p. 23.

19   World Bank, 'Life expectancy at birth, total (years), Central African Republic', 2019. Available at: https://data.worldbank.org/indicator/ SP.DYN.LE00.IN?locations=HT-CF (accessed 2 June 2021).

20   WHO, '9 out of 10 people worldwide breathe polluted air, but more countries are taking action', WHO, 2018. Available at: who.int/news/ item/02-05-2018-9-out-of-10-people-worldwide-breathe-polluted- air-but-more-countries-are-taking-action (accessed 9 June 2021).

21   Reproduced from Joe Earle, Cahal Moran and Zach Ward-Perkins, *The Econocracy: The Perils of Leaving Economics to the Experts* (Manchester: Manchester University Press, 2017), p. 38.

22   In recent years, behavioural economics has highlighted the many bar- riers to and limits of rationality in economic decision-making and this has been incorporated into economics in the idea of bounded ration- ality while retaining the three prongs outlined above.

23   Earle, Moran and Ward-Perkins, *The Econocracy*, pp. 35–36.

24   'IS' stands for Investment-Savings, while 'LM' stands for 'Liquidity Preference-Money'.

25   Other approaches such as agent-based modelling attempt to model economies with heterogeneous agents. It has been suggested by Paul Krugman that economists have partly avoided the problem because inequality is hard to model mathematically in the style of neoclassical economics. See Paul Krugman, 'Economists and

inequality', *New York Times* [Online], 8 January 2016. Available at: http://krugman.blogs.nytimes.com/2016/01/08/economists-and-inequality/ (accessed 19 May 2021).

26 Marion Fourcade, 'The construction of a global profession: the transnationalization of economics', *American Journal of Sociology*, 112:1 (July 2006), 145–194, 161.

27 Ha-Joon Chang, *Economics: The User's Guide* (London: Penguin Books, 2014), p. 126.

28 *Ibid.*, pp. 126–127.

29 Becker, 1957, cited in Ingrid Harvold Kvangraven and Surbhi Kesar, 'Why do economists have trouble understanding racialized inequalities?', Institute for New Economic Thinking, 3 August 2020. Available at: www.ineteconomics.org/perspectives/blog/why-do-economists-have-trouble-understanding-racialized-inequalities (accessed 18 May 2021).

30 For a review, see Arrow, 1998, cited in Kvangraven and Kesar, 'Why do economists have trouble understanding racialized inequalities?'.

31 Bill Spriggs, 'Is now a teachable moment for economists? An open letter to economists from Bill Spriggs', Howard University Department of Economics, p. 2. Available at: www.minneapolisfed.org/~/media/assets/people/william-spriggs/spriggs-letter_0609_b.pdf?la=en (accessed 19 May 2021).

32 Kevin Lang and Ariella Kahn-Lang Spitzer, 'Race discrimination: an economic perspective', *Journal of Economic Perspectives*, 34:2 (2020), 68–89. Available at: www.aeaweb.org/articles?id=10.1257/jep. 34.2.68 (accessed 19 May 2021).

33 Lisa Tilley and Robbie Shilliam, 'Raced markets: an introduction', *New Political Economy*, 23:5 (2018), 534–543. doi: 10.1080/13563467.2017.1417366.

34 William Darity Jr, Darrick Hamilton, Mark Paul, Alan Aja, Anne Price, Antonio Moore and Caterina Chiopris, *What We Get Wrong About Closing the Racial Wealth Gap* (Samuel DuBois Cook Center on Social Equity and the Insight Center for Community Economic Development, 2018). Available at: https://socialequity.duke.edu/wp-content/uploads/2019/10/what-we-get-wrong.pdf (accessed 19 May 2021).

35 Kyle Moore, 'The economics of race', *Phenomenal World*, 27 February 2020. Available at: https://phenomenalworld.org/analysis/ stratification-economics (accessed 7 June 2021).

36 See Darity, 2005 and Darity *et al.*, 2015 cited in Kvangraven and Kesar, 'Why do economists have trouble understanding racialized inequalities?'.

37 See Michael Reich, David M. Gordon and Richard C. Edwards, 'A theory of labor market segmentation', *American Economic Review*, 63:2 (1973), 359–365. Available at: www.jstor.org/stable/1817097 (accessed 19 May 2021).

38 Joelle Gamble, 'How economic assumptions uphold racist systems', *Dissent Magazine* [Online]. Available at: www.dissentmagazine.org/ online_articles/how-economic-assumptions-uphold-racist-systems (accessed 19 May 2021).

39 James Politi, 'African-American economic gap remains despite US expansion', *Financial Times* [Online], 5 June 2020. Available at: www.ft.com/content/6b3e23cc-645d-49c5-a63d-040de86b3d75 (accessed 19 May 2021).

40 Kvangraven and Kesar, 'Why do economists have trouble understanding racialized inequalities?'.

41 For critiques of this approach, see David Ruccio, 'Economics of poverty, or the poverty of economics', *Real World Economics Review Blog*, 15 October 2019. Available at: https://rwer.wordpress.com/ 2019/10/15/economics-of-poverty-or-the-poverty-of-economics/ (accessed 19 May 2021); Ingrid Harvold Kvangraven, 'Impoverished economics? A critical assessment of the new gold standard', *World Development*, 127 (2020), 104813, doi: 10.1016/j.worlddev.2019.104813; and Naila Kabeer, 'Women's empowerment and economic development: a feminist critique of storytelling practices in "randomista" economics', *Feminist Economics*, 26:2 (2020), 1–26, doi: 10.1080/ 13545701.2020.1743338. Economists' surprise that body cams don't reduce police brutality is another example, by Jennifer L. Doleac, 'Do body-worn cameras improve police behavior?', *Brookings Up Front* blog. Available at: www.brookings.edu/blog/up-front/2017/10/25/ do-body-worn-cameras-improve-police-behavior/ (accessed 19 May 2021). Recently, two heterodox economists summarised the problems

of attempting to address structural racism with micro-oriented and behavioural interventions. See Anastasia Wilson and Casey Buchholz, 'Abolition will not be randomized', *Developing Economics: A Critical Perspective on Development Economics* (15 June 2020). Available at: https://developingeconomics.org/2020/06/15/abolition-will-not-be-randomized/ (accessed 19 May 2021).

42 For example, a shop (the economy) has two pineapples and two mangoes and two people (customers). Person A likes pineapples, whereas Person B likes either. The Pareto optimal would be when Person A buys the two pineapples and Person B buys the two mangoes.

43 Amartya Sen and James Foster, *On Economic Inequality* (Oxford: Clarendon Press, 1997), p. 16.

44 For a more comprehensive critique of SWFs, see Peter Self, *Econocrats and the Policy Process* (London: Macmillan, 1975), pp. 14–25.

45 Robert Cooter and Peter Rappoport call these economists 'welfarists' and list Francis Edgeworth, Alfred Marshall, Irving Fisher, Arthur Pigou and John Bates Clark in Robert Cooter and Peter Rappoport, 'Were the ordinalists wrong about welfare economics?', *Journal of Economic Literature*, 22:2 (June 1984), 507–530.

46 This view didn't have much success when he published it in 1906 or his lifetime but was revived in the 1930s. This theory was later challenged and widely discredited but still plays a fundamental role in neoclassical analysis of redistribution and in university economics education.

47 See Lionel Robbins, *An Essay on the Nature and Significance of Economic Science*, second edition (London: Macmillan, 1935).

48 In addition, in the short run a residual (economic rent) is earned by the firm's owners who might be the entrepreneur or people who have invested money in the firm.

49 Gamble, 'How economic assumptions uphold racist systems'.

50 Joan Robinson, quoted in Rod Hill and Tony Myatt, *The Economics Anti-Textbook* (London: Zed Books, 2010), p. 179.

51 Josh Ryan-Collins, Toby Lloyd and Laurie Macfarlane, *Rethinking the Economics of Land and Housing* (London: Zed Books, 2017), p. 166.

52 *Ibid.*, pp. 52–57.

53 David Bentley, 'Reform of the land compensation rules: how much could it save on the cost of a public-sector housebuilding

programme?', CIVITAS – Institute for the Study of Civil Society, 2018, p. 2. Available at: www.civitas.org.uk/content/files/reformof thelandcompensationrules.pdf (accessed 19 May 2021).

54 Ryan-Collins, Lloyd and Macfarlane, *Rethinking the Economics of Land and Housing*, p. 39.

55 Brett Christophers, 'The PPE debacle shows what Britain is built on: rentier capitalism', *Guardian* [Online], 12 August 2020. Available at: www.theguardian.com/commentisfree/2020/aug/12/ppe-britain-rentier-capitalism-assets-uk-economy (accessed 19 May 2021).

56 Christophers, 'The PPE debacle'.

57 John Sloman and Alison Wride, *Economics*, seventh edition (Harlow: Pearson, 2009) p. 10. Loosely speaking, equity is fairness or equality.

58 Sloman and Wride, *Economics*, p. 304.

59 HM Treasury, *The Green Book: Central Government Guidance on Appraisal and Evaluation*, 2018. Available at: https://assets.publishing.service.gov.uk/government/uploads/system/uploads/attachment_data/file/938046/The_Green_Book_2020.pdf (accessed 19 May 2021).

60 Cahal Moran, 'Take care of the people, and the economy will take care of itself', *Open Democracy*, 12 March 2020. Available at: www.opendemocracy.net/en/oureconomy/take-care-people-and-economy-will-take-care-itself/ (accessed 19 May 2021).

61 Moran, 'Take care of the people, and the economy will take care of itself'.

Chapter 4 Whitewashes history

1 Jason Hickel, *The Great Divide: A Brief Guide to Global Inequality and its Solutions* (London: Penguin Random House, 2017), p. 3.

2 Melissa Dell, 'The persistent effects of Peru's mining *mita*', *Econometrica*, 78:6 (November 2010), 1863–1903. Available at: https://doi.org/10.3982/ECTA8121.

3 Nathan Nunn, 'The long-term effects of Africa's slave trades', *Quarterly Journal of Economics*, 123:1 (February 2008), 139–176. Available at: https://doi.org/10.1162/qjec.2008.123.1.139.

Notes

4   Stelios Michalopoulos and Elias Papaioannou, 'The long-run effects of the scramble for Africa', *American Economic Review*, 106:7 (July 2016), 1802–1848. Available at: 10.1257/aer.20131311.

5   The Core Team, *The Economy*, 'Unit 1: the capitalist revolution'. Available at: www.core-econ.org/the-economy/book/text/01.html#figure-1-1a (accessed 3 June 2021).

6   The Core Team, '1.3 History's hockey stick: growth in income', in *The Economy*. Available at: www.core-econ.org/the-economy/book/text/01.html#13-historys-hockey-stick-growth-in-income (accessed 7 June 2021).

7   Gerald Horne, 'The apocalypse of settler colonialism', *Monthly Review*, 69:11 (2018), p. 1. doi:10.14452/MR-069-11-2018-04_1. See also David Olusoga, *Black and British: A Forgotten History* (London: Macmillan, 2016).

8   Walter Johnson, 'To remake the world: slavery, racial capitalism, and justice', *Boston Review*, 20 February 2018. Available at: https://bostonreview.net/forum/walter-johnson-to-remake-the-world (accessed 7 June 2021).

9   Eric Williams, *Capitalism and Slavery* (Chapel Hill: The University of North Carolina Press), 1994.

10 Johnson, 'To remake the world: slavery, racial capitalism and justice'.

11 See Chapter 3 'Cross-continental nooses: catalyzed cotton and industrial wealth' in Donald E. Grant Jr, *Black Men, Intergenerational Colonialism, and Behavioral Health* (US: Palgrave Macmillan, 2019), p. xiv. doi: 10.1007/978-3-030-21114-1_3.

12 Walter Johnson, 'To remake the world: slavery, racial capitalism, and justice'.

13 *Ibid.*

14 *Ibid.*

15 Philip Roscoe, 'How the shadow of slavery still hangs over global finance', *The Conversation*, 21 August 2020. Available at: https://theconversation.com/how-the-shadow-of-slavery-still-hangs-over-global-finance-144826 (accessed 19 May 2021).

16 Angus Madison, *The World Economy: A Millennial Perspective* (Paris: Development Studies Centre of the OECD, 2001). Available at:

http://theunbrokenwindow.com/Development/MADDISON%20 The%20World%20Economy--A%20Millennial.pdf (accessed 19 May 2021).

17 Walter Johnson, 'To remake the world: slavery, racial capitalism, and justice'.

18 Holocaust Museum Houston, 'Genocide of Indigenous Peoples', HMH, n.d. Available at: https://tinyurl.com/1a36mbmp (accessed 19 May 2021).

19 Holocaust Museum Houston, 'Genocide of Indigenous Peoples'.

20 Hickel, *The Great Divide*, p. 72.

21 Denis Cogneau and Alexander Moradi, 'British and French educational legacies in Africa', *VoxEU and CEPR*, 17 May 2014. Available at: https://voxeu.org/article/british-and-french-educational-legacies-africa (accessed 20 May 2021).

22 Three examples of economic research cited in Yannick Dupraz and Valeria Rueda, 'There is no "case for colonialism": insights from the colonial economic history', Africa at LSE blog, 17 October 2017. Available at: https://blogs.lse.ac.uk/africaatlse/2017/10/17/there-is-no-case-for-colonialism-insights-from-the-colonial-economic-history/ (accessed 19 May 2021).

23 Dupraz and Rueda, 'There is no "case for colonialism"'.

24 While not formally colonised, Liberia was founded by the American Colonization Society as a colony for freed African American slaves in 1821. See Bhattacharyya, *Rethinking Racial Capitalism*, p. 80. In return for their apparent 'independence', Liberia and Ethiopia were forced to give up territory, agree to differing degrees of European economic control, and become participants in European spheres of influence. See Alistair Boddy-Evans, 'Countries in Africa considered never colonized', ThoughtCo., 2020. Available at: www.thoughtco.com/countries-in-africa-considered-never-colonized-43742 (accessed 3 June 2021).

25 Gurminder Bhambra, *Imperial Revenue and National Welfare: The Case of Britain*, paper given at the Imperial Inequalities conference, [YouTube], Tax Justice Network. Available at: www.youtube.com/watch?v=suo2mQ129FY&list=PLPle_vPYGn5znpobLMCgRqois-vSHpg7C&index=6 (accessed 7 June 2021).

Notes

26 BBC Bitesize, 'Why the Liberals introduced social welfare reforms', History (Higher). Available at: www.bbc.co.uk/bitesize/guides/z83ggk7/revision/5 (accessed 22 May 2021).

27 Guppi Bola, *Reimagining Public Health* (UK: CommonWealth, June 2020). Available at: https://tinyurl.com/2budba45 (accessed 22 May 2021).

28 See also Franz Fanon (1961), *Wretched of the Earth* (Harmondsworth: Penguin, 1967); Ranajit Guha and Gayatri Chakravorty Spivak, *Selected Subaltern Studies* (Oxford: Oxford University Press, 1988).

29 Walter Rodney, *How Europe Underdeveloped Africa* (London: Bogle-L'Ouverture Publications, 1972).

30 Gurminder K. Bhambra, 'Colonial global economy: towards a theoretical reorientation of political economy', *Review of International Political Economy*, 28:2 (2021), 307–322, p. 12. doi: 10.1080/09692290.2020.1830831.

31 Ann Laura Stoler, *Carnal Knowledge and Imperial Power: Race and the Intimate in Colonial Rule*, second edition (London: University of California Press, 2002), p. 47. doi: 10.2307/j.ctv15d80x0.8.

32 Nancy Folbre, *The Rise and Decline of Patriarchal Systems* (London: Verso, 2020), pp. 126–127.

33 *Ibid.*, pp. 126–127.

34 *Ibid.*

35 Stoler, *Carnal Knowledge and Imperial Power*, pp. 47–48.

36 *Ibid.*, p. 48.

37 *Ibid.*, p. 48.

38 John Maynard Keynes, 'J.M. Keynes reflected on that "happy age" of international commerce and freedom of travel that was destroyed by the cataclysm of the First World War (1920)', Online Library of Liberty. Available at: https://oll.libertyfund.org/quotes/88 (accessed 19 May 2021).

39 Dani Rodrik, *The Globalization Paradox: Why Global Markets, States and Democracy Can't Coexist* (Oxford: Oxford University Press, 2011), p. 37.

40 Thomas Piketty, *Capital in the Twenty-First Century* (Cambridge: Harvard University Press, 2014), p. 69.

41 *Ibid.*

Notes

42   Dani Rodrik, *The Globalization Paradox: Why Global Markets, States, and Democracy Can't Coexist*, (Oxford: Oxford University Press, 2012), pp. 38–39.

43   *Ibid.*

44   Daron Acemoglu and James Robinson, *Why Nations Fail: The Origins of Power, Prosperity and Poverty* (New York: Crown, 2012).

45   Catherine Hall, Nicholas Draper, Keith McClelland, Katie Donington and Rachel Lang, *Legacies of British Slave-ownership: Colonial Slavery and the Formation of Victorian Britain* (Cambridge: Cambridge University Press, 2016), pp. 19–20.

46   Dupraz and Rueda, 'There is no "case for colonialism"'.

47   Daron Acemoglu, Simon Johnson and James A. Robinson, 'The colonial origins of comparative development: an empirical investigation', *American Economic Review*, 91:5 (2001), 1369–1401. Available at: https://economics.mit.edu/files/4123 (accessed 20 May 2021).

48   For example, this paper considers how lack of control of the financial sector has limited the economic sovereignty of post-Independence Ghana and Senegal: Kai Koddenbrock, Ingrid H. Kvangraven and Ndongo S. Sylla, 'Beyond financialisation: the need for a longue durée understanding of finance in imperialism', *OSF Preprints*, 2020. Available at: doi:10.31219/osf.io/pjt7x.

49   Tax Justice Network, 'Tax havens and secrecy jurisdictions', n.d. Available at: www.taxjustice.net/topics/tax-havens-and-secrecy-jurisdictions/ (accessed 20 May 2021).

50   Vanessa Ogle, '"Funk money": the end of empires, the expansion of tax havens, and decolonization as an economic and financial event', *Past & Present*, 249:1 (November 2020), 213–249, 246. Available at: https://doi.org/10.1093/pastj/gtaa001.

51   *Ibid.*, pp. 228–230.

52   *Ibid.*

53   *Ibid.*

54   *Ibid.*

55   *Ibid.*, pp. 241–242.

56   *Ibid.*, p. 248.

57   Mark Bou Mansour, '$427bn lost to tax havens every year: landmark study reveals countries' losses and worst offenders', Tax Justice

Network, 20 November 2020. Available at: www.taxjustice.net/2020/11/20/427bn-lost-to-tax-havens-every-year-landmark-study-reveals-countries-losses-and-worst-offenders/ (accessed 24 May 2021).

58 Olusoga, *Black and British*, pp. 230–231.

59 Naomi Fowler, 'Britain's slave owner compensation loan, reparations and tax havenry', Tax Justice Network, 9 June 2020. Available at:www.taxjustice.net/2020/06/09/slavery-compensation-uk-questions/ (accessed 19 May 2021). Note that research builds on UCL's Centre for the Study of the Legacies of British Slavery's *British Slave-ownership* project (2009–2012), and the *Structure and Significance of British Caribbean Slave-ownership 1763–1833* project (2013–2015), available at: www.ucl.ac.uk/lbs/ (accessed 19 May 2021).

60 Naomi Klein, 'Democracy born in chains', 13 February 2011. Originally published in Naomi Klein, *The Shock Doctrine: The Rise of Disaster Capitalism* (Toronto: Alfred A. Knopf, 2007). Available at: https://naomiklein.org/democracy-born-chains/ (accessed 23 May 2021).

61 *Ibid.*

62 Mansour, '$427bn lost to tax havens every year'.

63 Marion Fourcade, 'The construction of a global profession: the transnationalization of economics', *American Journal of Sociology*, 112:1 (July 2006), 145–194, 166.

64 Rodrik, *The Globalization Paradox.*

65 Wolfram Elsner and Gerhard Hanappi, *Varieties of Capitalism and New Institutional Deals: Regulation, Welfare and the New Economy* (Cheltenham, UK: Edward Elgar, 2008).

66 The Core Team, '1.6 Capitalism defined: private property, markets and firms', in *The Economy.* Available at: www.core-econ.org/the-economy/book/text/01.html#16-capitalism-defined-private-property-markets-and-firms (accessed 7 June 2021).

67 Sven Beckert, *Empire of Cotton* (Harlow: Penguin Books, 2015).

68 Cited in Suse Steed, 'How can you do an economics degree in Britain without learning about the British Empire? Thoughts on the toxic combination of the violence and denial of empire'. Available at: https://susesteed.medium.com/how-is-it-possible-to-do-an-economics-degree-without-learning-about-britains-role-in-the-slave-aa5449937429 (accessed 20 May 2021).

69 Rodrik, *The Globalization Paradox.*

70 The Core Team, '1.6 Capitalism defined: private property, markets and firms'.

71 Josh Ryan-Collins, Toby Lloyd and Laurie Macfarlane, *Rethinking the Economics of Land and Housing* (London: Zed Books, 2017), pp. 16–29.

72 Rodrik, *The Globalization Paradox*, p. 6.

73 *Ibid.*, p. 9.

74 *Ibid.*, pp. 10–11.

75 '[t]he question of genocide is never far from discussions of settler colonialism', cited in Patrick Wolfe, 'Settler colonialism and the elimination of the native', *Journal of Genocide Research*, 8:4 (2006), 387–409. doi: 10.1080/14623520601056240.

76 David Harvey, *A Companion to Marx's Capital* (London: Verso, 2010), p. 284.

77 Mari Marcel Thekaekara, 'A huge land grab is threatening India's tribal people. They need global help', *Guardian* [Online], 25 February 2019. Available at: www.theguardian.com/commentisfree/2019/feb/25/land-grab-tribal-people-india-adivasi (accessed 20 May 2021).

78 Walter Fernandes, 'Indian tribes after sixty years – a study', 27 November 2008. Available at: http://sanhati.com/articles/1094/ (accessed 14 June 2021).

79 See Global Witness, 'Defending tomorrow: the climate crisis and threats against land and environmental defenders', *Global Witness*, June 2020. Available at: www.globalwitness.org/en/campaigns/environmental-activists/defending-tomorrow/ (accessed 20 May 2021).

80 See Pesticide Action Network International for more information. Available at: http://pan-international.org/ (accessed 20 May 2021).

81 D. R. Williams *et al.*, 'Proactive conservation to prevent habitat losses to agricultural expansion', *Nature Sustainability*, 4 (2021), 314–322. doi: 10.1038/s41893-020-00656-5.

82 Karl Polanyi, *The Great Transformation: The Political and Economic Origins of Our Time*, 2nd edition (Boston: Beacon, 2001), pp. 75–76.

83 Katharina Pistor, *The Code of Capital: How the Law Creates Wealth and Inequality* (Princeton, NJ: Princeton University Press, 2019), p. 2.

84 *Ibid.*, p. 3.

85 *Ibid.*, p. 4.

86 *Ibid.*, p. 20.

87 Rose Deller, 'Book review: *An Anthropology of Marxism* by Cedric J. Robinson', *LSE Blog*, 14 May 2019. Available at: https://blogs.lse.ac.uk/lsereviewofbooks/2019/05/14/book-review-an-anthropology-of-marxism-by-cedric-robinson/ (accessed 20 May 2021).

88 Robin D. G. Kelley, 'What did Cedric Robinson mean by racial capitalism?', *Boston Review*, 12 January 2017. Available at: http://bostonreview.net/race/robin-d-g-kelley-what-did-cedric-robinson-mean-racial-capitalism (accessed 20 May 2021).

89 Walter Johnson, 'To remake the world: slavery, racial capitalism, and justice'.

90 Fowler, 'Britain's slave owner compensation loan, reparations and tax havenry'.

91 Bhambra, 'Colonial global economy', pp. 307–322.

92 Suse Steed, 'Why I can't teach economics anymore'. Available at: https://susesteed.medium.com/why-i-cant-teach-economics-anymore-55c67c90a5fe (accessed 20 May 2021).

93 Ingrid Harvold Kvangraven and Surbhi Kesar, 'Why do economists have trouble understanding racialized inequalities?', Institute for New Economic Thinking, 3 August 2020. Available at: www.ineteconomics.org/perspectives/blog/why-do-economists-have-trouble-understanding-racialized-inequalities (accessed 18 May 2021).

Chapter 5 Undermining democracy and development

1 Grieve Chelwa, 'Pop developmentalism in Africa', in Godwin Murunga and Ibrahim Ogachi, *Randomised Control Trials and Development Research in Africa – Special Issue*, The Council for the Development of Social Science Research in Africa, Number 1, 2020, p. 3.

2 Albert Hirschman, *The Essential Hirschman* (Princeton, NJ: Princeton University Press, 2013). Cited in Grieve Chelwa, 'Pop developmentalism in Africa', p. 4.

3 Thandika Mkandawire and Charles Soludo, *Our Continent, Our Future: African Perspectives on Structural Adjustment* (Dakar: CODESRIA, 1998). Cited in Grieve Chelwa, 'Pop developmentalism in Africa', p. 4.

4 Grieve Chelwa, 'Pop developmentalism in Africa', p. 4.

5   *Ibid.*
6   See, for example, Ha-Joon Chang, *Kicking Away the Ladder* (London: Anthem Press, 2002).
7   Thandika Mkandawire, 'Thinking about development states in Africa', *Cambridge Journal of Economics*, 25 (2001), 289–313, cited in Grieve Chelwa, 'Pop developmentalism in Africa', p. 5.
8   Seán Mfundza Muller, Grieve Chelwa and Nimi Hoffmann, 'How randomised trials became big in development economics', *The Conversation*, 9 December 2019. Available at: https://theconversation.com/how-randomised-trials-became-big-in-development-economics-128398 (accessed 23 May 2021).
9   In this section we draw significantly on Ingrid Harvold Kvangraven, 'Nobel rebels in disguise – assessing the rise and rule of the randomistas', *Review of Political Economy*, 32:3 (2020), 305–341.
10   Naila Kabeer, 'Women's empowerment and economic development: a feminist critique of storytelling practices in "randomista" economics', *Feminist Economics* 26:2 (2020), 20, cited in Ingrid Harvold Kvangraven, 'Nobel rebels in disguise', p. 314.
11   This point was made by Timothy Mitchell, 'The work of economics: how a discipline makes its world', *European Journal of Sociology*, 46 (2005), 297–320.
12   Nimi Hoffman, 'Involuntary experiments in former colonies: the case for a moratorium', *World Development*, 127 (2020). Cited in Ingrid Harvold Kvangraven, 'Nobel rebels in disguise', p. 327. Ingrid Harvold Kvangraven, 'Nobel rebels in disguise', p. 328.
13   *Ibid.*
14   Arthur Jatteau, 'The success of randomized controlled trials: a sociographical study of the rise of J-PAL to scientific excellence and influence', *Historical Social Research / Historische Sozialforschung*, 43: 3 (2018), 95.
15   Seán Mfundza Muller, Grieve Chelwa and Nimi Hoffmann, 'How randomised trials became big in development economics'.
16   *Ibid.*
17   John Gapper, 'Lunch with the FT: Esther Duflo.' *The Financial Times*, 17 March 2012. Available at: www.ft.com/content/81804a1a-6d08-11e1-ab1a-00144feab49a (accessed 13 June 2021). Cited in Ingrid Harvold Kvangraven, 'Nobel rebels in disguise', p. 320.

18 Polly Hill, *Development Economics on Trial: The Anthropological Case for the Prosecution* (Cambridge: Cambridge University Press, 1986).

19 The flaws in the theoretical treatment of collective choice in economics, or in the way those treatments have been interpreted and used, have been demonstrated by Amartya Sen, 'The possibility of social choice', *American Economic Review*, 89:3 (June 1999), 349–378, and Hugh Stretton and Lionel Orchard, *Public Goods, Public Enterprise, Public Choice: Theoretical Foundations of the Contemporary Attack on Government* (London: Macmillan Press, 1994).

20 John Alford, 'Defining the client in the public sector: a social-exchange perspective', *Public Administration Review*, 62:3 (2002), 339.

21 Paul Studenski, 'Government as producer', *Annals of the American Academy of Political and Social Science*, 206:1 (1 November 1939), 34.

22 Perfect competition occurs when all producers sell identical products and none can influence the market price of their product which is solely determined by demand from consumers. Perfect competition is assumed to hold for analysis of the basic supply and demand diagram we saw in Chapter 3.

23 Shoshana Zuboff explores how this phenomenon is an example of a deeper shift in capitalism in Shoshana Zuboff, *The Age of Surveillance Capitalism: The Fight for a Human Future at the New Frontier of Power* (New York: Public Affairs, 2019).

24 This organisation has an interesting, if strange, history: it started life as a government institution, but now describes itself as a social purpose company, jointly owned by the UK Government, Nesta (the innovation charity) and its employees.

25 Behavioural Insights Team, 'Who we are: the Behavioural Insights Team'. Available at: www.behaviouralinsights.co.uk/about-us/ (accessed 23 May 2021).

26 James C. Scott, *Seeing Like a State: How Certain Schemes to Improve the Human Condition Have Failed* (New Haven: Yale University Press, 1999).

27 Dani Rodrik, *The Globalization Paradox: Why Global Markets, States and Democracy Can't Coexist* (Oxford: Oxford University Press, 2011), pp. 180–181.

28 Rodrik, *The Globalization Paradox*, pp. 180–181.
29 Naomi Klein, 'Democracy born in chains', 13 February 2011. Originally published in Naomi Klein, *The Shock Doctrine: The Rise of Disaster Capitalism* (Toronto: Alfred A. Knopf, 2007). Available at: https://naomiklein.org/democracy-born-chains/ (accessed 23 May 2021).
30 *Ibid.*
31 *Ibid.*
32 *Ibid.*
33 *Ibid.*
34 *Ibid.*
35 *Ibid.*
36 *Ibid.*
37 Rodrik, *The Globalization Paradox*, pp. 179–180.
38 Klein, 'Democracy born in chains'.
39 *Ibid.*
40 See, for example, John Huston and Roger Spencer, 'The wealth effects of quantitative easing', *Atlantic Economic Journal*, 44:4 (2016), 471–486, and Fredj Jawadi, Ricardo M. Sousa and Raffaella Traverso, 'On the macroeconomic and wealth effects of unconventional monetary policy', *Macroeconomic Dynamics*, 21:5 (2017), 1189–1204.
41 Treasury bonds are seen as low risk as a government can always service its debts through the income it receives from taxes.
42 See for example Fredj Jawadi, Ricardo Sousa and Raffaella Traverso, 'On the macroeconomic and wealth effects of unconventional monetary policy', *Macroeconomic Dynamics*, 21:05 (2016), 1189–1204. Henning Hesse, Boris Hofmann and James Weber, 'The macroeconomic effects of asset purchases revisited', *Journal of Macroeconomics*, 58, 2018, pp. 115–138. Luiz Lima, Claudio Foffano Vasconcelos, Jose Simão and Helder Ferreira de Mendonça, 'The quantitative easing effect on the stock market of the USA, the UK and Japan: an ARDL approach for the crisis period', *Journal of Economic Studies*, 43:6 (2016), 1006–1021.
43 Rakesh Kochhar and Richard Fry, 'Wealth inequality has widened along racial, ethnic lines since end of Great Recession' Pew Research Center [online], 2014. Available from: www.pewresearch.org/fact-tank/2014/12/12/racial-wealth-gaps-great-recession/ (accessed 14 June 2021).

44 Karuna Jaggar, 'The race and gender wealth gap', *Race, Poverty & the Environment*, 15:2 (2008), 79–81.

45 Gregory Sharp and Matthew Hall, 'Emerging forms of racial inequality in homeownership exit, 1968–2009', *Social Problems*, 61:3 (2014), 427–447.

46 Ngina Chiteji, 'The racial wealth gap and the borrower's dilemma', *Journal of Black Studies*, 41:2 (2010), 351–366.

47 Stephanie Seguino, 'Engendering macroeconomic theory and policy', *Feminist Economics*, 26:2 (2019), 27–61.

48 See, for example, Marco Casiraghi, Eugenio Gaiotti, Lisa Rodano and Alessandro Secchi, 'A "reverse Robin Hood"? The distributional implications of non-standard monetary policy for Italian households', *Journal of International Money and Finance*, 85:C (2018), 215–235.

49 Raoul Martinez, *Creating Freedom: Power, Control and the Fight for our Future* (Edinburgh: Canongate Books, 2017), p. 159.

50 The term EDC was introduced by two economists to describe social conflicts born from the unfair access to natural resources and the unjust burdens of pollution. See Joan Martinez-Alier and Martin O'Connor, 'Ecological and economic distribution conflicts', in Robert Costanza, Joan Martinez-Alier and Olman Segura (eds), *Getting Down to Earth: Practical Applications of Ecological Economics* (Washington, DC: Island Press/ISEE, 1996).

51 Visit the website Environmental Justice Atlas, available at: https://ejatlas.org/ (accessed 24 May 2021) or see Leah Temper, Daniela del Bene and Joan Martinez-Alier, 'Mapping the frontiers and front lines of global environmental justice: the EJAtlas', *Journal of Political Ecology*, 22 (2015), 255–278.

52 See Central Electricity Authority, '2018 Report of the Central Electricity Authority', Government of India, 2018. Available at: https://cea.nic.in/old/reports/annual/annualreports/annual_report-2018.pdf (accessed 10 June 2021).

53 See Ilmi Granoff *et al.*, 'FAQ: coal, poverty and the environment', ODI, n.d. Available at: https://odi.org/en/about/our-work/climate-and-sustainability/faq-coal-poverty-and-the-environment/ (accessed 24 May 2021).

54 Aruna Chandrasekhar, 'Jharkhand villagers ask why should they lose land for Adani project supplying power to Bangladesh', *Scroll.in*, 13 June 2018. Available at: https://scroll.in/article/882342/jharkhand-villagers-ask-why-should-they-lose-land-for-adani-project-supplying-power-to-bangladesh (accessed 24 May 2021).

55 Newsclick Report, 'India: protesting > 40K trees cut for mine, police crack down', Housing and Land Rights Network/ Habitat International Coalition, 12 December 2019. Available at: www.hlrn.org/activitydetails.php?id=pm1maA==#.YKtoRahKg2w (accessed 24 May 2021).

56 Chitrangada Choudhury, 'We believe 15,000 trees have already been cut', People's Archive of Rural India, 18 December 2019. Available at: https://ruralindiaonline.org/en/articles/we-believe-15000-trees-have-already-been-cut/ (accessed 24 May 2021).

57 See Amnesty International, cited in Rina Chandran, 'India's coal mining ambition hurts indigenous group, Amnesty says', *Reuters*, 13 July 2016. Available at: www.reuters.com/article/india-coal-displacement-tribals-mining-idINKCN0ZT0YP (accessed 24 May 2021).

Chapter 6 Reforming academia

1 University of Cambridge, 'Meaning of diversity in English', Cambridge Dictionary. Available at: https://dictionary.cambridge.org/dictionary/english/diversity (accessed 22 May 2021).

2 Originating as a concept from Maria Stewart's writings in 1831, Sojourner Truth's 1851 'Ain't I a woman?' speech, among many other influential early Black feminists, the idea of 'intersectionality' is not a new concept. Savitribai Phule's advocacy of gender and caste oppressions in India can also be considered as early advocacy of the concept. See F. Tormos, 'Intersectional solidarity', *Politics, Groups, and Identities*, 5:4 (2017), 707–720, doi: 10.1080/21565503.2017.1385494; Avtar Brah and Ann Phoenix, 'Ain't I a woman? Revisiting intersectionality', *Journal of International Women's Studies*, 5:3 (2004), 75–86. Available at: https://vc.bridgew.edu/jiws/vol5/iss3/8 (accessed 22 May 2021). The term 'intersectionality' was officially coined by lawyer Kimberlé Crenshaw in 1989 as a critique of the US legal system that failed to recognise the complexities

Notes

of discrimination against Black American women. To Crenshaw, this system saw racism and sexism as exclusive of one another and not interlocking or cumulative structures of oppression. See Kimberlé Crenshaw, 'Demarginalizing the intersection of race and sex: a black feminist critique of antidiscrimination doctrine, feminist theory and antiracist politics', *University of Chicago Legal Forum*, 1:8 (1989), 139–167. Available at: http://chicagounbound.uchicago.edu/uclf/vol1989/iss1/8 (accessed 22 May 2021). Intersectionality is a powerful analytical tool to understand overlapping identities and their impacts on power relations resulting in inequalities and injustices. See also Supurna Banerjee, 'Intersectionality and spaces of belonging: understanding the tea plantation workers in Dooars', Occasional Paper No. 46, Institute of Development Studies Kolkata, March 2015. Available at: http://idsk.edu.in/wp-content/uploads/2015/07/OP-46.pdf (accessed May 2021).

3   Promoting Economic Pluralism, 'What is a pluralist approach to teaching economics?'. Available at: https://economicpluralism.org/accreditation/what-is-economic-pluralism/ (accessed 13 June 2021).

4   Fanta Traore, '19 Black economists to celebrate and know, this Juneteenth and beyond', *Fortune* [Online], 19 June 2020. Available at: https://fortune.com/2020/06/19/black-economists-fixing-systemic-racism-juneteenth/ (accessed 5 June 2021).

5   J. Morgan and W. K. Olsen, 'Aspiration problems for the Indian rural poor: research on self-help groups and micro-finance', *Capital and Class*, 35:2 (2011), 189–212. Available at: https://tinyurl.com/r6ahvfa5 (accessed 5 June 2021).

6   Quoted in Edwin Dolan, 'Austrian economics as extraordinary science', in Edwin Dolan (ed.), *The Foundations of Modern Austrian Economics* (Kansas City: Sheed & Ward, Inc., 1976).

7   Clearly, Western empires are not the only empires with presence and significance in world history. While they are the most relevance reference point for the context of the work we are doing, in other contexts there will be multiple legacies to contend with. 'Decolonisation' as a project is something that is necessarily context-specific in terms of its aims and practices, as evidenced by the variety of thought and action taking place in the UK, South Africa, South America, Australia and former Soviet Republics.

8   Colorado Funders for Inclusiveness and Equity, *The Four 'I's' of Oppression*, 2010. Available at: www.coloradoinclusivefunders.org/uploads/1/1/5/0/11506731/the_four_is_of_oppression.pdf (accessed 22 May 2021).

9   Here we refer to Sam Moyo. His strong commitment towards autonomous knowledge production from the South was particularly important. Indeed, according to the book editors, Moyo's intellectual journey laid down the principle of epistemic sovereignty. See Dzodzi Tsikata, 'Sam Moyo: a life of prodigious scholarship, institution building and strategic activism', *Development and Change*, 48:5 (2017), 1154–1167. doi: 10.1111/dech.12335.

10   Miriam Lang, 'Prologue: the crisis of civilisation and challenges for the left beyond development', pp. 5–14, in M. Lang and G. Mokrani, *Beyond Development: Alternative Visions from Latin America* (Amsterdam/Quito: Transnational Institute / Rosa Luxemburg Foundation, 2013). Available at: www.tni.org/en/publication/beyond-development (accessed 22 May 2021).

11   Indigenomics Institute (n.d.), 'About Indigenomics'. Available at: http://indigenomicsinstitute.com/about-us/ (accessed 13 June 2021).

12   The Alternative UK, 'A startling new book from Australia – "Sand Talk: How Indigenous Thinking Can Save The World" – gives lessons in complexity', *The Alternative UK*, 18 July 2020. Available at: www.thealternative.org.uk/dailyalternative/2020/7/19/sand-talk (accessed 22 May 2021).

13   Nayantara Sheoran Appleton, 'Do not "decolonize" … if you are not decolonizing: progressive language and planning beyond a hollow academic rebranding', *Critical Ethnic Studies Blog*, 4 February 2019. Available at: www.criticalethnicstudiesjournal.org/blog/2019/1/21/do-not-decolonize-if-you-are-not-decolonizing-alternate-language-to-navigate-desires-for-progressive-academia-6y5sg (accessed 5 June 2021).

14   See E. Tuck and K. W. Yang, 'Decolonization is not a metaphor', *Decolonization: Indigeneity, Education & Society*, 1:1 (2012), 1–40. Available at: https://jps.library.utoronto.ca/index.php/des/article/view/18630/15554 (accessed 22 May 2021) and Decolonising SOAS Working, 'Decolonising SOAS Learning and Teaching Toolkit for Programme and Module Convenors Group', School of Oriental

and African Studies, London, May 2018. Available at: https://blogs.soas.ac.uk/decolonisingsoas/files/2018/10/Decolonising-SOAS-Learning-and-Teaching-Toolkit-AB.pdf (accessed 22 May 2021).

15 Katharina Pistor, *The Code of Capital: How the Law Creates Wealth and Inequality* (Princeton, NJ: Princeton University Press, 2019).

16 Lang and Mokrani, *Beyond Development*.

17 Erik S. Reinert, Jayati Ghosh and Rainer Kattel (eds), *Handbook of Alternative Theories of Economic Development* (Cheltenham: Edward Elgar Publishing, 2018).

18 Ingrid H. Kvangraven, 'A prize to be expected', Twitter post, 14 October 2019. Available at: https://twitter.com/ingridharvold/status/1183722222118166529?lang=en (accessed 5 June 2021).

19 See P. McIntosh, 'White privilege and male privilege: a personal account of coming to see correspondences through work in women's studies', [Online] Working Paper 189 (Wellesley, MA: Wellesley College Centre for Research on Women, 1988). Available at: www.wcwonline.org/images/pdf/White_Privilege_and_Male_Privilege_Personal_Account-Peggy_McIntosh.pdf (accessed 5 June 2021).

20 Joe Earle, Cahal Moran and Zach Ward-Perkins, *The Econocracy: The Perils of Leaving Economics to the Experts* (Manchester: Manchester University Press, 2017).

21 Appleton, 'Do not "decolonize" … if you are not decolonizing'.

Chapter 7 Everyday democracy

1 This research is summarised in Johnny Runge and Nathan Hudson, 'Public understanding of economics and economic statistics', Economic Statistics Centre of Excellence Occasional Paper, 3 November 2020; and David Leiser and Yhonatan Shemesh, *How We Misunderstand Economics and Why It Matters – The Psychology of Bias, Distortion and Conspiracy* (Abingdon: Routledge, 2018).

2 Runge and Hudson, 'Public understanding of economics and economic statistics'.

3 Ali Norrish, *What's the Economy? Exploring How People Feel About Economics and Why We Need to Improve It* (UK: Economy, 2017).

Available at: www.ecnmy.org/wp-content/uploads/2017/11/Exploring-How-People-Feel-About-Economics-Research-Report-2017-ecnmy.org_.pdf (accessed 23 May 2021).

4   New Economy Organisers Network, *Framing the Economy – How to Win the Case for a Better System* (UK: NEON, 2018). Available at: https://neweconomics.org/uploads/files/Framing-the-Economy-NEON-NEF-FrameWorks-PIRC.pdf (accessed 23 May 2021).

5   Anna Killick, *Rigged: Understanding the Economy in Brexit Britain* (Manchester: Manchester University Press, 2020) and Anna Killick, 'Impersonal forces versus a rigged economy: a political ethnographic study of everyday actors' understanding of "the economy" in post-crisis Britain', 2018. Available at: www.psa.ac.uk/sites/default/files/conference/papers/2018/Impersonal%20forces%20versus%20a%20rigged%20economy.pdf (accessed 23 May 2021).

6   The top-down and bottom-up distinction is drawn from Runge and Hudson, 'Public understanding of economics and economic statistics', p. 172.

7   Anna Killick, 'Do people really lack knowledge about the economy? A reply to Facchini', *The Political Quarterly*, 88:2 (2017), 265–272.

8   Runge and Hudson, 'Public understanding of economics and economic statistics', pp. 174–175.

9   Killick, 'Do people really lack knowledge about the economy?'.

10   Runge and Hudson, 'Public understanding of economics and economic statistics', p. 176.

11   A history explored in Joe Earle, Cahal Moran and Zach Ward-Perkins, *The Econocracy: The Perils of Leaving Economics to the Experts* (Manchester: Manchester University Press, 2017).

12   Kate Raworth, *Doughnut Economics: Seven Ways to Think Like a 21st Century Economist* (London: Penguin Random House, 2017).

13   We draw here on ideas from The Foundational Economy Collective, *Foundational Economy: The Infrastructure of Everyday Life* (Manchester: Manchester University Press, 2018).

14   Paolo Freire, *Pedagogy of the Oppressed* (New York: Herder and Herder, 1972).

15   By scrolling out from this link you can see a global map of where mutual aid groups are based: https://covidmutualaid.org/local-groups/

(accessed 13 April 2021). Another example of community responses to this crisis is the C19 People's Coalition group in South Africa. Available at: https://c19peoplescoalition.org.za/about-us/ (accessed 6 June 2021).

16 Luca Calafati, Julie Froud, Colin Haslam, Sukhdev Johal and Karel Williams, *Meeting Social Needs on a Damaged Planet: Foundational Economy 2.0 and the Care-ful Practice of Radical Policy* (Foundational Economy Collective, 2021). Available at: https://foundationaleconomycom.files.wordpress.com/2021/01/fe-wp8-meeting-social-needs-on-a-damaged-planet.pdf (accessed 23 May 2021).

17 This section draws on the argument made by James Scott, *Seeing Like a State: How Certain Conditions to Improve the Human Condition Have Failed* (New Haven: Yale University Press, 1998).

18 Scott calls this knowledge Metis. Scott, *Seeing Like a State*, p. 311.

19 Scott, *Seeing Like a State*, pp. 319–323.

20 *Ibid.*, p. 336.

21 *Ibid.*, pp. 337–338.

22 In the UK, the Royal Society of the Arts (RSA) ran a Citizens' Economic Panel Programme and the final report summarises work in this space and makes recommendations. RSA, *Building a Public Culture of Economics* (London: RSA, 2018). Available at: https://web.archive.org/web/20190119095954/https://www.thersa.org/globalassets/pdfs/reports/building-a-public-culture-of-economics.pdf (accessed 23 May 2021).

23 Paul Griffin, *The Carbon Majors Database: CDP Carbon Majors Report 2017* (London: CDP UK/Climate Accountability Institute, 2017). Available at: https://tinyurl.com/28f4mxzp (accessed 6 June 2021).

24 Fernando Belinchón and Qayyah Moynihan, '25 giant companies that are bigger than entire countries', *Business Insider* [Online], 25 July 2018. Available at: https://tinyurl.com/bha9vpyy (accessed 6 June 2021).

25 For ideas about how to influence where your pension funds are invested, see for example the international fossil free divestment campaign at: https://gofossilfree.org/divestment/what-is-fossil-fuel-divestment/ (accessed 6 June 2021).

26 Jeroen Veldman and Hugh Willmott, 'Statement on management', The Modern Corporation. Available at: https://themoderncorporation.wordpress.com/management-and-msv/ (accessed 23 May 2021).

27 A more detailed argument for social licensing can be found in Julie Froud and Karel Williams, 'Adding value', in Rachel Reeves (ed.), *Everyday Socialism: How to Rebuild Britain* (London: Fabian Society, 2019). Available at: https://fabians.org.uk/wp-content/uploads/2019/09/FABJ7429-Socialism-Pamphlet-0819-WEB-002.pdf (accessed 23 May 2021).

28 For ideas about ethical standards that corporations could develop and uphold, see company ratings developed for over thirty years by Ethical Consumer, 'Ratings categories and sub-categories'. Available at: https://research.ethicalconsumer.org/corporate-research-database/our-ethical-ratings-system/ethical-ratings-categories-sub-categories (accessed 6 June 2021).

29 Maggie Gaston, 'The power battle between media and tech companies', *PR Week* [Online], 28 April 2020. Available at: www.prweek.com/article/1681573/power-battle-tech-giants-media-companies (accessed 23 May 2021).

30 For more information see Decolonising Economics on Twitter: https://twitter.com/Decolonising or its website: https://decolonisingeconomics.org/ (accessed 6 June 2021).

31 Global Fund Community Foundations, 'An open letter to International NGOs who are looking to "localise" their operations', 5 March 2020. Available at: https://globalfundcommunityfoundations.org/news/an-open-letter-to-international-ngos-who-are-looking-to-localise-their-operations/ (accessed 23 May 2021).

32 *Ibid.*

33 *Ibid.*

34 Global Fund for Community Foundations, 'Manifesto for change', 5 June 2019. Available at: https://globalfundcommunityfoundations.org/news/announcing-the-pathways-to-power-symposium-london-18-19-november-taking-shiftthepower-to-the-next-level/ (accessed 23 May 2021).

Notes

35 Arundhati Roy, 'We need a reckoning', YouTube, 9 June 2020. Available at: www.youtube.com/watch?v=bhDo_nl-h2U (accessed 23 May 2021).

36 Economy, *The Case for Economic Literacy for Everyone* (Economy, 2018). Available at: www.ecnmy.org/wp-content/uploads/2018/10/The-Case-for-Economics-for-Everyone-Online.pdf. Economy, 'What is economic literacy?' (2018). Available at: www.ecnmy.org/literacy/ (accessed 23 May 2021).

Chapter 8 For future generations

1 Damian Carrington, 'Coronavirus: "Nature is sending us a message", says UN environment chief', *Guardian*, 25 March 2020. Available at: www.theguardian.com/world/2020/mar/25/coronavirus-nature-is-sending-us-a-message-says-un-environment-chief (accessed 22 May 2021).

2 Centers for Disease Control and Prevention, 'Zoonotic diseases'. Available at: www.cdc.gov/onehealth/basics/zoonotic-diseases.html (accessed 8 June 2021).

3 Elliot Teperman and Maria Lettini, 'An industry infected: animal agriculture in a post-COVID world', FAIRR Initiative. Available at: www.fairr.org/article/industry-infected/ (accessed 8 June 2021).

4 Social Science Analytics Cell (CASS), 'The impacts of the COVID-19 outbreak response on women and girls in the Democratic Republic of the Congo', UNICEF, n.d., p. 1. Available at: www.unicef.org/drcongo/media/5416/file/COD-CASS-impacts-COVID-response-women-girls.pdf (accessed 22 May 2021).

5 Emily Janoch, *Evolving Trends: Women in COVID-19* (UK: Care International, 2020), p. 3. Available at: https://insights.careinternational.org.uk/images/in-practice/RGA-and-measurement/GiE_Learning_RGA-Global-Trend-Update_July2020.pdf (accessed 22 May 2021).

6 *Ibid.*, p. 3.

7 Bina Agarwal, 'Livelihoods in COVID times: gendered perils and new pathways in India', *World Development*, 139 (March), Article:105312, 1–7. doi: 10.1016/j.worlddev.2020.105312.

8 *Ibid.*

9 Marion Sharples, 'Covid-19 has shown the economy isn't working. But for women, it never has', *Huffington Post* [Online], 24 April 2020. Available at: www.huffingtonpost.co.uk/entry/care-work-women-care-home-coronavirus_uk_5e9ef20bc5b6b2e5b8382447 (accessed 22 May 2021).

10 Fawcett Society, 'Coronavirus: making women visible', n.d. Available at: www.fawcettsociety.org.uk/coronavirus-making-women-visible (accessible 22 May 2021).

11 UNDP/UN Women, 'Covid-19 Global Gender Response Tracker', Version 1 (28 September 2020), p. 2. Available at: www.undp.org/publications/covid-19-global-gender-response-tracker-fact-sheets#modal-publication-download (accessed 22 May 2021).

12 *Ibid.*, p. 9.

13 *Ibid.*, p. 9.

14 Though the understanding of vulnerability may/does not incorporate a historical oppression and racialised/gendered/socioeconomic lens of the sort we develop in Chapter 1 and would be improved if it did.

15 Jayati Ghosh, 'Covid-19 in India – profits before people', *Social Europe*, 27 April 2021. Available at: www.socialeurope.eu/covid-19-in-india-profits-before-people (accessed 22 May 2021).

16 Jayati Ghosh, 'Vaccine apartheid', *International Politics Society*, 23 November 2020. Available at: www.ips-journal.eu/topics/democracy/vaccine-apartheid-4813/ (accessed 22 May 2021).

17 *Ibid.*

18 Ownership is through the World Trade Organization's TRIPS agreement (Trade-Related Aspects of Intellectual Property Rights), implemented in 1995 which WTO member countries enforce and abide by.

19 Civil society letter, 'Supporting proposal by India and South Africa on waiver from certain provisions of the TRIPS agreement for the prevention, containment and treatment of Covid-19', 2020. Available at: www.globaljustice.org.uk/wp-content/uploads/2020/10/csoletter_supportingwaiverfinal.pdf (accessed 22 May 2021).

20 Kate Raworth, *Doughnut Economics: Seven Ways to Think Like a 21st-Century Economist* (London: Random House, 2017), pp. 35–36.

21 *Ibid.*, p. 36.

22 Tim Gore, 'Confronting carbon inequality: putting climate justice at the heart of the COVID-19 recovery', Oxfam Media Briefing, 21 September 2020, p. 9. Available at: www.oxfam.org/en/press-releases/ carbon-emissions-richest-1-percent-more-double-emissions-poorest-half-humanity (accessed 22 May 2021).

23 Samir Amin, 'Underdevelopment and dependence in Black Africa – origins and contemporary forms', *Journal of Modern African Studies*, 10:4 (1972), 503–524. doi: 10.1017/S0022278X00022801.

24 C. Dorninger *et al.*, 'Global patterns of ecologically unequal exchange: implications for sustainability in the 21st century', *Ecological Economics*, 179, Article 106824 (January 2021), 1–14. doi: 10.1016/ j.ecolecon.2020.106824.

25 KILN, 'The Carbon Map'. Available at: www.carbonmap.org/#Historical (accessed 22 May 2021).

26 KILN, 'The Carbon Map'. Available at: www.carbonmap.org/ #PeopleAtRisk (accessed 22 May 2021).

27 Jubilee Debt Campaign, 'IMF loan to Mozambique following Cyclone Idai "shocking indictment" of international community', JDC Press Release, 23 April 2019. Available at: https://jubileedebt. org.uk/press-release/imf-loan-to-mozambique-following-cyclone-idai-shocking-indictment-of-international-community (accessed 22 May 2021).

28 Guppi Bola, *Reimagining Public Health* (UK: CommonWealth, June 2020). Available at: https://uploads-ssl.webflow.com/ 5e2191f00f868d778b89ff85/5efc68de5bcaea188e5d3d88_CW_ Reimagining%20Public%20Health_Bola.pdf (accessed 22 May 2021).

29 Leon Sealey-Huggins, '"1.5°C to stay alive": climate change, imperialism and justice for the Caribbean', *Third World Quarterly*, 38:11 (2017), 2444–2463. doi: 10.1080/01436597.2017.1368013.

30 *Ibid.*

31 *Ibid.*

32 Institute for Economics and Peace, *Ecological Threat Register 2020: Understanding Ecological Threats, Resilience and Peace* (Sydney: Institute for Economics and Peace, September 2020). Available

at: https://reliefweb.int/sites/reliefweb.int/files/resources/ETR_2020_web-1.pdf (accessed 13 June 2021).

33 Instituto Nacional de Estadística y Geografía, 'Ciudad de México (09)', INEGI. Available at: https://en.www.inegi.org.mx/app/areasgeogra ficas/?ag=09 (accessed 22 May 2021).

34 Office for National Statistics, 'Estimates of the population for the UK, England and Wales, Scotland and Northern Ireland', 24 June 2020. Available at: www.ons.gov.uk/peoplepopulationand community/populationandmigration/populationestimates/datasets/ populationestimatesforukenglandandwalesscotlandand northernireland (accessed 22 May 2021).

35 Stats SA Department: Statistics South Africa, 'City of Johannesburg', Stats SA, 2011. Available at: www.statssa.gov.za/?page_id=993&id=city-of-johannesburg-municipality (accessed 22 May 2021).

36 Action Aid, 'Climate change and gender', 5 March 2021. Available at:www.actionaid.org.uk/our-work/emergencies-disasters-humanitarian-response/climate-change-and-gender (accessed 22 May 2021).

37 Care USA, 'Far from home: the 13 worst refugee crises for girls', Care USA, 2021. Available at: https://care.exposure.co/far-from-home (accessed 22 May 2021).

38 Senay Habtezion, *Gender and Climate Change* (New York: UNDP, 2016), p. 4. Available at: www.undp.org/content/dam/undp/library/ gender/Gender%20and%20Environment/UNDP%20Linkages%20 Gender%20and%20CC%20Policy%20Brief%201-WEB.pdf (accessed 22 May 2021).

39 Chidiebere J. Onwutuebe, 'Patriarchy and women vulnerability to adverse climate change in Nigeria', *SAGE Open* (January–March 2019), 1–7. doi: 10.1177/2158244019825914.

40 Tahnee Prior and Leena Heinämäki, 'The rights and role of Indigenous women in the climate change regime', *Arctic Review on Law and Politics*, 8 (2017), 193–221. doi: http://dx.doi.org/10.23865/ arctic.v8.901.

41 *Ibid*.

42 Steve Keen, 'The appallingly bad neoclassical economics of climate change', *Globalizations* (2020), 14. Available at: 10.1080/ 14747731.2020.1807856.

43 SEI, IISD, ODI, E3G, and UNEP, *The Production Gap Executive Summary*, 2020. Available at: https://productiongap.org/wp-content/uploads/2020/12/PGR2020_ExecSum_web.pdf (accessed 22 May 2021).

44 See Rainforest Action Network *et al.*, *Banking on Climate Chaos: Fossil Fuel Finance Report 2021*, RAN, 2021, p. 4. Available at: www.ran.org/wp-content/uploads/2021/03/Banking-on-Climate-Chaos-2021.pdf. Rainforest Action Network *et al.*, *Banking on Climate Change: Fossil Fuel Finance Report 2020*, RAN, 2020, p. 4. Available at: www.ran.org/bankingonclimatechange2020/ (both sources accessed 22 May 2021).

45 Patrick Greenfield, 'World's top three asset managers oversee $300bn fossil fuel investments', *Guardian*, 12 October 2019. Available at: www.theguardian.com/environment/2019/oct/12/top-three-asset-managers-fossil-fuel-investments (accessed 22 May 2021).

46 Greenpeace, *It's the Finance Sector, Stupid* (Greenpeace, 2020), p. 4. Available at: https://storage.googleapis.com/planet4-international-stateless/2020/01/13e3c75b-greenpeace_report_wef_2020_its-the-finance_sector_stupid.pdf (accessed 22 May 2021).

47 These sectors are: forestry and non-food forest commodities; fossil fuels; food production and agricultural commodities; metals and minerals mining; tourism; relocation of goods and people; and infrastructure. Portfolio Earth, *Bankrolling Extinction: The Banking Sector's Role in the Global Biodiversity Crisis* (Portfolio Earth, 2021), p. 20. Available at: https://portfolio.earth/wp-content/uploads/2021/01/Bankrolling-Extinction-Report.pdf (accessed 22 May 2021).

48 World Meteorological Organization, '2020 on track to be one of three warmest years on record', WMO, 2 December 2020. Available at: https://public.wmo.int/en/media/press-release/2020-track-be-one-of-three-warmest-years-record (accessed 22 May 2021).

49 Barbara Buchner *et al.*, *Global Landscape of Climate Finance 2019* (London: Climate Policy Initiative, 2019), p. 3. Available at: www.climatepolicyinitiative.org/wp-content/uploads/2019/11/2019-Global-Landscape-of-Climate-Finance.pdf (accessed 13 June 2021).

50 *Ibid.*, p. 6.

51 Rathin Roy, 'Decolonising climate action', ODI Insight Blog, 9 December 2020. Available at: https://tinyurl.com/z8fzw95v (accessed 22 May 2021).

Notes

52 *Ibid.*

53 *Ibid.*

54 *Ibid.*

55 Bola, *Reimagining Public Health.*

56 *Ibid.*

57 Raworth, *Doughnut Economics.*

58 Keston Perry has argued for climate reparations in the form of a global climate stabilisation fund and resilience fund programme for loss and damage in marginalised and former colonised societies. Keston Perry, 'Realising climate reparations: towards a global climate stabilization fund and resilience fund programme for loss and damage in marginalised and former colonised societies', 1 March 2020. Available at: https://dx.doi.org/10.2139/ssrn.3561121 (accessed 8 June 2021).

59 Stanford University, 'Equality of outcome', n.d. Available at: https://edeq.stanford.edu/sections/equality-outcome (accessed 22 May 2021).

60 Robert Nozick, *Anarchy, State and Utopia* (USA: Blackwell Publishing, 1974), pp. 149–182.

61 Learn Liberty, 'Immanuel Kant: philosopher of freedom', 2 November 2017. Available at: https://tinyurl.com/y6hbr3ha (accessed 22 May 2021).

62 Amitav Ghosh, *The Great Derangement: Climate Change and the Unthinkable* (Chicago: University of Chicago Press, 2016), p. 128.

63 One example is Paul Collier's 'hard centrism' in his recent book: Paul Collier, *The Future of Capitalism* (London: Penguin Books, 2019). Another is Dani Rodrik's criticism of globalisation while basically defending the fundamental correctness of neoclassical economics which we explored earlier in the book: Dani Rodrik, *The Globalization Paradox: Why Global Markets, States and Democracy Can't Coexist* (Oxford: Oxford University Press, 2011).

64 For real-time updates on the numbers of those who have participated in strikes since 2019, see Fridays for Future, 'Strike statistics'. Available at: https://fridaysforfuture.org/what-we-do/strike-statistics/ (accessed 22 May 2021).

65 Rosanna Wiseman, 'Colonialism + capitalism = climate crisis', Global Justice Now, 7 October 2019. Available at: www.globaljustice.org.uk/blog/2019/oct/7/colonialism-capitalism-climate-crisis (accessed 22 May 2021).

353

Notes

66   The Wretched of the Earth collective, 'Our house has been on fire for over 500 years', speech given at the London Climate Strike on 20 September 2019. Available at: https://wretchedotearth.medium.com/our-house-has-been-on-fire-for-over-500-years-79de7d11f810 (accessed 8 June 2021).

67   *Ibid.*

68   *Ibid.*

69   *Ibid.*

Appendix

1   The US has intersectional data on women and people of colour in economics.

Acknowledgements

The collective effort that went into this book is illustrated not only by its contributors, but by Maeve Cohen who initiated it, Laurence Jones-Williams who helped steer it through choppy waters, Ali Al-Jamri who led Rethinking's early work on decolonising economics and Juliet Michaelson who from start to finish was always there to provide invaluable support. They each, in their own way, made this book possible.

Without the help of many economics students and recent graduates worldwide who conducted peer-to-peer interviews, this book would lack some of the voices and stories behind the statistics. A big thank you to Adam Catt, Alby Berticević Nicols, Sandra Delgado, Maria Georgouli Loupi, Taïs Real, Mayada Hassanain, Liam Mullany, André Pedersen Ystehede, Matthew Yu, Marie Meyle, Veronica Mrvcic, Ben Newey, Chuchen Pan and Lizzie Friesen.

We appreciate all of the interviewees for sharing their stories about studying and working in economics. While we could not include everything you said, your experiences helped to shape the book's arguments.

Thank you also to Ali Norrish for helping to conduct focus groups in schools, to the teachers who let us into their classrooms and to the students who welcomed us.

Acknowledgements

Special thanks to those who have advised us since the very beginning: Eshe Nelson, Marion Sharples, Ayeisha Thomas-Smith, Polly Trenow, Susanne Hofmann, and to those who provided constructive feedback on earlier drafts: Charu Agrawal, Rafael Galvão de Almeida, Louise de Gaudemaris, Bill Golden, Isbat Ibn Hasnat, Kavitha Ravikumar, Judy Seymour. Advice about diversifying and decolonising economics from Carolina Cristina Alvez and Ingrid Kvangraven was particularly appreciated and so too was guidance about economics and the living world from Kate Raworth.

RE's international staff team also receive a special mention for their support since research for the book began.

We owe a big thanks to Jayati Ghosh for her patience and writing the foreword for this book. Seeing the work you do to diversify and decolonise economics is hugely inspiring. We are in debt to Paula Clarke Bain for wonderful copyediting and indexing and to our editor Tom Dark for his support and diligence.

We are also immensely grateful for the funding provided by the Women's Rights Program of the Open Society Foundations, without which this book would not exist.

The people who have supported the creation of this book come from a variety of backgrounds, life experiences and with a range of ideas about what economics is, how it can be taught and practised, and by whom. Each of them is reclaiming economics in their own way and for this we are grateful.

We know that this book is just a small part of a much wider movement that is on a long journey towards a world where racial and social justice, gender equality and sustainable coexistence with the living world are a reality. Rethinking Economics will take this work forward working closely with allies across the world. We hope you will join us.

Index

Note: Page references with 'n' indicate endnote numbers. Page numbers in *italic* refer to illustrations.

Index

Index

Index

Index

Index

Index

Index